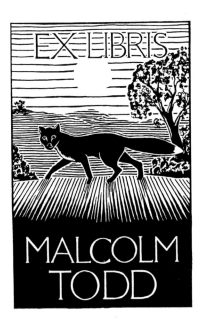

EX LIBRIS

MALCOLM
TODD

MAN OF MANY TALENTS

MAN OF
MANY TALENTS

An Informal Biography
of
James Douglas 1753-1819

by

RONALD JESSUP

PHILLIMORE

1975

Published by
PHILLIMORE & CO., LTD.,
London and Chichester
Head Office: Shopwyke Hall,
Chichester, Sussex, England

ISBN 0 85033 199 4

Thanks are due to the Marc Fitch Fund
for its generous help which enabled
this book to be published

Text set in 11/12pt. Journal
Printed by Unwin Brothers Limited,
Old Woking, Surrey.

On Chatham Downs . . . the Engineer, Captain Douglas, who is just entered on the study of Antiquity, and is as complete an Enthusiast as ever I met with in my life . . . He seems beginning where he should leave off . . .

Edward Hasted, the Kentish historian, 1780.

The account [of Roman remains] is drawn up in the Abbe's best style of pomposity and laboured obscurity, so that one cannot help comparing him to a magician who vanishes in a cloud of smoke of his own raising.

John Hawkins to Samuel Lysons, 1812.

The variety of his talents evaded description.

The Sun, *20 November, 1819.*

Faussett's error brings out however into clearer light the perspicacity of his fellow-worker, Douglas . . . who regards these and allied phenomena with the eyes of an enlightened archaeologist of to-day. In matters of detail also he is refreshingly modern.

Professor G. Baldwin Brown, 1915.

LIST OF CONTENTS

List of Illustrations   ix

Foreword   xi

Part I   1

Chapter

 1   Dreams and Realities: Les Chongs Clotiers   ...   3

 2   Realities: A Narrative Reconstructed   12

 3   Travellers' Tales   30

 4   The Complete Enthusiast   47

 5   Dissertation   64

 6   Further Dissertations   77

 7   Disquisition   92

 8   Minor Pleasures   115

 9   The Sussex Pad   122

10   The Last Decade   142

11   Epilogue   166

Part II 179

Chapter

12 Selection of Letters to Henry Godfrey Faussett
  of Heppington, 1781-1794 182

13 Selection of Letters to Major Hayman Rooke,
  1784, 1787 230

14 Selection of Letters to the 3rd Lord Egremont
  and his Agent, 1803-1806 243

15 Selection of Letters to William Cunnington,
  1809-10 251

16 Selection of Letters to Sir Richard Colt Hoare,
  1812-1814 271

17 Notes on the Plates 283

18 Bibliography 293

19 Index 305

ILLUSTRATIONS
(between pages 282 and 283)

1   Portrait of James Douglas by T. Phillips, R.A., F.S.A.

2   'Les chongs clotiers', Tournai Cathedral

3   Procession de la Peste, Tournai

4   Sand-pit, Ash, 1773, 1783

5   Chatham Dockyard from Fort Pitt, *c.* 1828
    The Great Lines, Chatham from the Keep of Rochester
    Castle, 1973

6   Plan of the City of Tongres, 1773

7   Ruins of *Atuatuca*, 1773

8   A Swiss Boy

9   Monsieur Varelst

10 Roman barrows at Koninksem

11 Roman walling at Tongres

12 Tongres: the Basilica and statue of Ambiorix

13 Piringen near Tongres: Roman barrow excavated by
    Douglas, 1733

14 Antiquities excavated at Chartham, Kent, 1730

15 Anglo-Saxon antiquities from East Kent

16 The Faussett Pavilion, Heppington, Kent

17 Proof pull of a drawing used as letter paper, 1787

18 Portrait of Francis Grose, 1785

19 Coston church, Leicestershire, 1791

20 Roman ceremonial bronze axe found near Canterbury, and another of unknown provenance

21 The Old Parsonage, now Glebe House, Chiddingfold, Surrey

22 Richborough Castle from the Amphitheatre, 1787

23 Barrows in Greenwich Park, 1784, 1973

24 Barrows at St. Margaret's-at-Cliffe, near Dover, 1782, and facsimile entry from the Common-Place Book of Lord Winchilsea, 1720

25 Plan of Tumulus I, Chatham Lines, 1779

26 Contents of Tumulus II, Chatham Lines, 1779

27 Contents of Tumulus II, Chatham Lines, in the Ashmolean Museum

28 Glass vessels from Roman and Anglo-Saxon graves, East Kent

29 Roman pottery and glass from Tongres by the Abbé Van Muyssen

30 A Van Muyssen drawing and Douglas's version

31 Group of Barrows south of Stonehenge, c. 1806

32 The Goldstone, Hove Park, Sussex

33 Preston near Brighthelmston, 1873

34 Kits Coty House, Aylesford, Kent

35 Roman pottery from Tongres and Douglas's snuff-box

36 Memorial inscription to Douglas in Preston church near Brighton

FOREWORD

THE LONG but pleasant task of writing this book has been lightened by most generous help from friends and official authorities here and abroad. In February 1934 after my Admission as a Fellow of the Society of Antiquaries of London the late Reginald Smith, then Director of the Society, showed me an untidy bundle of papers which included letters from James Douglas to Henry Godfrey Faussett and suggested that they were worth more attention than I had hitherto given Douglas as an antiquary and excavator of barrows. These papers were misplaced during the removal of the Society's library during the War and were only recovered from an obscure basement room several years later by the persistent searching of our present Librarian, Mr. John H. Hopkins, to whom I am grateful for much help. At the suggestion of Council I was invited to study and make brief notes on these most interesting papers which were then mounted and bound to form MS. 723 which I formally exhibited to the Society in 1953. It was then hoped that more could be discovered about Douglas's life and the papers published. This book —and a detailed study of Roman burial mounds in northern Europe—are the formal result.

It is to the archivists and those in charge of official records that my particular thanks are due for most courteous and detailed replies to what, to many of them, must have seemed almost elementary enquiries. At the Royal Commission on Historical Manuscripts, the Secretary, Mr. Roger Ellis, at the War Office the Librarian,

Mr. D. W. King, and at the National Army Museum, Mr. Boris Mollo, Keeper of Records, gave me much help, as did the Keeper of Archives of the City of Leicester, Miss Jean Kennedy, the City and County Archivist of Norwich and Norfolk, Dr. Mary Finch of the Lincolnshire Archives Committee, Mr. W. R. Sargent of the Ipswich and East Suffolk Record Office, Mr. C. R. Davey, Deputy County Archivist and Diocesan Record Officer of Hampshire, Miss Margaret Swarbrick of the Westminster Library Archives Collection, my old friend Francis W. Steer, Maltravers Herald Extraordinary and formerly County Archivist for West Sussex (to whom I owe many kindnesses), and his successor in Sussex, Mrs. Patricia Gill, through whose introduction I was able to read certain letters from the Petworth House archives by kind permission of Lord Egremont; and I should also like to thank another old friend, Dr. Albert E. J. Hollaender, for receiving enquiries about military archives in Europe with kindness and equanimity. To the incumbents of most of the benefices held by Douglas I am obliged for permission to read church records and entries made by him in various parish registers. The Registrar of the Royal Archives at Windsor graciously answered several enquiries. For some long time I could not trace Douglas's marriage: it was noted for me, by chance, by Sir George Bellew, lately Garter King of Arms.

The Douglas Collection in the Ashmolean Museum at Oxford I described and partly illustrated at the suggestion of the Keeper of Antiquities, the late Edward Thurlow Leeds, but the manuscript was destroyed in the early days of the War. I record my most grateful recognition of his help and for the generous assistance I received later from Dr. D. B. Harden, Miss Joan Kirk (Mrs. Joan Clarke) and more recently from Mr. P. D. C. Brown. At Liverpool Miss Elaine Tankard and latterly Mr. T. A. Hume, then Director of the City Museums, gave me much help with the Faussett-Mayer material.

I should like also to thank Mr. Kenneth Woodbridge for calling my attention to letters between Douglas,

Cunnington and Colt Hoare, which I had not been successful in tracing, and to the Wiltshire County and Diocesan Archivist at Trowbridge, Mr. Maurice Rathbone, for allowing me to read them and print certain examples. I am also very grateful to the present custodians of the few of Douglas's own hand-coloured copies of *Nenia Britannica* for permission to study them in detail.

In my Sussex enquiries I have also been helped by Messrs. George Holleyman and Norman F. S. Norris: the latter has generously presented two photographs for this book.

When the work was almost ready for press I was fortunate to meet Mr. Eric G. Vasmer of Caldecote, Bushey Heath, Hertfordshire, who kindly allowed me unrestricted access to his family documents which include papers relating to James Douglas's father and the successive owners of his estate. Mr. Vasmer also gave me much helpful information about its topography.

In Belgium the late Baron Ph. de Schaetzen gave me welcome access to his magnificent private collection which is now incorporated in the Gallo-Roman Museum at Tongres and much information about the Abbé Van Muyssen. The late Professor Jacques Breuer of the Service national des Fouilles and Dr. H. Roosens the present Director, Dr. Marcel Amand, Dr. Paul Janssens, Professor Antoine De Schryver, Monsieur Englebert, Attaché at the Belgian Embassy in Vienna, Dr. Georges Colin, Conservateur of the Bibliothèque Royale, Brussels, and Mademoiselle Paule Spitaels have variously guided me—and sometimes accompanied me—in following the routes of Douglas's travels and activities in their own country, in examining archaeological collections, and in suggesting possible sources for his military records. In Vienna, Dr. Kurt Peball most kindly checked contemporary military records in detail. In the Archaeological Institute of the University of Göttingen Dr. Charles Boehringer gave me much appreciated help in a study of Roman bronze ceremonial axes.

I must also record my devotion to the memory of the

late Thurlow Leeds and my grateful thanks to Sir Thomas Kendrick, always most generous and helpful of friends, and I remain dutifully and gratefully indebted to the Society of Antiquaries.

Above all I am most grateful for a generous Grant from The Marc Fitch Fund which has enabled this book to be published.

RONALD JESSUP

London, W.1.

PART I

1

DREAMS AND REALITIES: LES CHONGS CLOTIERS

LET THE READER be introduced to James Douglas in a rather unorthodox manner—by means of a little essay about a splendid day which he spent in a Flemish city.

For long years afterwards he could recall in detail and with pleasure the events of the day at Tournai when, at the age of 20, he had come to a decision which was to change the whole course of his life.

That famous city, once the cradle of France and key to the Kingdom, with its noble five-steepled cathedral (Plate 2) said to be the finest building of its sort north of the Alps, its picturesque Romanesque, Gothic, Renaissance and Baroque churches and houses, its collections of pictures, books, tapestries and antiquities, its still warm regard for the English, and above all the spirit of its people described in the popular saying *Le Tournaisien s'amuser* and manifest in scholarship, art and music had always had for him a particular and devoted attraction. As in the days when he was but a cadet in the École Militaire at Ghent, and now in 1773 as a full Lieutenant of Hussars to Majesty of Austria, he was more than glad for a chance to return yet again.

From Ghent on this brilliant day in September he had set out at first light with part of his squadron and come

the long way round by Oudenaarde and Avelghem along
the Schelde so as to avoid the crowds of pilgrims and
tourists travelling by the Courtrai road to see and take part
in La Grande Procession de Tournai. The long ride of more
than 65 kilometres was inclined to be rough in places, but
there were few travellers and fully adequate watering and
rest for the horses at Oudenaarde. Here, too, as a soldier
he was glad of an excuse to pay his *devoir* to the gilded
figure of lucky *Jean le Guerrier,* Little John the Warrior,
on the cupola of the Hotel de Ville, and as an antiquary
to buy for his collection two dishes of fine red Roman
pottery fished up from the bed of the Schelde, each
marked with its maker's name. From one well-remembered
place on the road approaching Tournai it was now possible
to see the five square towers of the Cathedral, affectionately known locally as *les chongs clotiers,* rising in the
hard brilliant light of what in those seemingly far-off
days in Hertfordshire his father would have called the
Harvest Moon. Here, he thought, was a suitable place for
a final short briefing of his squadron's duties and place
in the procession before they clattered away down into
the city and across to their lines on the *champ de
manœuvres.*

  With Tongres, Tournai was the most ancient town in
Flanders and similarly had a long and varied history
stretching far back into its days as a Roman military and
trading centre. In both places relics of the Romans were
often brought to light, walls of houses, pottery, fine
glassware bottles, trinkets and even jewellery, traces even
of the canals and aqueducts by which a regular supply of
water was assured. From where he rode he could see
part of the Roman town wall and only a year before it
was possible to see a piece of a Roman road complete
with its paving not far under the ground. In 1090 Tournai
suffered greatly from a plague which stayed as
though by the intervention of a miracle. To commemorate
the deliverance and the recovery of the city's prosperity
there had been instituted a vast procession of witness and
thanksgiving, *La Grande Procession de l' Exaltation de la*

Sainte-Croix or, more simply, *de Notre Dame de La Peste,* or colloquially in two words, *La Peste.* It was most carefully organised year by year early in September with the backing of high civil, ecclesiastical and military authority, and to it came the professional religious, other religious orders, members of many wealthy guilds and associations, pilgrims both solemn and gay, tourists with gaping mouths, and all those providers of special foods and amusements which the city with its greatly increased temporary population would find difficulty in providing.

The general route he had no difficulty in recalling from previous attendances at *La Peste*, and again briefed his squadron warning them not to canter in the precincts of the Cathedral or on the bridges over the River Schelde. The procession would form in the Grand' Place, go by the Cathedral, rue des Orphèvres, Grand' Place again, rue St. Martin, de France, to aux Poids, Vieil Marché aux Bêtes, and then perhaps a diversion to Barre St. Brice, rue de Pont, rue de la Tête d'Or and so eventually back to the Grand' Place where the squadron could assume double open order and dismount. Lines were at midnight, but late entry by Le Mot was permissible and would never either in Tournai or back in Ghent be subject to enquiry. But at all times it was to be remembered that certain churches and places with long-established practices of local devotion—he would remind them only of the Annunciation sculpture in St. Marie-Madeleine, the venerated Notre Dame d'Alsemberg in St. Piat and the memorials in St. Nicholas—must receive the quiet veneration of the squadron as it passed by. The Ensign would please remember his special duties: *souveraine naturelle* Highness might well be called and regarded as an idol of the people, but the Governor-General was also a man of good sense and a good soldier as everyone knew, and Ensign must therefore take great care to assure the perfect behaviour of his troops while they were on official duty. Afterwards, there would be amusements, naturally enough. Already by the early hours of the next morning small shrines and images ringed with flowers and lighted candles appeared in the

windows and above the doorways of many private houses.
Circles of lighted candles and stands of specially-grown
roses were being placed along the roadsides. Fine brightly-
coloured carpets and more solemn tapestries decorated
with religious scenes, products of an industry for which
Tournai had become well known, hung from windows of
official buildings and of well-to-do citizens. Peals of church
bells rung with skill and precision filled the morning air,
while from some far-off convent a single heavy tenor
added its monotonous clang. He sat his horse with comfort
and pleasure, a little warm in full-dress uniform after the
three beakers of an excellent wine provided by members
of the Cathedral Chapter for leading officials of the
city and of the procession. As always, his note-book was
in a pannier pocket within easy reach and it was not
thought at all strange, but taken rather as a compliment,
that he should draw what he saw. The already large
crowds were steadily increasing, but *luronne* and *paresseux*
alike, these pleasant Tournaisiens knew how to behave
on such a solemn occasion. Were they not now to give
solemn thanks for the passing of *La Peste*? The familiar
clack-clack of the heavy iron bricolet ball, the strange
cries of the players, the singing of age-old dialect songs,
folk-dancing in the Grand' Place and no doubt some other
distracting but less decorous activities would follow later.

Here came a band of drums and fifes leading a parade
of 50 local mousquetaires and at least as many members
of the Compaynée of St. Antoine, followed by a troop
of red-coated and green-hatted *cannonieres* and the archers
of St. Sébastien, *les Arbalétriers de St. Georges* in their
picturesque old-fashioned uniforms and carrying their
weapons on display, and representatives of several other
societies of archers four of whom carried an enormous
dish or platter of Tournai porcelain finely decorated in
blue with the crest of their own Society. Slowly, two by
two, came the Children of Charity raised in their special
school, les Sœurs Clarisses, les Noires, les Grises, les
Ursulines, les Sœurs de Marie réparatrice, all known for
their good works, or so it was said. After a gap as though

to emphasise their very different social background there walked with great pose a small group of sisters from a Béguinage, the 'steadfast support of the needy and care of the sick', in their well-kept robes of blue and spotless white linen headgear and one, a novice, with a wreath round her head. Then there followed 20 members of the Austrian cavalry in their doublets of rose-coloured satin, tunics of pale green and epaulettes of silver and gold with the Imperial arms, sitting firmly on their mounts and looking neither to right nor left.

A gap again and then one could see the members of the Cathedral Chapter in full canonical dress leading Monsieur Chanoine and Monsieur l'Evêque himself in mitre and sumptuously embroidered cope bearing in a gilded monstrance *Sainte Sacrement*. Next on the shoulders of six minor canons was borne a wonderful Virgin of carved ivory with her affectionately smiling Child, a Mother and Child who really lived and shone with radiance and glory. Quickly following were the monks and friars, Mendicants, Dominicans, Capuchins, Augustinians, Redemptorists and the rest, no doubt in some especially significant order but one which made no sense to the English Lieutenant of Austrian Hussars who here led his part of the troop in their assigned place in the procession. It was common knowledge that some orders were greatly unpopular and some of the contemplatives appearing here apparently by special permission might soon have to find homes elsewhere. In any case it was none of his business.

What did interest him, and interest him greatly, were the reliquaries which now came into view. Normally they were impossible to see unless one could have rare privileged access to the Treasury of the Cathedral, but he had taken special care to make drawings of these remarkable artistic treasures as the procession was arranging itself earlier in the day. There was La Châsse des Damoiseaux (Plate 3) made in 1571 at Bruges for Les Confrères de Notre-Dame dit les Damoiseaux, an aristocratic legal Brotherhood of Tournai who, led by their cross-bearing steward and dressed formally in white gloves, stiffly-

laundered white shirts and white ties, gowns of black
silk adorned with richly-embroidered gold facings and
wearing black flat-topped caps, carried the carefully
supported shrine on their shoulders, the four carriers
being closely guarded and attended by their Brethren.
Then came the three-foot-long gilded copper Châsse de
Notre-Dame Flamande, sometimes said to be of St.
Ursula, a work of great richness and beauty made in 1205
by Nicolas de Verdun. Even as he dared to look backward
for a moment he could appreciate the fine quality of its
enamel and filigree decoration, the skilled enrichment of
the chiselled repoussé. How many craftsmen would have
assisted at its making; how long was spent on its design?
The third and by far the best loved was the beautiful
silver-gilt Châsse de Saint Eleuthère (Plate 3), the heavy
rectangular gabled shrine of Tournai's own Saint, he who
in 1247 founded the first church on the site of the Cathedral. This shrine, nearly five feet in length and three-and-a-
half feet high as he had measured, was carried by clergy
of the Foundation in their white wide-sleeved habits and
black hooded scapulas. Earlier he had sketched details of
the magnificent enamel and filigree work, the figures of
the Apostles, John the Baptist, the Annunciation, the
Church and the Synagogue, and the brilliantly rendered
figure of the Saint himself holding in his left hand a
representation of the Cathedral with its characteristic five
steeples. Never, one heard, had the shrine been opened.
It certainly needed repair, but even so in its present
condition eight priests were required to lift it from the
ground.

There were many other groups of young girls and boys
carrying flower-garlanded and torch-lit statues of various
saints from the local churches, St. Brice, St. Piat, St.
Quentin, St. Jacques and St. Nicolas among them. Each
group had its distinctive confraternity uniform, a long
gown of blue, black, red or occasionally white, carefully
washed and newly pressed. Of the statues, two carved in
a remarkably naturalistic style in the local slate-coloured
marbles of Tournai were the only examples of antique art.

The rest, in modern plaster, showed to the Lieutenant's mind but little taste. Still the procession continued. Here now to the jingle of harness and trappings on their well-draped horses, were certain biblical, historical and mythological characters closely followed by others on foot. One could recognise Alexander the Great, Hector and Achilles, Julius Cæsar, Pompey, Judas Maccabaeus, David and Goliath, Roland and Oliver, a beautiful Judith from Ghent and her Holofernes already somewhat drunk, even King Arthur of Britain. Many had colourful tabards and satin gold-trimmed robes while some carried bright heraldic banners making a fine show. A tall gigantic Hercules with bare arms, legs and feet wore only an antique corselet polished as sunlight. And to end it all there danced and pirouetted five characters who were said to represent the Senses, though judging by the shouts of encouragement and approval from the crowd their broad and bawdy antics were rather to be regarded as a sign that seriousness was now finished and that the *kermesse* could begin.

The Lieutenant found a stable for his horse, moved to his favourite café and sat outside on the pavement of the Grand' Place. Lefebure, his Ensign and a man of Tournai, paid a duty visit to an aged aunt, and now was the time and place for reflection.

Should he continue to stay in Flanders or perhaps in Austria in court circles? He went over the ground again in his own mind: but no, he had to go back much further than that, and at the same time think much into the future. Pay was quite good, social life as rewarding as one wanted or could care to afford, there was much to see in both town and country, antiquities, architecture, sculpture, painting, not least the very face of the land itself with all its interesting variations, but all travel even on army service cost money. Then there was the rent of his comfortable rooms near the Lieverkai in Ghent which seemed always to be due. Certainly there would be a fee to come, and quite a substantial one, for the translation into English of Comte Hippolyte de Guibert's classical book on warfare and tactics which he had now almost completed, and surely some of the many sketches and drawings taken upon his travels would sell, especially if he could work them up from his extensive notes into a book of travelling anecdotes, a sort of sentimental journey in the fashion of Mr. Sterne. Money, he reflected, had always been difficult and his mind went back to the days when the thud of the Lancashire looms had brought a fortune to his brother William at Pendleton and nothing but loathing to himself. He had no mind for business and had told the family so. But money he must have and perhaps a change to a more settled career, though it might have to be a military one where his real experience would count. In this very year there were rumours of a war with the Turks, but Hapsburg man or not his head spiked on the gates of Constantinople would not make a becoming sight.

Perhaps there was a possible solution. Gossips in the Mess talked about the plan of His Highness of Liechtenstein-in-Saxony to buy remounts for his cavalry in England. A well-placed word or two in the right quarter, and Highness was by no means unapproachable, might result in a journey back home. There was also Baron Friedrich von der Trenck with whom he had talked much in Vienna, a soldier-diplomat who remembered his own entry into the Prussian Guards as a cadet of only 16, and at any rate it might be a priceless advantage to meet the Baron who would soon be in Ghent again, and seek his influence to set a way upon a new career. The Baron was certainly a man full of intrigues and notions: his knowledge of Britain and British ways was profound and in some quarters it was hinted that he was an agent in 'The Service'. There were vague rumours that he had helped an English colonel of Guards in the Austrian army to find a new career away back home. His thoughts ran on, stimulated by a good claret wine. The best of the cavalry horses, Leicester crosses with the Yorkshire Cleveland Bays, were still reared on the broad pastures of Leicestershire, and it might be that he could see once again old Doctor Burnaby, that diligent antiquary of Baggrave, and pay duty to Margaret Oldershaw, one of the pretty twin daughters of the eminent surgeon at Leicester. Relatives and friends there were in these Midland counties, and friends moreover of influence. It might be the means towards a new life, a commission perhaps for a presentable officer in the English forces or even a living in the Church, for which his constant reading in the classics would be no disadvantage, with money and the leisure for excursions, writing, painting and above all for the study of antiquity. In any event his experience in the construction of fortifications and his wide knowledge of all kinds of soils might ensure an appointment with the Board of Ordnance who were now improving the defences of the River Medway against the French, and who knows what relics of antiquity might not be found in digging in such a place, the ancient Gateway of England in the south east?

There were matters for careful consideration indeed, he thought, as Liselotte, chattering away, took the money for his wine. As he and his horse threaded their way slowly from the Grand' Place to the Place de Lille between draperies, food-booths, pedlars, dancers and mountebanks of all descriptions away down to the cavalry lines there came the clatter and squeak of the last wagons of the procession homeward bound, and outside St. Marguerite the last faint mutterings of an Ave to Notre Dame des Malades. Midnight sounded from the great cracked Bancloque, the monotone dying slowly over the fields, and a bugler blew for 'Lights out' along the lines. But *les chongs clotiers* stood out even brighter in the hard light of the Harvest Moon. It seemed a good omen for the future. In this mind he paid a round of imaginary social calls: the past and the future, the dream and the memory, all mingled together.

2

REALITIES: A NARRATIVE RECONSTRUCTED

JAMES, SON OF JOHN and Mary Douglas, was born on 7 January 1753 and baptised on 24 January of that year in the church of St. George, Hanover Square in the growing and fashionable London district of Mayfair. It was to be an interesting world into which the youngest Douglas child was carried in the hard frost of that winter day. It was the fourth birthday of Charles James Fox, and Fanny Burney was also a babe in arms. Goldsmith would not arrive in London for another three years, and barely a decade was to pass before Boswell met Johnson. Meanwhile there were Hume and Garrick and Gray, the fantasy of Strawberry Hill and the death of George II in the middle of the Seven Years War. The stars told well for this fortunate little boy, but it was perhaps prophetic that according to one almanac Mercury was then too close to the Sun for proper observation.

The famous and now more than ever fashionable St. George's built in 1724 by the well-known architect John James is still one of the most distinguished and well-cared-for churches of its kind, but the nearby houses of the nobility are now recalled only by the preservation of their names while the homes of the smaller gentry and prosperous tradesmen have with one or two exceptions long since disappeared leaving no trace even in the names of their replacements. A notable exception is Half Moon Street laid out in 1730 on the north side of Piccadilly where, according to the contemporary Rate Books, the only John Douglas registered in the parish lived and where there are still several good 18th-century terrace houses remaining. The street leads to the pleasant unsuspected hinterland of Shepherd Market.

Of the occupation and business residence of John the father of James Douglas there is no doubt. Local Poor Rate records, the Poll List of voters in the Outer Ward of St. George's, Hanover Square, at the by-election of 1749, and his own Will proved in 1766 describe him as a victualler or innholder of the *Hercules Pillars* in Hyde Park Road, or as it was sometimes called, Hide Park corner. It was a well-known inn, demolished in 1771 to make room for the Adams brothers' Apsley House, 'No. 1 London', now the Wellington Museum. Its reputation is preserved in Fielding's classic novel *Tom Jones* of 1749, for it was here that the irascible Squire Weston accompanied by his parson sought advice about lodgings while in pursuit of Sophia, his run-away daughter, and found the landlord 'an excellent third man' who over a bottle of wine 'could inform them of the news of the town, and how affairs went; for he knows a great deal since the horses of many of the quality stand at his house'. It was also described as a comfortable low inn where the horses and grooms of gentlemen were put up, a waiting-place for chairmen and as a well patronised resort of farmers and graziers. It was evidently profitable, and its income was sufficient to meet the payment of several family annuities bequeathed under the Will of John Douglas when after his death in 1762 it came into the legal possession of his widow, and the Will also mentions monies held by the eldest son and elsewhere, though there are no details. The testator was evidently not without considerable means. The name of the inn, derived from that of the twin rocks at the entrance to the Mediterranean at the Straits of Gibraltar, was not uncommonly given to inns situated as was this house on a main approach road to a town.

Mayfair, as its name suggests, was not without its lighter and popular side. James, as a small boy, could have watched the Guards in their riding-house, stables and grounds in Curzon Street. He could have seen, or heard talk of, the May Fair which lasted at least all the month of May, with its theatre, toy-men, jugglers, prize-fighters, mountebanks, the open-air cattle market, and the barbarous cruel sport of duck-hunting on a pond in Hertford Street. Before the notorious Shepherd Market was officially suppressed at the end of the century as a public scandal he may even have heard of the Frenchwoman of Sun Court who, lying naked on a bed supported an anvil on her breasts, singing loudly while two farriers brought from nearby White Horse Street forged on the anvil a set of horse shoes from red-hot iron. The butchers' and greengrocers' shops lasted for some years, and so did the periodical visits of Tiddy Doll in his white silk gold-laced suit whose famous gingerbread cake James may well have tasted. In his later years James was often to stay in Little Stanhope Street off Curzon Street where at its first rating in 1762 there were but three houses, and where only six more were to be built during the ensuing century.

The family was to be well recorded by later genealogists from information given largely, it would seem, by two particularly successful members. It was of the Morton branch of the distinguished Douglas house that Alexander, the first ancestor to settle in England, came in 1603 to Yorkshire as a supporter of James I on his accession to the crown of England. There followed his son Alexander, a Royalist of the Civil War, Thomas, a barrister-at-law in the reign of Charles II, whose fourth son John was to become in 1753 the father of our James. John is recorded in Burke's *Commoners* as having lived in the parish of St. George's, Hanover Square, and John Warburton, Somerset Herald recognised him in 1754 as a 'gentleman'.

As a small boy James also had the advantages of a pleasant country home. Some years before his birth his father had bought from the estate of an impecunious meadman, a close neighbour at Hyde Park Corner, the

Rook House 'or by what other name or names it was called or known' at Caldecotte Hill, then in Aldenham parish some three miles north of Harrow and just over the county boundary between Middlesex and Hertford- shire. The house and 13 acres of meadow and pasture cost £572 in 1744. It was the sort of small country estate which would appeal to a London tradesman, not too far from town in quiet and calm with wide views over heaths, woods and the Vale of St. Albans on one side and, on the other, in fine weather as far as the hills of Sydenham in Kent where later was to appear the glisten- ing Crystal Palace. It was a charming place and the greatest of contrasts to Shepherd Market and Mayfair, and even now as part of Bushey Heath it is hidden from the nearby M1 Motorway and the Watford by-pass. Could it be a coincidence that both owners were connected with the brewing trade, and they settled here to be near to the famous Aldenham School, a very old foundation endowed by the Brewers Livery Company? The remaining incom- plete Registers give no indication. The history of the property is recorded in deeds and documents owned by Mr. Eric G. Vasmer whose family has been established in the neighbourhood for many years.

The outline is clear. Here John Douglas died in 1762. By his Will, apparently undated, proved in Doctors' Commons and in the Prerogative Court of Canterbury on 13 May 1766 the Rookery estate was bequeathed to his wife Mary for her life. She was Mary Gardiner, daughter of a landed Surrey family—and this is perhaps why John Douglas, as we have noted, was described as a 'gentleman' by Somerset Herald in a Gardiner pedigree—whom he had married in 1731 and by her had nine children, three of whom survived, Thomas, the eldest, born in 1732, William, the seventh child, born in 1745, and James, the youngest, born 22 years after the marriage. The executors and administrators of the Will were Mary, Thomas and William Douglas, and it was proved by Mary and Thomas. Mary evidently died intestate within a short time after and Letters of Administration of her goods and property

were granted on 2 October 1766 by the Prerogative
Court of Canterbury to Thomas the eldest son described
as of the parish of St. George, Hanover Square. The Rook
House estate was let until Thomas sold it with 11 acres of
land in 1786 for £500 to a saddler who was also a parish-
ioner of St. George's, Hanover Square, and it so passed out
of the Douglas family. The subsequent story of the
property, which is not strictly the concern of this book,
is interesting. It was affected by the Enclosure Acts of
1800-03, and by 1820 had become part of the grounds
of the attractive Regency-style Berkeley Cottage which
is now in a sad state of repair. For many years the name
of the Rook House or the Rookery still appeared on
estate maps and in documents to denote the site of the
older establishment usually referred to as an old enclosure.

It is here necessary to say a little about James's brothers.
Thomas, the elder by 21 years, was originally engaged in
mercantile pursuits, and afterwards acquired considerable
property in Lincolnshire of which county he was High
Sheriff in 1776. He died in London in 1787 by which
time James was well advanced in his career, a career in
which Thomas was to have some influence. Of James's
cousins, the boy died on military service in the West
Indies while the three girls married into the nobility, the
army and the Church. Between James and his eight-year-
older brother William there was a closer relationship. At a
very early age William had been sent to Manchester by his
father as an apprentice in the cotton industry where he
did exceptionally well, became a noted manufacturer and
exporter of fustian, a cotton spinner and merchant, a
Constable of Manchester in 1780, and in due course
bought for his home the Old Hall at Pendleton where
he died in 1810. Both Thomas and William Douglas enter
the history of British cloth-making for they were the
leading members of the trade to give evidence against the
desirability of Sir Richard Arkwright continuing his
patents for yarn manufacture. In 1785 the letters patent
were set aside by the Court of King's Bench and although
Arkwright went on to build better and more important

mills all of the many existing machines which incorporated his hitherto patented features were freed of monopoly with very great benefit to the national trade. William's son John took success even further. He was a notable Old Boy of the Manchester Grammar School, became one of the original members of the Manchester Assembly Rooms, a Deputy Lieutenant for Lancashire, a banker, and as of Gyrn, Flintshire, was granted arms and became the subject of a main entry in Burke's *Commoners.*

When at the age of nine James was left without parents it would seem that William, although rather less than a decade older, but experienced in a hard Manchester business and the ways of the world and already in possession of part of his father's funds, undertook the responsibility for his brother's upbringing. He was to assist James, chiefly with money, almost throughout his life. On 5 August 1765 there was admitted to the Manchester Grammar School at the age of 12 'James, son of John Douglas, innkeeper of London, Middlesex'. There is no further information about James Douglas or his progress but this is not surprising as the records tend to concentrate on the careers of boys who went straight from the School to Oxford or Cambridge. It is abundantly evident, however, from the works he was to study and from those he himself to write later in life, that James Douglas benefited greatly from the high classical standards set by Charles Lawson the then High Master. Not only did he absorb the discipline of classical studies, valuable enough in its own right, but he also acquired an ease and great enjoyment in reading Greek and Latin texts, though such pleasures were not immediately to his advantage.

A background of classical learning was indeed useless in the Manchester trade to which James was now put under his brother. The clatter of the mills and the rigour of the cotton trade did not suit him, nor he it. According to private information given very many years later to David Elisha Davy who made manuscript collections for a parochial history of Suffolk in which county, at Kenton,

Douglas was to hold the vicarage (British Museum *Add. MS.* 19097), he was at first employed abroad in the business of William's manufactures but having abused the credit he had received for his expenses the arrangement was cancelled and he was left at Leghorn or elsewhere in Italy without resources. This would scarcely be surprising in view of the complete lack of a sense of money values which James was often to show later in his life. He was now reduced to such difficulty, it was said, that he offered his services to the Emperor of Germany and was employed for some time as a cavalry officer. There is no proof. Another account suggests that his family, recognising his inaptitude for a business life arranged for his admission to a military college in Flanders, most probably, at Ghent, whence he entered the Austrian army as a cadet in Vienna. The military records available in Brussels, Ghent, Malines and Vienna throw no light on any of these matters—while there are detailed records of the regular army there are none of the foreigners serving with it—but Douglas's own later writings provide evidence enough of his Flemish and Austrian travels (there is more than one reference many years later to the German Emperor's Collection of National Curiosities in Vienna), and for Flanders, its art and its antiquities, he retained a knowledge and an affection which lasted until his death. It was there, too, that he learned to exercise a considerable talent in his own pencil drawing, and kept well-filled notebooks which were to be of great use later on.

In the humdrum of the boy's Manchester life there was one important happening. Somehow he managed to gain the acquaintance of Sir Ashton Lever, a noted naturalist and ardent collector who was forming at Alkrington Hall a museum which on its removal to Leicester Square, London, in 1774 was to become one of the recognised sights of the Capital. James assisted with taxidermy and browsed among the varied collections of fossils, shells, stuffed birds and natural curiosities. The friendship thus started was to last until Lever's death in 1788. Lever in due course was to be the principal sponsor for Douglas's election to a Fellowship of the Society of Antiquaries and Douglas in his turn made many gifts to the Museum, particularly beads from graves at Ash in Kent, of fossils from the London Clay of the Isle of Sheppey in Kent, and of fossil teeth of mammoth and other extinct animals from the gravels of the Medway near Rochester. He was often to recall fossils in the Museum or Holophusikon as Lever called it when he wished to illustrate a point of research, and he lived long enough to deplore the disposal of Lever's treasures by lottery and the final public auction of 7,879 lots lasting 65 days in 1806 after the Trustees of the British Museum had refused their purchase. A devotion to natural history and especially to fossils and antiquities of all kinds remained with him all his life. It was during this period of his early life that Douglas found near the Castle Field in Manchester a piece of finely-decorated samian pottery which he was to illustrate many years later (Plate 30). Many other Roman relics, pottery, a tessellated pavement and coins came from this place which, he says, he visited occasionally. He and Bryan Faussett in East Kent some 35 years earlier must surely be the two earliest schoolboy archaeologists in Britain: by an amazing chance a few years later the younger was to make practical use of the discoveries and field-work of the elder.

Some uncertainty surrounds James Douglas's movements in the Austrian army but his life was far from uneventful. There was menace of war against the Turks and as he was to say later, he thought 'the possibility of my head grinning on the gates of Constantinople was not a very becoming sight'. It is said that he was sent on the orders of Prince John of Lichtenstein to England to buy remounts for the cavalry and once home he did not return. Again, no official records of his army career appear to be preserved in the places where they might be expected. But of two matters there can be no doubt. At Tongres, in 1773, on a long journey from Maestricht into the heart of Germany, the 20-year-old officer met the Abbé P. G. Van Muyssen, an established and well-known antiquary and collector, with whom he travelled and excavated in the richly-

furnished Roman barrows of the surrounding countryside
and with whom for many years he was to maintain a lively
correspondence and exchange of relics of antiquity. This
was the very satisfactory outcome of Douglas having
noted the barrows and Roman roads on approaching
Tongres and the frequent occurrence of fragments of
Roman pottery in a valley by the road side. The story is
told in partly fictional form in Douglas's own first book,
Travelling Anecdotes. And at about this same time in
1781 he translated into English as *A General Essay on
Tactics* one of the many works of a military writer,
Comte J. A. Hippolyte de Guibert. The original is a long
and learned work which was of considerable reputation
in its field: it is difficult to imagine, for anyone who has
had the good fortune to read them, that this could have
been the writer of the marvellous love-letters to Mademoiselle de Lespinasse.

The original book, with its review of the current political
scene and the art of war in addition to a detailed account
of tactics as exercised by the infantry, cavalry and
artillery, is full of highly technical matters. The translator
made an excellent job of his task; he followed the exact
sense both of a draft and of the published text; he also
put argument and instruction into a form which could
be understood by the English military authorities. Even
today it makes for interesting reading in the by-ways of
military study. The translation was both accurate and
competent, but Douglas under the pseudonym of 'An
Officer' excuses any inaccuracies which may have arisen
from his adapting French army regulations into recognis-
able English forms and pleaded in extension his long
distance from the press and that 'several Years Absence
from my Country in the Service of a foreign and distinguished military Power has been greatly injurious to me
in the sound Principles of my Mother Tongue'. He need
not have worried. By the time of its publication in
London in 1781, the translator was back in his homeland.
The book gained for him respect and a reputation in
military circles and, with his ability to draw plans no doubt

helped his subsequent employment by the Board of Ordnance and Corps of Royal Engineers at Chatham in Kent.

On his return to England, it is said, Douglas obtained a commission as a Lieutenant in the Leicester Militia. The Muster Rolls which would have contained his name do not commence until 1780. But on 22 October 1779 an Ensign by the name of James Douglas was commissioned in the Independent Company at Sheerness, Kent. In the Army List of 1779 in the Independent Company of Invalids at Dover it would seem, though it is not clear, that James Douglas was Ensign or Lieutenant by 2 November of that year. Yet by September 1779 Captain James Douglas by his own account had appeared on the staff of Colonel Debbieg at the fortification of Chatham Lines within a short distance of Sheerness. Again, his name does not appear in the early Commission Books of the Corps of Engineers or in any Registry of Warrants or records of Leave of Absence. There was friendly influence enough for him to have secured a commission in the Leicester Militia had he wished to do so: for the rest, family patronage, talk of his *Tactics* translation and his experience abroad could well have secured for him one of the new commissions in the Corps of Engineers.

The Royal Corps was officially established in 1787 from members of other military organisations, even from qualified civilians, and it quickly became a recognised branch of the service. At the beginning it was a Staff Corps composed of officers only and here Douglas would have met with no difficulty.

There was one other interesting happening not long after his return from the Continent. Douglas is sometimes erroneously described as a Master of Arts of the University of Oxford. In fact on 22 October 1777 'Jacobus Douglas Middlesaxiensis e Scholâ de Manchester annum agens vicesimum secundum admittitur ad mensam Sociorum' was in the words of the Admission Book admitted as a Fellow Commoner at Peterhouse, Cambridge. He matriculated in Easter Term in the following year but there is

no evidence in the books of the University that he ever
took a degree. 'He was a man of most varied talents' says
a later member of this College in an account of its
Members, and with that masterly understatement no one
can disagree. But what led this travelled student, mature
in age, a fine classical scholar and a military man of
experience and account, to seek entry at Cambridge at
such a time? Was it fear of a lack of success in a career
in the British army—there certainly looked like being a
period of peace, and consequently half pay for many
officers, not far ahead—or the hope of a soft option, a
financially helpful marriage and time for the comfortable
study of antiquity if he read for Holy Orders. All that
can be known for sure is that at Peterhouse he started to
prepare a book of what he called Travel Anecdotes and
that as the author of a book on sermons published in
1792 he described himself as of St. Peter's College,
Cambridge.

So much for reconstructed narrative. It is now time to
consider something of the broader realities.

The Peace of Paris had lasted for 12 years. The powers
of France and Spain moved by ambition and united in
perfidy had been almost everywhere frustrated, said a
member of the Government, and their fleets and armies
forced to return in disgrace. The Opposition declared that
Divine Providence was a powerful ally; there was still
unpreparedness, and the degeneracy and veniality of the
times were much· to be lamented. The Gordon Riots and
the cry of No Popery, the mobs 'committing the most
violent outrages, by forcing open, burning and destroying
private Houses and property, and publick Prisons, and
setting the Criminals and Prisoners therein at Liberty',
made advisable the adjournment of the Society of Antiquaries, so the Secretary recorded in his Minutes. But
learned life went on with discussions of such varied matters
as equal and apparent time, Hannibal's passage through the
Alps, the different modes of taking degrees in our two
Universities, the causes of hurricanes in the West Indies,
accounts of New Zealand, the cruelty of the slave trade

and, of course, criticisms of Virgil and Shakespearean obscurities. Drury Lane and Covent Garden presented full and attractive programmes, even in mid-winter: *School for Scandal* and *Fortunatus, Way to keep Him* and *Flitch of Bacon* gave variety to the fairly constant presentation of Shakespeare. Within London, life pursued a fairly normal course. In the previous year 16,500 children were baptised and 20,500 people died. Fever, old age, dropsy, smallpox, bad teeth and coughs took their toll, and in that order. There were no deaths from diabetes, rickets or scalded heads, but one from 'Rising of the Lights' and 10 people succumbed to grief. Many were found drowned. Deaths from over-eating and over-drinking were far out-numbered by those due to the French Pox. Only five murders had been satisfactorily detected.

At Chatham Dockyard in Kent a midshipman of the Royal Navy had caused the death of a sailor by beating him in a cruel manner and stabbing him with a sword, for disobedience. In the Yard fees, or bribes called fees, were the motive power. Security was tighter than it had been during the Seven Years War, but visitors with friends at court could still see the men-of-war in building, the vast rope house and sail-lofts, approve the long tiers of guns in storage and the pyramids of cannon-balls, and exclaim at the glowing fury of the furnaces in the smithy. Outside the Yard, in 1779, they could see, on the hill-top, the building of the Amherst Redoubt and repairs and additions to the earlier defences, a line of fortifications enclosing the peninsula of the Dockyard between the Chatham and Gillingham Reaches of the Medway, which were at last being undertaken as a result of public pressure of opinion. Many discoveries of antiquities had already been made here during the works of previous years often on the sites of army kitchens though the relics were not saved and now there were visible graves with decayed bones, rusted spears and swords, pots and glass vessels, Roman coins and the foundations of a Roman house with its brilliantly-coloured wall plaster, all discoveries which, thanks first to the benevolent interest of the Chief Engineer, Colonel

Hugh Debbieg, an irascible individual who delighted in fighting his own private war against the authorities had become a cadet-gunner at the age of 12, had, like Douglas, served in Flanders and in the East been on secret missions to France and Spain, all of which gave him a sympathy towards Douglas, were in due course to become important items in the published history of archaeology in Britain.

Fortunately Douglas realised the significance of the relics unearthed by labourers and soldiers in opening new ditches and throwing up bulwarks, and with his Colonel's agreement—'to whose liberal taste in literary pursuits I am indebted for the civilities with which he facilitated my discoveries', he thought it wise to say some years later (by which time the Colonel had become a Major-General) he supervised the excavations (Plate 5). By 1782 something like 86 barrows or levelled graves had been opened and their contents described and sometimes carefully drawn; measurements and notes of their relative positions were recorded in a field note-book. The relics all passed into Douglas's own hands. For the present he made records: speculation was to follow later in his lengthy writings. In all, if we may depend on later topographers such as G. A. Cooke in the 1819 edition of his *Pocket County Directory of Kent,* Douglas opened no less than 100 graves. The sites were along the ditches of the Lines fortifications and also on the hill-side now officially known as the Great Lines (Plate 5) a short distance north-east of the prominent Naval War Memorial. The scars of excavations, possibly those of Douglas's barrow-diggings, and some slight mounds, could still been from the air in 1941.

At the same time in Rochester Thomas Fisher, alderman and bookseller, had lately set up the first printing-press in his city. He had already become noted for two scholarly books, *The History and Antiquities of Rochester,* 1772, and *The Kentish Travellers' Companion,* 1776; his circle of antiquarian friends included John Thorpe the younger, 'on antiquarian topics almost an enthusiast' and later to edit the famous *Custumale Roffense,* Samuel Denne, a prolific writer, and Edward Jacob, the antiquarian, bibliophile and naturalist of Faversham. Not yet was his younger son born, the Thomas Fisher who was to work in the India House and become a pioneer in lithography and one of the most famous of antiquarian draughtsmen ever to work in Britain. Now to the sensibility and taste of this city well known for its literary climate and hospitality to travellers on the Dover Road was to be added Captain James Douglas of the Corps of Engineers, an expert engaged in the building of the new fortifications on Chatham Lines. Here, first at St. Margaret's and then in the comfort of a quiet and commodious house in the shadow of the Cathedral he thought much about the antiquities he had recently uncarthed at Chatham, found a wife, and between times made up the proofs of a travel book, which was shortly to be printed and published by his friend Thomas Fisher. This sojourn at Rochester, did he but know it, was once more to change his whole way of life.

From his house in College Yard—it no longer exists but was close to the well-known College or College Yard Gate, still the entry from the High Street to the cathedral precincts—Captain James Douglas moved easily to and from his professional work on the new fortification of Chatham Lines. The city of Rochester he found commodious and much to his mind in point of situation. Letters should still be addressed to him at the Office of Ordnance on Chatham Lines, he advises a friend, for his own letters can be officially franked and by that means he can save the cost of postage, an early example of the petty meanness which was to be a marked feature of his life. Now he began to collect and study in detail the many relics of antiquity discovered by the Engineers in the course of their excavations and to make skilled drawings of the most interesting items. More quickly he entered into Rochester and county society, making friends among the dilettanti, the clergy and the antiquaries. This is what Edward Hasted the well-known county historian had to say about him at that time (the letter is printed in John Nichol's Illustrations of the *Literary History of the*

Eighteenth Century, Vol. IV (1882), p. 58): '. . . there
have been many more Roman remains lately dug up at
the Lines at Brompton near Chatham, which I have just
had a relation of from the Engineer, Captain James
Douglas, who is just entered on the study of Antiquity,
and is as complete an Enthusiast as ever I met with in
my life; for he despises all the Romain remains in this
Country so late as Caesar's time, before which, you know,
there was none here. He seems beginning where he should
leave off, and talks much of criticising Bryan Faussett,
who was, I do think, as capable and learned a man in
that way as this country ever had, or will produce . . .'.

Hasted was a little generous in his tribute to Faussett
but he failed completely to understand the novel chronological points which Douglas with good sense was trying
to make and he obviously knew nothing of his scientific
curiosity. For his part, and even at a convivial antiquarian
dinner, Douglas found Hasted shy and withdrawn and
wondered whether 'perhaps in the walk [*sic*] of an antiquary visiting Kent' he had inadvertently given the
historian some unguarded offence. It is a pity that each
found the other to be tolerated rather than respected, but
Douglas was not alone in his inability to make friends
with the often ill-tempered Hasted.

The Engineer was also moving in an expanding and
wider social circle. On 6 January 1780 he married Margaret
Oldershaw, the twin daughter of John Oldershaw, M.D.,
an eminent surgeon of Leicester now settled in Rochester.
The marriage did not take place with ceremony in
Rochester as might have been expected but without the
benefit of a licence and in the presence of two frequently-
serving professional witnesses by John Jefferson, Officiating Minister, at the parish church of St. Marylebone in
London. Almost certainly it was a run-away match, the
circumstances of which and its possible Leicester connection can only be guessed at. She brought with her £1,000
worth of Government stock, but it was so carefully tied
up legally that her husband could not touch a penny.
Margaret's twin sister Martha became Lady (Richard)

Glode, wife of a wealthy Sheriff of the City of London and of Middlesex, one brother a doctor of medicine practising in Stamford, Lincolnshire, another learned and respected brother was to be appointed Archdeacon of Norfolk and a Fellow of the Royal Society: all were to give James Douglas much advice and material assistance in his later life.

In the same year that he was married, James Douglas Esquire of Stratton Street, Piccadilly—the London house of his well-to-do sister—was elected into a Fellowship of the Society of Antiquaries, the learned Society founded in 1707 and with a Royal Charter in 1751 which by its Statutes was empowered to elect a strictly limited number of 'Persons Excelling in the Knowledge of the Antiquities and History of this and other Nations'. He had the personal recommendation of his friends Sir Ashton Lever, Edward Jacob of Faversham, Colonel Robert Melville and Dr. Michael Lort, a well-known antiquary-about-town and a founder-member of the first Dining Club to be associated with the Society at whose meetings he was a most regular attendant. The meeting on 8 June 1780 at Somerset House at which Douglas should have been elected had to be adjourned as the Gordon Riots, with their gang of crazy and ferocious hooligans was reducing London to temporary panic. The Minute Book of the Society records that: 'The riotous & incendary Mobs, which with unrestrained Fury, and now subsisted for some Days, committing the most violent Outrages, by forcing open, burning & destroying private Houses & Property . . . & threatening further Mischief and Destruction to Collective Bodies, as well as private Individuals; the Vice-President . . . & other Members of this Society . . . thought it advisable under these Circumstances to adjourn to Thursday next, without entering upon Business'. George III, 'Farmer George', had not lost his nerve and by the following week matters were again normal. Douglas was elected and properly admitted with the formal words still in use, and for many years after until his personal fortunes decreed otherwise he regularly attended the

Society's weekly meetings, exhibited there a wide range of antiquities, read several papers to the assembled Fellows and communicated his discoveries and his thoughts, as was then the custom, in letters to the Secretary to be published in *Archaeologia,* the Society's Journal. His exhibits and communications included drawings of his own discoveries at Chatham and elsewhere, a silver object found near Penrith (described in the margin of the Minute Book 'Supposed to be a broach' and clearly from Douglas's fine drawing pasted in the Minute Book a remarkably fine 10th-century long pin penannular brooch) and two amulets, one of which had been worn by Mary, Queen of Scots. He read an important paper on the origin and significance of the 'brass Instruments called Celts', sent communications on the language of the Gypsies (here Douglas is described as 'Doctor of Divinity'), a Roman sword from Kingsholm near Gloucester, Roman remains from Kent and, quite outstanding for his time and the first study of its kind, remarks on the real significance of the bones of fowls discovered in Roman burials. More will be said about some of these contributions later in this book.

Here and there we find a more popular note. On 4 February 1785 he wrote to his friend Henry Godfrey Faussett: 'The Antiquarian Society is conducted on a very extensive plan and it is now become one of our most fashionable weekly rendésvous's. Instead of old square toes you now behold smooth faces, and dainty thin shoes with ponderous buckles on them'.

Those who have been honoured to act as Scrutators at an Anniversary Meeting of the Society of Antiquaries will enjoy reading a letter written on 25 April of that same year (see p. 204 for the letter in full):

> . . . we have had much serious business debated at our Society on this last Council election, and I was honored with a *Scrutatorship* and kept seven hours without my dinner casting up votes 'till my eyes struck fire and the colic seized my bowels for the want of food—this aerial repast you may say is bad for an hungry antiquary—but what of that, my zeal, my zeal! and o' my patience under such

affliction of long and fustian speeches. amply rewarded my labours—we set down at ½ past eight I should say 9 to a good dinner and plenty of wine carousing 'till ½ past one at the Devil tavern and as a certain wit replied on one occasion, that the Society *was broke up and gone to the Devil.*

Many of these letters, important for the sidelight they throw on the history of the Society, may be read in Part II of this present book. This occasion was the first Presidential election to be contested in the Society's already long and not trouble-free history. At the weekly dinners Douglas kept in touch with the leading antiquaries of his day, discussed publications of all kinds and exchanged information about current discoveries and theories. At all times he held the Society in great regard and when, with Council's approval, he withdrew one of his papers for publication elsewhere, he took particular care to say that 'I will ever hold it my duty however feeble the endeavour as a Member desirous of supporting a body of learned men by such testimony of zeal for their welfare, most cordially to communicate my discoveries'. In all he thus made eight communications, most of which had value.

3

TRAVELLERS' TALES

CERTAINLY AT ROCHESTER as he sat making up the pages of his travel book Douglas was perplexed and unsettled about his future. The Preface had been written, he says, in the retired precincts of a College in Cambridge; he will not write a second volume although a second had been promised, 'as my avocations are now of a more serious turn . . . Youth is sometimes permitted to risque many things which men, in riper years, have no plea for circulating'. More will be said later about his avocation, but meanwhile it may be noted that in 1783 he spent 10 days in London 'to get an iron out of the fire: the second volume of *Travelling Anecdotes*'. It never appeared and the signed preface to an edition of the first volume published in Dublin in 1787 explains why. On his return from abroad he had much leisure while at Peterhouse to amuse himself in scribbling over the desultory matters which perhaps he might too wantonly have circulated. The book was intended for certain persons who have leisure and who could afford the time for such digressions, people who had already been amused with its perusal. As he had been received with very great courtesy at the Court of Vienna he could not bring himself to circulate anecdotes which 'when related fancifully have a greater effect and perhaps a more pointed tendency than when gravely or methodically told'. He must be restrained by civility and a sense of gratitude. What the contents of the second volume were to be, we can but guess.

The *Travelling Anecdotes through various parts of Europe,* an octavo volume sold at six shillings, first printed and published in Rochester in 1782 by his good friend Thomas Fisher, appeared anonymously; in the second edition published in London in 1785 the author's name is printed as J.D., and thus it appeared in a third London edition in the following year. The book has character, a good deal of atmosphere, a little of scenery and history; its author was a humane and civilised person. There is certainly no deep insight, but here and there sympathy and imaginative touches suggest that the author was not prepared to put all on paper. Douglas makes good use of his own experiences in Flanders and Austria and sometimes of the experiences of others, basing fiction on fact. Although he disavows any Shandean manner, the stories of the *guinguette* on the road, Rose, the little country girl, of Poussine, a 16-year-old French nun, and of a stuffed buck rabbit mounting a hen in the Royal Menagerie at Brussels are hardly free of suggestiveness and a delightful veiled impropriety.

The nine plates which Douglas drew and himself etched are in a dark brown aquatint, relieved only by the red nose of a German postillion. An antique ring with an intaglio of Diomede which he bought from a Jewish pedlar for three ducats, a Roman coin, a plan of the city of Tongres (Plate 6) and a drawing of the ruins of the Roman station of Atuatuca (plate 7) there find place with modern, 16th-century Flemish and Greek women, a Swiss boy (Plate 8), the German postillion, a celebrated collector of antiquities, one Monsieur Varelst (Plate 9) who had not left his house for 14 years, and a curious Surinam toad in the Royal Menagerie. That the drawings are unselfconscious is not to say that they are graceless. Obviously they tend to be wooden and solid for the sake of the engraver, but they are from direct observation and carry conviction. The Swiss and the German have a vague feeling of Hogarth: just possibly Douglas could have seen Livesey's etchings for the *Peregrination.*

His own peregrination starts, of course, at Calais and proceeds by Lilliers (Lillers), Lisle (Lille) and Courtray (Courtrai) to Ghent, thence by Mell (Melle) and Aloest (Aalst) to Brussels, after which follow Louvain, Tongres, Maastricht and Aix. Travel over the 180 miles is by *diligence,* and the routes followed by these public stage-coaches were still indicated in the early editions of Karl Baedeker's handbooks. Douglas made many journeys in Flanders, as I have in following his travels, but most of his notes for this book were made in 1773 during the course of a long excursion deep into Germany. He was much at home at a village *kermesse* and knew

> *Nobilibus Bruxella viris, Antwerpia nummis,*
> *Gandavum laqueis, formosis Bruga puellis,*
> *Lovanium doctis, guadet Mechlinia stultis*

The allusions to the plight of Ghent, the pretty girls of Bruges, and the story of the citizens of Malines who tried to douse the moonlight shining into their cathedral with fire-pumps were already part of his wide appreciation of the Flemish background.

Here are his opening pages

> When an Englishman sets out to make his tour on the Continent, he closets himself up in the post-chaise, and sleeps to Dover; nay, it frequently happens—I have seen it myself—that he slumbers his passage over in the same vehicle. When he arrives at Calais, the first thing he enquires for, is, Bergundy from Mr. Dessein, and horses for St. Omers. If it is the first time of his *trajet,* he laughs at the *bidets* and postillions, and talks bad French with the master of the house; if the second, he shuts himself up in une voiture Anglais bien etoffée, and is dying of the hyp till his arrival at Paris, unless he meets with a countryman at the Hôtel de Bourbon at Lisle, and fancies the Burgundy excellent—I speak of the generality of travellers; who, by their fortune purchase ease at the expence of information and amusement. Sleep on then, my torpid countrymen!—lounge with ease in your voluptuous lined chaises.—I will mount the diligence, and study the spirit of the nation I travel through.—'Tis true, it has no such easy springs as those you swing upon—it jolts confoundedly; but what of that? Surely my ------- can bear it as well as the ----- of the Carmelite Nuns before me.

And as the rattling coach runs off the confounded pavé
on to the smooth sandy road towards Lilliers he begins a
gentle conversation with the nuns. La Briole and La
Fauvette, one of whom squeezed his hand—'perhaps she
was afraid of falling!' One of the nuns beguiled the time
spent in putting right a broken axle-tree with a long and
amusing story of Poussine, a beautiful and enchanting
16-year-old nun and her lover, a Franciscan friar who, by
most ingenious labour removed a stone, rescued her from
the dreaded punishment cell and took her to live in The
Hague where they were both respected 'in the first
companies'. It is a charmingly told little story, no less
attractive because it is not original and its source obvious.
A serious conversation about paintings and other art-
treasures in the churches of Flanders jogged along at the
same time. There is something very affected in frequent
quotations from authors, he remarks, and 'it is a species
of impertinence'. Yet how many there are in this short
book, and how many more sometimes even to the point
of boredom were to appear in his subsequent works.
But there was every excuse for passages of interest and
importance. More to the matter were his cutting remarks
about the young on the Grand Tour and their bear-leaders,
especially in the field of art. Of the Rubens Virgin—he
meant the celebrated altar-piece in the Rubens chapel at
St. Jacques in Antwerp—he had heard the talk of Sir and
his Leaders: '. . . It's a daub, the man was only painting
for money and not for fame—the Virgin is the portrait
of Rubens' kitchenwench—there is no sublimity in the
composition: and, instead of having a religious veneration
for the Mother of Christ, I should be thinking of the
fishmarket at Antwerp'. And so for 13 pages Douglas
words his disgust at the jog-trot connoisseurs.

His language is harsh and sometimes pompous, and
his remarks on the Grand Tour, essentially the completion
of a liberal education, are tinged with a querulous jealousy
which was to become more marked in his later years.
Perhaps he was unfortunate in his personal contacts with
the almost professional bear-leaders. He must surely have

known of and delighted in Walpole and Gray's famous Tour of 1739, and heard something of Lord Burlington's Tour in 1715 at the age of 20 with a band of servants, two personal artists and of course a bear-leader, from which he returned with more than 800 cases of pictures, antiquities, musical instruments and books. Richard Boyle, third Earl of Burlington, was to become one of the greatest and enlightened patrons of learning and the arts in early Hanoverian times. The early Burlington House, his family seat in London, and the delightful villa at Chiswick in the design of which he collaborated with William Kent, are his memorials, and Douglas must have known well enough the primary sources of Lord Burlington's inspiration. Certainly in the 18th century there were notable critics of the Grand Tour, Adam Smith and Lord Chesterfield among them, but their castigations were rather against a lack of experience among the young travellers and, of course, against harlotry and Popery. With Douglas, on the other hand, criticism was loaded with envy.

But this was not all. There had to be a long and pompous sermon to English travellers. It was written partly tongue-in-cheek, with the inaccuracies and inconsistencies in orthography and spelling which were ever to mark his work. Let us borrow his 'species of impertinence'.

> When your equipages arrive in a town on the Continent, the rascals of trades-people, and much greater knaves of inn-keepers, are laying plans to plunder you; and troops of famished wretches, devoted to any office that travellers think proper to employ them upon, like starved Tyrolian wolves prowling for rapine, surround you on every side—for they conceive your riches to be immense, and your ostentatious extravagance still more excessive: they first flatter you on the known liberality of your character as Englishmen, and then they subscribe in the most servile manner to all your absurd ridiculous caprices. The police and shop-keepers have in pay the scoundrels of lay-lackays, who surround your hotels; the former to learn your history (perhaps) from your thick-headed looby of an English valet, who probably may smatter just enough of the language, to perplex you on all occasions; and the latter, to cozen you in their boutiques, where you pay cent. per cent. more than the natives. The inhabitants

of distinction invite you into their circles fo filch you at their card parties.—A pert coquet, of some beauty and fashion, shams an intrigue with you, to wheedle you to lose your money at piquet; who, while you are racking your imagination to tell her some dull story, and to play off some piece of gallant witticism, is counting her game, and under the mask of nonchallant badinage, studying how to capot you. You suffer your purses to be drained with a grace, in hopes of acquiring the name of Madame's *bien amiê*; while the hussey smiles at your bad imitation of foreign intrigue, and supremely ridicules your English *fadaise*. She will admit you to her toilet in the morning, when you may see her in dishabille; and, because the customs of your country are more discreet and becoming than foreign ones, you fancy, that a nasty creature's dressing room, will furnish you with a story, to display your gallantry when you return from your travels.

Men, who have been trained from their earliest infancy, under the hands of a *frisseur,* to wear their bags, solitaires, and brocades, with magnanimous dignity, look contemptuously on your affected ease in the manœuvres of your snuff boxes, and your awkward carriage in sporting your persons.

Do not, therefore, my dear countrymen, when you travel for improvement; and when you should travel as respectable representatives of a body of people; who, as long as ever civil society has been known to flourish, have been courted and esteemed, do not attempt to imitate any other nation than your own; you have virtues and refinements among yourselves, sufficient to render you compleatly amiable as men; and understandings, to put you on an equality with the most enlightened of mankind; in short, you have talents within yourselves, when properly exerted, which command the esteem of all the world: let the end then of your visits among foreigners be, to enhance the blessings of your own country; to glean that species of information, which may teach you how to prize the comforts you possess at home; and by learning the distinct qualities of men, to secure to yourselves private happiness, that may last you all your lives; to bring back with you the laws of different empires; politics to serve your king in a national exigency; improvement in the arts to benefit your countrymen; and an universal benevolence to carry you through life without rubs to yourselves, and with happiness to those who have any commerce with you. Suffer not the light character of Frenchmen, the absurd hauteur of the German Baron, of the sixteenth generation, or, the vain-glorious insolence of a romantic Italian, to brand you with ridicule.—If you perceive virtues in either, that will mend your hearts, or be of national benefit in the application

of them to your country at large—treasure them in your
memory: but leave their vices where they were first engen-
dered, to secure to you that ascendancy you have always
had over them: for, by these exotic acquisitions, you return
home with a poison more fatally administered than by the
hands of your enemies:—and which, in succeeding commotions
with your neighbours, will be a remote conquest, which you
have drawn upon yourselves. Show yourselves therefore
liberal, but avoid the character of magnificent fools; whose
greatness is only manifest in the superior faculty of squander-
ing riches, more profusely than the natives you are associating
with.

I have seen you laughed at, and my heart has bled for
you. I have seen, when your backs have been turned, an
insolent foreigner speak with contempt of you, who has
flattered you with a most egregious irony of praise before
your faces. Assert your solidity of character, and even your
deficiences in the agremèns, with an Englishman's dignity.
Consider your characteristic qualities in a physical sense; do
not balance them against those of the foreigner; and, believe
me, that your natural character, joined with your early and
substantial educations, will make you ever respected. — But
O, my countrymen! suffer not your fame to be tarnished with
the affected imitation of foreign buffoonery, and the cursed
folly of boasted extravagance.

Then there are several lightly-drawn word sketches of
people seen by an artist's eyes. Character, in words, is
scarcely his strong point: he is himself a shade too amiable
and at 20 years of age perhaps a little too impatient to
observe with an acute personal detachment. The diminu-
tive landlord has a long scarlet plush waistcoat with
sleeves reaching below his knees, the arthritic Monsieur
Varelst—of whom there is the striking picture we have
already noted—in his silk bedgown, a white beribboned
nightcap with a tuft of real Brussels lace on its summit, a
cravat with the same kind of lace at its knot and ruffles
of the same high quality. His dress never varied and as he
regarded the open air as quite fatal he had not been outside his house for 14 years and spent all his time with his
remarkable cabinet of paintings and antiquities which he
loved to show to visitors. Then the *diligence* was joined
by Rose, a pretty country girl who parted in tears from

her mother and sisters. The narrator in his kindly way used the excuse of seeing a Swiss boy with his fiddle and performing marmoset—the boy whom he had sketched—to draw her into a friendly conversation, and she showed him a parting-present from her lover, a tooth-pick of ivory. They held hands, kissed warmly, and afterwards, since 'I could not again make her sprightly' the narrator fell to musing on the beauty of the unusual carved ivory case and, of all things he might have chosen, on the situation of the Portus Itius of the Romans. It must be at Calais, he thought, not at St. Omer or Boulogne and his musings here put in a long footnote were to be used again as part of an antiquarian dissertation 14 years later. But Douglas can be tender enough in his feelings when the occasion demands. At Aloest he had witnessed the execution of a boy on a stone gallows for stealing a coat of his master in which he intended, as a jest, to visit his mistress to whom he was to be married the following day. ''Tis true, we have not many thieves but we have many executions to deter them' said a bystander, a decent odd-looking quiz of a mechanic. The author said he was not ashamed to shed tears and felt that the memory could only be alleviated by a good application of a flesh brush. It was a *trepas* which did not reflect honour on humanity. Even under bright clouds the present day road at Aalst, long and straight lined with car-breakers' yards and the factories and ribbon-development at nearby Hofstade, belie the centuries of history evinced by the Grote Markt and the unhappily ruined church of St. Martin with its famous Rubens and a magnificent early 17th-century tabernacle and, what ought to have appealed particularly to Douglas, an epitaph by Erasmus.

Inevitably there are military anecdotes, and in view of Douglas's professional background it would be surprising if there were not. There is mention of Prince Charles's famous Guard of Hussars in Brussels, of the manoeuvres of the Austrian Les Rois regiment drawn up on the Square in Ghent with discipline and severity, defenders

of their own country of course and not wanton butchers
of an enemy of their own creating—'ah! ah!, excellent
apology indeed'. A French officer describes on the spot
the seige of Lisle, citadel, bastion, hornworks and the rest
with details of Vauban's systems of defence. He wanted
glory, not commerce, but Douglas, tongue-in-cheek again,
argues well for trade and does not come off badly.
Prussian officers on a recruitment campaign profess to
admire the English army but a dialogue between them and
a travelling English Colonel turned out to be but a poor
dish of military discourse.

Fact and fiction built on it are now more than ever
intermingled. There is a background of good antiquarian
learning and appreciation against which the antics of a
surly English Colonel of Infantry who shared the travellers'
barouche from Louvain to Maastricht are set in light
relief. Near Tongres Douglas recognised the well-preserved
track of a Roman road raised clear above the fields and
tried to interest the Colonel in Roman tactics but he,
who scarcely comprehended the formation or duties of a
squadron of cavalry, persisted in chattering to the point
of boredom of tactics at the Battle of Lausselt in which
he had been engaged. He meant the Battle of Lawfeld
or Laaffelt south-west of Maastricht where in 1747 the
French secured a victory over the Allied forces of
Dutch, British auxiliaries and Austrians under the command of the Duke of Cumberland. At a critical moment
some British regiments were thrown into disorder as the
Dutch in the centre of the line gave way and Cumberland
had to retire on Maastricht, the British cavalry sacrificing
themselves to secure the protected retreat of the infantry.
At this distance of time one can feel some sympathy
with this veteran Colonel of Infantry and his criticism of
the way in which the battle was fought; he would have
approved, one likes to think, of the stone cross with its
inscription in Gaelic (or Erse) to the memory of the
Irish Brigade which fought with the Allies erected in 1964
on the site of the battle, and he would have enjoyed, as
one can still enjoy, a walk across the heights of Herderen

towards the once-fortified villages of Vlijtingen and
Laaffelt and so to Maastricht, reconstructing in his
mind's eye the course of the battle and the retreat.
Douglas saw some large barrows at a distance from the
road—possibly they were three of the Roman barrows at
Tirlemont or, as seems much more likely, the two massive
barrows at Koninksem (Plate 10), the larger some 52 feet
in height and 140 feet in diameter, which are still outstanding features in the landscape—and much to the
Colonel's disgust, delayed the barouche to. make a visit
of inspection. Perhaps the Colonel would have viewed
the proceedings with more interest had he known that
the barrows were pillaged by French soldiers in 1747.
What Douglas wanted was the 'rummaging of the inside
of a *hypogeum* or hanging with greedy veneration over
a fragment of some Roman pot . . . I thought we had
sprung a mine'. In the event the Colonel regained his
patience and Douglas found his wish. At Tongres they
made acquaintance with a sociable Abbé, a fictional
character based upon the famous Abbé Van Muyssen who
was to become one of Douglas's good friends, who
took them home to view his collection, 'a few bagatelles'
as he called it. The meeting is worth recording in full:

> It was morally impossible to contain myself any longer:—
> Now, Colonel, you see the famous town of Tongres—it had
> no effect—he was enumerating the regiments and commanders
> names who were employed in the battle.—Then, confound
> me, if I ever mention the battle of Lausselt again, was it to
> save your heart from bursting with choler or impatience.
>
> It is a common saying, when a man is desirous of finding
> the thing he is immediately in want of, that the said thing
> is not to be found; or else takes him a plaguy long while
> in seeking after; the following incident will show that there
> are exceptions to this rule.
>
> No zealous Catholic, whose soul was on the brink of
> eternity, was ever more desirous to see an Abbé, than I was
> at Tongres.—The very instant the Barouche stopped to change
> horses, I enquired with a most rapid emphasis for one: my
> enquiry was addressed to a little dry looking man, who was
> standing close to the carriage to reconnoitre our persons; he
> was dressed in a reddish brown coat, with short powdered

hair curled tight up to his neck.—I had no sooner mentioned the word Abbé than a similar impetuosity sprung up in his countenance.

'Monsieur wants an Abbé', says he making a half flexion of a bow. Before I could put my enquiries into some form, I that instant perceived that I had addressed myself to the very being I was in search after—for a blue binding above his stock, convinced me that he was the very man. He desired to know my *business*; whether some religious office he had to perform—'a la confession, peut-être?' The very thing, I said to the Abbé, smiling.

But my smile was too ironical to give weight to the answer.—The Abbé said, he was willing to serve me, and once more desired to know my business.

I prefaced my discourse, by observing, that as persons of his cloth, were in general possessed of liberal knowledge, and therefore informed of many particulars which escape the ignorant multitude, I presumed to address him on a subject which related to the old town of Tongres—here, I remember, he fixed a most penetrating look on me, and I am sure, in three seconds of time, he distinctly surveyed the whole features of my face. To finish my preliminary chapter, and not to belye my first answer, I confessed to him, the great desire I had to find a person, who had taste enough for antiquity, to survey the spot where the ancient town of Atuatuca stood.

'Aça', exclaimed the Abbé, drawling out the last syllable as long as the inflation of his lungs would permit him,—'Monsieur est Amateur'.

We shall not arrive at Lausselt, cried the Colonel, if you dangle after that Jacobite-looking scoundrel—with a promise of only staying until the horses were put to, I prevailed on him to follow us.

The little Abbé, with the most eager and satisfactory look in the world, led us into a clean, but small house, which we traversed to his study; where, by books and loose papers I saw lying on the table, I was well persuaded he merited the compliment I had just paid to his learning . . .

He opened his Cabinet—Just Heavens! what are the feelings of the Dilitanti!—urns, vases, lachrymatories, paterae, fibulae, coins, &c &c, burst on my enraptured sight—it was richer to me than the Duke of Tuscany's cabinet, or all the cabinets in the world—for I had been so pleasingly wound up for it . . .

At that instant, I would not have changed station with a king, an emperor, or a perpetual dictator of the whole universe, were I to have sacrificed the delightful sight which appeared before me.

What Douglas would have said of later discoveries such as that of a fine barrow of a second-century artist fully equipped with all his treasures, furniture and professional equipment excavated in 1898 at Herne-Saint-Hubert-les-Tongres, and the subsequent scientific analysis of his remaining paints and pigments, can only be imagined. How greatly, too, would he have appreciated Maurice Frère's paper on the Tungrian collectors and collections in *Tongres Point de Recontre Romain* (1958) which accompanied an exhibition of outstanding local archaeological material in that year. Most of all he and the Abbé Van Muyssen would have enjoyed an evening stroll round the newly-exposed Roman town walls, considering the excavation of a military barracks outside the town walls, viewing the lines of an impressive Romano-Celtic temple with its characteristic square portico already in existence in the first century and restored in the second, and arguing in a friendly way about the significance of the god there honoured, whether Mercury of whom fragments of a statue were found, or Jupiter represented by pieces of a Giant's Column emblematic of the triumph of light over darkness, or life over death. But the skill and assiduity of Professor Merten's recent excavations, his much-admired reconstruction drawing, and a sight of his plan as compared with their own would have left them speechless.

> There passed by the room door, a clean and pretty black-eyed *grisette*, whom the Colonel espyed, and with an oath exclaimed, there's a piece of modern rarity, worth all your coins or Roman antiques, as you call them! If I had, continued he, all the curiosities of the world, I would not freely part with them for a kiss of the Parson's maid. The Colonel, who spoke only an atrocious German, bounced after her. At that moment the embarrassed Abbe opened his cabinet.

There followed long conversations on antiquity, on painting and, rather surprisingly, on the medicinal qualities of the mineral springs at Tongres which were known to Pliny: the Fontaine de Pline in the Park is indeed still visible. Much of this Douglas was to use later in his major

work, *Nenia Britannica*. Then came a promenade round
Tongres (Plate 11), the Roman station of *Atuatuca* (still
to be warmly recommended), of which Douglas made a
plan and a sketch, and a sly dig in a nearby barrow.
Surprisingly he makes no mention here of the magnificent
Gothic basilica of *Onze Lieve Vrouw* which he admired
greatly. The more modern statue of Ambiorix, leader
against Caesat's troops in 57-54 B.C., mounted on a mock
megalith (Plate 12) might well have appealed to his fancy.
The Van Muyssen collections unfortunately do not grace
the present magnificent Provincial Gallo-Roman Museum
at Tongres—they were sold in Amsterdam in 1788 for
only 800 francs—but the contents of the Museum give the
visitor of the present day an idea of what riches the collections may have contained. A tree-clad barrow with its
typical conical profile at Piringen (Plate 13) close to
the Roman road from Tirlemont to Tongres is still to
be seen and there are traces of an old excavation in
its side, probably it was that made by Douglas but
French troops here in 1747 also looted barrows for
treasure. Nearby is the 'Beukenberg', the Roman aqueduct, a prominent feature in the landscape and its
route now lined with beech trees, which surely cannot have escaped Douglas's eye though he does not
mention its existence. The Colonel still wanted to see
his battlefield but they stayed late in the evening until
the horses were put to. Then by moonlight and after
much good hock the party was on its way to
Maastricht, singing with the roar of sound health, good
lungs and true vigour until the Colonel fell asleep and
Douglas a-musing. Had the journey been in daylight they
could not have failed to see another fine Roman barrow
on the line of the Roman road near Herderen, the road
which the barouche followed. It is still visible and worth
seeing, just inside the entrance to a private park on the
north side of the modern main road almost opposite Hove
Malpertuus, where Yvo Molenaers cooks one of the best
dishes of Croque-Monsieur in Belgium. Douglas could not
sleep. This extraordinary letter addressed 'To the spirit of

the great Camden' and much seasoned with the humanity of archaeology as we know it was the result:

Maestricht

I am heartily glad of this opportunity of testifying my peculiar happiness in having a friend like yourself, who has a taste for antiquity, and whose bosom is at all times a sanctuary for the foibles of a fellow creature—foibles—wherefore foibles?—surely the name is unjustly applied.—Is not the world to blame, when it derides the pursuits of men which help to fill up the dreary vacuum of life, and conduct them smoothly thro' all its strange meanders?

I grant that antiquity is an useless study, unless it tends to throw light on ages, from whence little or no information has been handed down to us; unless it impresses some awful truth, illustrative of the virtues of past ages; a monument of their vices, or a record of their customs, which may serve the moderns as a model to imitate, or an example to steer clear of.

Wherefore should we pore with wonder and immoderate regard over some antient remain, without reason for the pleasure we feel? The mind may be amused: but this argues puerility. But when the laws, customs, virtues, and vices of remote ages, do constitute part of our studies; when we select those materials from the ruins of vast empires, which point out to us those errors which occasioned their overthrow; when they thus become the awful monitors of a succeeding people; when by their fatal example they show them how to establish a more permanent existence; when they amend their legislature, and confer that salutary knowledge, which could not possibly be other ways attained; the veneration for antiquity becomes respectable and highly beneficial to society.

The faculties of men are capable of expansion; and they are fruitful in their inventions, but their lives are of too short a period to bring their plans to perfection; — by selecting therefore the useful from antient vestiga, they can in part make amends for the shortness of life, and produce to their companions in society, the happy effects of their own industry, and the united labours of a once flourishing people —examples of virtue for the happiness of the individual, and a combination of useful knowledge for the general welfare.

The reflecting antiquary when he views the dilapidated altar, recalls to his mind the sane or depraved government of the Emperor to whose memory it was erected; he praises or condemns the most striking passages in his life; and he endeavours by his example to amend his own heart, or to propagate to his brethren a species of knowledge to awaken their feelings as patriots, or to stimulate their actions as men,

Here a coin enables him to throw splendour on the historic page, or a variety of other reliques to correct the wandering spirit of a Godfrey of Monmouth, and to transmit to the world those data from whence truth and information may be drawn.

The mind of man is prone to the marvellous, and dwells with a secret pleasure on things that are deeply concealed within the womb of time; hence some men are fond of courting dark and mysterious things, without other aids than the strength of their own imaginations; of these, we may say with Plautus

> . . . piscari in ære,
> Venari autem rete jaculo in medio mari.

Simple and plain truth is not their reward; but in its stead, they array the insubstantial vapour they have caught in a plausible form, which circulates abroad, bewildering the rigid enquirers after truth, and furnishing matter of ridicule to less serious investigators.

I have sent you a plan and drawing of Atuatuca, or Aduatica, Tungrorun, or Tongres. [See Plates 6 and 7.] The drawing represents the ruins of the walls. You must not rely on the accuracy, since my few hours grubbing on the spot would not admit of a Stukeley's precise investigation, or the classical detail of a Whittaker's *Mancunium.*

Atuatuca derives its name from a castle, which I conjecture from Caesar's expression, to have been built by the Tungri, or Eburones, before Caesar's conquest of that people; it is situated on the banks of the little river Jecker, about 10 miles W. from Maestrict, and as many to the N.W. from Liege. Like the station at Manchester, Chesterford, and Ivelchester, it seems to have had its angles rounded; as near as I could well judge by my eye, it concenters upwards of fifty acres of ground, and is of the parallelogrammic form. Vegetius describes the nature of these works to be more beautiful, as they approach in their length to a third more than their breadth: Atuatuca, if my eye has not deceived me (for I had no time to measure it) greatly partakes of this property.

The town plan recorded in recent excavation by Professor J. Mertens for the Service national des Fouilles has yielded vastly more information than Douglas's few hours of grubbing: but Douglas was not wholly inaccurate.

The author continues his Anecdotes with some remarks on the pharo-table at Aix-la-Chapelle where the stakes ran high, but has nothing to say about its famous hot baths, sweating-chambers and cold plunges despite his interest in the mineral waters of Tongres. Viscount Bolinbroke had been there in 1723, Robert Clive in 1768, and here was another travelling Englishman given this advice by his doctor:

> I bid him go into the country out of the sight of any women and find out some very cold spring or river where he should first plunge overhead, then put on his shirt, coat and hat to prevent catching cold from the wind and air and sit up to the waist for an hour at least, night and morning, and for a month drink nothing but milk twice a day sweetened with sugar of roses; at noon eat well-roasted mutton with cold salets, as cucumbers, lettice, purstane etc and drink nothing but spring water with a little claret wine and at night wrap up his whore-tackle in a linen cloth wet in strong vinegar and claret wine, and so to sleep.

This treatment was a successful specific against the French disease but Douglas, whose official tastes forbade him even to hang paintings depicting female nudes on his walls, could scarcely be expected to add such matters to his *Travelling Anecdotes.* His book ends with a little tail-piece about the love affairs of a young Prussian officer.

The *Anecdotes* attracted considerable attention and were well received. Reviews were favourable and despite the high price of six shillings, sales were good. There were one or two querulous voices. A titled Antiquary asked the Director of the Society for the author's name as the book was not without some merit and this was the first writer who had courage enough to hint at the not very amiable character of the King of Prussia. In the *Monthly Review* an anonymous reviewer thought it showed learning, some knowledge of the world. It was affected and fantastic but sentiment was sometimes hit off very happily, and one or two stories were told with vivacity and acuteness. The author, he supposed, was a person of fortune, of some distinction and perhaps superior to the general run of dealers in travels, tours, etc. With great propriety he might rank among the 'mob of gentlemen who write with ease'. In fact the *Anecdotes* had nothing in common with *Paradise Lost.*

It is easy to criticise the book for what it is not. Here was no Boswell on the Grand Tour, but the present-day reader must nevertheless regret that there is relatively little of Douglas's own reactions to the landscape and topography of the country through which he passed, no word of the art and antiquities of Courtrai, Ghent, Brussels and Louvain, matters on which he was well qualified to speak. The change of horses and a long wait at Courtrai, for example, took place within sight of the magnificent church of Nôtre Dame, the outstandingly fine Belfry and the Béguinage, but of these remarkable old buildings there is no mention. But had he been gifted with foresight how greatly he would have appreciated such modern excavations as at Tongres, the antiquities museum and the Roman remains under the Grand Bazaar at Courtrai, still more the archaeological museums of the University of Ghent, and the Cinquantenaire in Brussels. The travel journal had become a sort of minor novel but it was, after all, intended only as a book of *Travelling Anecdotes,* and as such it happily succeeds.

4

THE COMPLETE ENTHUSIAST

TO THE CAPABLE AND LEARNED Bryan Faussett of whom Hasted had spoken we shall return, but we may digress for a few moments to consider briefly the wide literature of Anglo-Saxon antiquities which, in addition to its particular appeal to Faussett and Douglas, had in its own right a subjective interest. It is not in any way lessened by the fact that such relics were not at the time of their discovery attributed to our Germanic forefathers. While the mosaic pavements of Roman villas and circles of standing stones were familiar enough sights to the early topographers as they surveyed the countryside of Britain, the travellers were also acquainted with the coins, rusty spears and swords, the crumbling shield-bosses and the brooches which in some numbers were to be seen in the cabinets of their hosts, but which to their eyes were only further relics of the Roman or the Celt.

Perhaps the earliest record of Saxon relics is that contained in the Chronicles of Roger of Wendover, the first established historian of the Abbey of St. Albans, wherein is described the opening by the monks of St. Albans of one of a group of burial mounds called 'Hills of the Banners' in the village of Redbourn. One of the mounds was traditionally regarded as the burial-place of St. Amphibalus, the popular name being derived from the religious processions which in consequence gathered there and when the explorations of the monks uncovered a grave containing a human skeleton accompanied by iron weapons, it was at once adjudged to be that of the Saint and the bones carefully removed to the sanctuary of the Abbey. The event took place perhaps as early as A.D. 1178, and it is indeed interesting to wonder how far the contents of many a medieval reliquary may have come from a similar source.

It is in the stately prose of Sir Thomas Browne that we find the earliest mention of Saxon jewellery. 'Great examples grow thin', he remarks in the Epistle of May Day, 1658, which opened his *Hydriotaphia, or Urn Burial,* and the examples which he 'fetched from the passed world' to illustrate his essay came in fact from a Saxon cemetery found in a field close to his home at Old Walsingham in Norfolk. There were between 40 and 50 burial urns, one of which probably survived in 'Tradescant's Ark', the collection which in 1677 formed the basis of Elias Ashmole's bequest to the University of Oxford. The urns contained burnt bones, decorated combs, and 'handsomely wrought like the necks of Bridges of Musical Instruments, long brass plates overwrought like the handles of neat implements; brazen nippers to pull away hair . . . and one kinde of *Opale,* yet maintaining a blewish colour'. To Sir Thomas these were an eloquent reminder of the power and culture of Rome, but his reflections towards the end of his essay do not altogether exclude the claims of the Danes and the Saxons. For our part, we can quickly recognise in the relics the furnishings of a typical Anglian cremation cemetery, characterised by cruciform or square-headed brooches with prominent bows and elaborate decoration.

The same view was taken of objects unearthed in the barrows dug at an excavation party in 1730 at Chartham on the chalk downs of East Kent. The gathering itself, encouraged by the interest of a well-known country squire of his day, Charles Fagge of Mystole, was a remarkable one, for the digging was supervised by Cromwell Mortimer, a Charter Fellow of the Society of Antiquaries in 1751, an 'impertinent, assuming empiric physician' who became the second Secretary of the Royal Society, and it was eagerly watched by a 10-year-old boy called Bryan Faussett who was to distinguish himself in later years as a zealous antiquary and collector of the finest of Anglo-Saxon antiquities known until the discovery of the treasure at Sutton Hoo. Mortimer compiled a bland and laborious narrative of the proceedings; it is of note for the earliest detailed description of a piece of Saxon jewellery found in Britain, and both Faussett and Douglas were later to make use of the account in their own works. By a fortunate chance an excellent coloured drawing of the Chartham antiquities (Plate 14) was made some years later by Faussett's son and added to the blank pages at the end of his father's excavation Journal.

Bryan Faussett and his antiquarian researches deserve more than a passing reference. He was born at Heppington near Canterbury in 1720, and despite what might be inferred from his presence at Mortimer's digging at Chartham he was in no sense an infant progidy; indeed his only claim to notice in his early days seems to be that he survived being thrown on the nursery fire by a pet monkey. At Oxford he left a reputation as 'the handsome Commoner of University [College]', and little else, but here he acquired a taste for genealogy and skill in the art of heraldry, both of which, together with the care of his collection of some 5,000 coins, occupied much of his time when, at the age of 30 and without a benefice, he came home to live again in Kent. His real introduction to archaeology in the open air came on a midsummer Sunday evening in 1757 when, with the rector of Crundale, he walked to Tremworth Down in the latter's parish to observe the site of a Roman burial-ground mentioned by one of the Kentish topographers. The parish clerk, who had been employed as a labourer to assist in the uncovering of the graves some 50 years earlier remembered their location, and by nightfall had been set the germ of that enquiring and enthusiastic spirit which, in the next 16 years, was to be responsible for the opening of more than 600 graves and burial-mounds in East Kent.

In all Faussett's explorations there is evident a diligent quest for knowledge, and we do well to remind ourselves how much we owe to his careful and painstaking observations, manifested by his unfailing habit of keeping a daily Journal of work. His sense of mindful appreciation was acute. There is also a great deal that we now find entertaining. The hurried opening of as many as 28 graves in one day and nine barrows before breakfast to avoid spectators, as he did at Bishopsbourne, is not according to the modern archaeological book; and we smile at his encouragement to his workmen '. . . persuasion, and a little brandy, without which nothing, in cases such as the present, can be done effectually'. A nice literary style reflects the country background of this Journal which was kept by Faussett between the years 1757 and 1773 under the title of *Inventorium Sepulchrale.* In his simple but charming prose, a sword-pommel is the 'size of a middling walnut', a chain the 'thickness of a crow's quill', and fragments of iron the 'size of a goose-quill', but the records are exact enough in their way. And it does not under-rate their value to say that the author did not recognise among his treasures remains of the Saxons. To him they were tokens of Britons Romanised or Romans Britonised.

The famous collection of jewels, weapons and trinkets (Plate 15)—it contains some 400 jewels alone at a rough computation—remained for three generations in the Faussett home at Heppington, strictly tied by the terms of Bryan's will so as to be of no use to anyone, and almost forgotten. It was at one time offered to the British Museum but the then Trustees were unable to consider its purchase, and at length it was acquired in 1850 by Joseph Mayer, a liberal and wealthy Liverpool goldsmith, who presented this remarkable collection of arts and antiquities then valued at £80,000 to his native city. In recent years this unique collection has been cleaned and properly drawn at Oxford under the superintendence of Professor and Mrs. Christopher Hawkes, and it is much to be hoped that the rumour of its adequate publication in one of the new British Academy series of Reports proves to be correct. Although it is not strictly germane to the purpose of the present book it is worth noting that several letters from Charles Roach Smith to Mayer still preserved at Liverpool throw an interesting light on antiquarian affairs of the 19th century, and particularly interesting is a letter of 1847 from the Danish antiquary Worsaae who had seen the collections of Dr. Rolfe at Sandwich in Kent and of Boucher de Perthes (the French customs officer and archaeologist who demonstrated an evolutionary series of Palaeolithic flint tools in the Somme gravels), the latter being 'exceedingly kind and civil to me, gave me his books, etc., etc., and I liked him very much. Only the truth is, that he on one hand has many sound ideas and on the other hand gives too much way to fanciful theories'. Such could occasionally be said with truth about James Douglas.

The *Inventorium* manuscript was published by subscription in 1856 under the editorship of the well-known antiquary, Roach Smith. The original manuscript, contained in six vellum-bound notebooks with the author's diagrams and drawings is now with his collection in the City of Liverpool museum.

Faussett is also to be remembered for a charming pavilion (Plate 16) built between 1769-75 in his garden at Heppington but destroyed in the 1950s. The house itself, a building of very old foundation, had been pulled down and rebuilt completely in 1730. A variety of antiquities decorated the pavilion walls: a quern-stone used as the cover for a Roman cremation urn, the bowl of an early font from the nearby church at Kingston, sculptured corbels from Northbourne in Kent, a terracotta relief from Roman London, an effigy from the tomb of an ecclesiastic in St. Augustine's Abbey, Canterbury, and a remarkable piece of late Romanesque sculpture of a Biblical prophet, formerly part of the decoration of the first Almonry Chapel at Canterbury. All were accompanied by descriptions in elegant Latin carved on stone tablets. The font, regenerated, was returned to Kingston church in 1931. Most of the other pieces are in the Royal Museum at Canterbury,

and the Romanesque sculpture, in view of its great importance, has been lent to the Victoria and Albert Museum.
The pavilion with a later inscription of 1799 by Henry
Godfrey Faussett, the son, must often have been seen
by Douglas on his visits to Heppington.

The manuscript has a number of additional colour
illustrations (as in Plate 14) of a very high order by the
hand of the same Henry Godfrey Faussett. With Henry,
man-of-law, skilled draughtsman and careful collector of
pictures, James Douglas was now to make a long-lasting
friendship based on a mutual love of art and antiquity.
Henry succeeded to his father's estate at Heppington.
Since childhood days he had been his father's companion
in all his rambles and researches: he was born and bred
an antiquary. It was his claim throughout life that he
himself had discovered the famous gold and jewelled
brooch, the gem of his father's rich collection, at Kingston
as he directed the opening of the barrow on behalf of
his father who sat crippled with gout in a carriage nearby.
Bryan at once drove off with the obviously valuable
brooch, and by the next day there was a village rumour
that so filled with gold was the parson's carriage that
its wheels would scarcely turn. The Lord of the Manor
forthwith prohibited all further digging on the Downs.
All this was long ago, and Henry Godfrey Faussett now
travelled widely out and about the countryside to visit
his friends, was sometimes in London, very often in
nearby Canterbury and quite often with the literary circle
in Rochester. It was on a visit to Brompton and Chatham
Lines in 1779 or 1780 that he met Captain Douglas, and
although he did not possess Douglas's immediate enthusiasm he was well enough informed about antiquities and,
in the words of a learned contemporary, had great taste
and expertise in his own cabinet of tumuli treasures.
Douglas knew full well about the dust-laden cabinets at
Heppington to which he had greatly hoped to have
access; could it be used, he wondered, in a project
already turning itself over in his active mind, nothing
less than a major disquisition of the nature and significance

of burial customs in British antiquity based first on his own discoveries at Chatham. After a little initial coolness the two men got on well together, met often and corresponded at length. Of Faussett's letters to Douglas there is no trace, and although the correspondence is thus one-sided it does nevertheless brighten the lives of the two men with a degree of colour and vivacity, and moreover it is almost the only source of information about a busy and most interesting period of James Douglas's varied career. Of the 33 surviving letters dated between 1781 and 1794, six were published by Charles Roach Smith in 1836 as appendices to his edition of Bryan Faussett's *Inventorium Sepulchrale.* These letters belonged to Joseph Mayer who had doubtless bought them with the Faussett Collection; they are now preserved in MS. 723 in the Library of the Society of Antiquaries. A selection is included here in Part II.

The letters are often private and personal in their content. They were an ordinary correspondence never intended for posterity, and no one would have been more surprised and delighted than their writer to know that by chances he could never have foreseen his letters were to find a permanent home in the Library of the Society for which he had such a high regard and affection. Most of the letters were written in the earlier years, from Rochester, Blackheath, London, and Chiddingfold in Surrey, no less than 25 bearing dates between 1781-86, while, except for 1790, there is only one letter preserved for each year until 1794. Each is carefully docketed by Faussett who occasionally reckons his tithes and accounts on the back of the sheets. Occasionally, too, Douglas writes on the back of a proof pull of one of the aquatints (Plate 17) which was to be used in his great disquisition, *Nenia Britannica,* about which more will be said later. The letters are formal to begin with, then cordial in degree of hope for a view of the famous collection and favours to be obtained, but salutations move quickly from 'Your faithful and Obedient Servant' to 'With much sincerity your hearty and ready friend' and from the

formal 'Sir' to 'My dear Faussett'. It becomes abundantly
clear that one of Douglas's main intentions, and a
laudable one which he pursued with tenacity of purpose
over several years, was to secure permission to publish
some part at least of the Faussett Collection and the
manuscript account of the early excavations, and in this
he eventually succeeded. But he also showed a good and
wise general spirit of understanding. No great picture of
the contemporary world emerges, but there is much about
his adoption of a career in the Church and his anxiety
for preferment which reveals not only his own personality
but also something of the ecclesiastical circles in which
he moved. There is very much more of the plan and
progress of his great book. Next is up-do-date news of
his own and other antiquarian diggings and 'ransacks', of
discoveries and of doings at the Society of Antiquaries.
Then again, accounts of paintings and his dabbling in
picture-dealing occupy much space, and there are pleasant
domestic details of the day-to-day life of a parson-
antiquary who could discuss the purchase of pigs at a
country fair, ask after the health of the Faussett brats
and almost in the same breath comment on the reduction
of deaths from malaria in the garrison at Chatham
from eight a night to four as entertainingly as he could
describe his visit to Paris to see the splendid relics of the
Frankish King Childeric found at Tournai in 1653 in the
destruction of some old houses adjoining St. Brice, a
church which he knew well.

In the spring of 1785 Douglas had thoughts of introducing his wife to Flanders by way of a sojourn in France,
but if he doesn't go to Flanders he will go into the north
of England and have a touch at barrow-hunting. A few
years later he proposed another tour from a supposition
that 'your inclination leads you to the plan of touring it
about, than which nothing can be more delightful and
cheering to the mind as also wonderfully instructive'.
It seems likely that he and Faussett did travel together,
but no precise record remains.

The families often exchanged domestic visits. What

antiquarian gossip may not have been heard in the Chocolate House at Blackheath, and as a measure of his open-hearted sincerity but bravely unorthodox views there is Douglas's remarkable letter of sympathy on the death of Faussett's first wife Susan Sandys in 1789 (see page 223):

> There is nothing but time and a good constitution which can enable you to dull the edge of your grief; here I speak as one of the laity, but in the language of my cloth, I shall always assert that human wisdom or in other words human fortitude, is not equal to the severe task of expelling sorrow.
>
> Under this severe pressure (it was in a similar situation to your own) Johnson had recourse, by the advice of a friend, to religious duty and it was in that alone that his mental agony was mitigated. I know too well by repeated experience what the evils of life can produce, and sometimes by a kind of horrid anticipation I tremble for my own resolution: and to speak my mind freely I dare not promise myself even from that most glorious consolation, religion's voice, a perfect submission or resignation to the divine will; so forcibly do I well conceive the miseries which this life is teeming with.
>
> With these impressions you must well conceive how impossible it is for me to undertake the task of consolation. I can only offer up my prayers for perseverance in fortitude, and that you may be soon in some respect or other be restored to comfort and happiness.

The years between 1779 and 1782 were full of interest. The redoubt on Chatham Lines was still under construction and the site continued to reveal relics of antiquity, the greater number of which found their way into Douglas's quickly-growing collection after details of their discovery had been recorded in his note-books. In Rochester itself he made frequent searches for graves within the walls of the Roman town but was unsuccessful because the buildings of the later city had obliterated remains of earlier civilisations as many another antiquary until very recent times has had reason to note. At the foot of the city walls he collected much Roman pottery, and he obtained more when he excavated the whole area round Gundulph's Tower, the early Norman structure on the north side of the Cathedral. Excavation of a Roman house on Chatham Hill followed, with careful notes of the wall-plaster striped in red and black, of the samian pottery, glass-ware and a piece of carved ivory. By the summer of 1782 the pestilential malaria which troubled Chatham was dying down. He was then able to travel further afield, excavating barrows at St. Margaret's-at-Cliffe on the coast between Deal and Dover (Plate 24), and graves at Eastry near Sandwich in East Kent. At Chesterford near Cambridge he knew of 'a range of inhumed bodies—I had labourers on the spot to go through with a day's digging, but the weather prevented us'. Chesterford had been a Roman town and Stukeley had anathematised the workmen who in 1719 were pulling down its walls to mend the roads, but it was not until long after Douglas's death that the real military importance of the site with its nearby Celtic-type temple was realised. Douglas realised however that it was a place worth the antiquaries' time and attention.

But work in general had to be postponed for a while as the trend of international affairs began to make itself felt even in the Ordnance Office at Chatham. The redoubt was not finished when the Peace of Versailles was signed in September 1783. France and Britain had composed their differences, Spain was no longer an enemy, and there was to be a period of peace between Britain and America. The Captain of Engineers was likely to have more leisure on his hands than he cared to contemplate, and there would have to be a great change in his future life unless he remained permanently an Engineer. The Peace would make some revolution in his future condition of life he tells Faussett in February 1783. He had consulted much with his friends and had effectually decided to enter the Church for which he was making the most thorough and expeditious preparations. He was indeed sorry to have missed one of Faussett's visits to Rochester, he writes on 26 March 1783, and most of the letter is worth reading in full:

> . . . but when I inform you that the most important object of church preferment depended on the exertion of a moment to get into Orders, you will not I trust be surprised at my leaving

Rochester for such a purpose and so suddenly. And although I lost no time and was so fortunate in getting my testimonials and a demissory letter from a Bishop to expedite my pious intentions for admission to Orders last term, and on which my presentation to a living in lapse to the Lord Chanc: turned, I was not withstanding too late in my application four days . . . I have therefore entered the church and I shall preach my first sermon next Sunday: when my initiation is thus fairly compleated and the fever of novelty arising from my change of life somewhat abated, I shall think of that delectable study—antiquity: and reassume the subject of painting &c with you. My intention is to reside in this quarter of the world for some time longer . . . I think of taking a curacy for employment and placing a curate in the living my friends are now working hard to procure for me . . . the great opportunities which I have of pampering my antiquarian appetite in this quarter of Kent lures me much to take up my abode here . . .

He continues by saying that he would rather live at Canterbury for preference and asks Faussett if he hears of any vacant curacies please to send word at once.

But where and how was James Douglas ordained? The answer is somewhat surprising.

The Registers of the Bishop of Lincoln contain the full record. Thomas Thurlow, Bishop of Lincoln and Master of the Temple, ordained 18 deacons at a general ordination held in the Temple Church, London, on Sunday 16 March 1783, including 'James Douglas, a literate person, from the Bishops of Rochester and Carlisle'. The Bishop of Rochester had evidently satisfied himself with Douglas's 'title and conversation' which would not have been at all difficult, but the connection with the Bishop of Carlisle is not clear. The interesting letter to Faussett had been written 10 days after his ordination. The circumstances are not difficult to imagine. Once again Douglas had relied on the patronage of his family and although he never says so, it seems clear that he had sought aid from his elder brother Thomas who had also failed in his mercantile career but had managed to acquire valuable property in Lincolnshire and in 1776 had served as High Sheriff for the County. He was well known on the turf and moved in

exclusive circles so that an approach to the Bishop of
Lincoln on his young brother's behalf need not have been
a difficult matter. But above all Thomas Thurlow was
Dean of Rochester from 1775 until 1779, knew of Douglas
as an antiquary and was a powerful friend.

It was not to be an easy change from Engineer to Holy
Orders. He was able to find a temporary appointment at
Strood on the opposite bank of the Medway and to
serve also in Rochester, but some six months after his
ordination he writes to Faussett:

Rochester 14th Decr 1783

Dear Sir,

After having detached my mind from every other concern,
excepting the object of some church preferment, using much
interest and spending money in running backwards and for-
wards, I am at last obliged to sit down with disappointment.
I was a candidate for a vacant minor canonry of this
cathedral and till the Chapter has decided on the election
I thought it prudent to give some respite to Nenia Britannica
—but which I have now taken up with fresh vigour—indeed
my health has been for many months impaired by a slow
autumnal fever which many persons have had in this quarter
and which has occasioned an ineptitude in me to sit down
to business.

I have received two very large packets [see Plates 29 and
30] from the little Abbé of Tongres who I mentioned in my
Trav. Anecdotes—in which he has sent me an inventory of
his Cabinet which is formed from his own discoveries from
tumuli and what he has otherwise collected from that old
town of the Tungry. His collection is rich beyond your
conception and in Meddals he is rich indeed.

Now Doctor Faussett, I live in Rochester, I think I have
taken up my residence in it for some time longer. I should
ill have considered my own and family's interest had I left
it for Stamford when there was an opening here for me in
the Church—you know perhaps that I am officiating Minister
at Strood. Will you come and see me and bring a friend perhaps
your good brother-in-law Sands [sic] will come with you.
I have known you now long enough to regard you independent
of an antiquary, as a friend if you will permit me to call
you by that name. Antiquaries you know are interested dogs
and like each other for the *exugo* sake, come then as a friend.
I have a bed for you and your lady or friend when you

please—you owe me a visit—and I promise you Mrs Douglas whether *en chenille* or in *grande gala* will not deny herself again, I have much to say to you but more to show you: I improve in my drawings and to satisfaction in the aquatints as you shall see.

Entre nous I have found Church duty very hard I assure you, two Churches I have had for some weeks past—Rochester and Strood and sermons my friend have fagged me. I believe I shall lay in a stock of printed ones for ease sake . . .

P.S.   I have ransacked Pliny for the origin of Pliny's pearl—do you know how it got that name?

It is not surprising that some of the authorities at Rochester had but little time for this newly-ordained deacon who had perhaps dared to say in conversation as he was soon to say to no less an authoritative body than the Royal Society that man existed in the valley of the River Medway before the Flood, and that fossil fruits and the fossil remains of tropical animals were not brought to this corner of Kent by the Flood but represented life as it did in fact exist at a very remote period indeed. But meanwhile, though Douglas went a little slowly with his writing he did not wholly neglect his study of antiquity. We read of the 'clandestine' opening of a few barrows, and of plans to visit Canterbury where a hill near the well-known Dane John had disclosed a burial. There was also a visit to Leicestershire where he was promised the 'ransacking' of a decent range of tumuli, time for long correspondence with antiquarian friends in Cornwall and Nottingham and with the Abbé P. G. Van Muyssen at Tongres in Flanders. In two long summer days he opened some 20 burial mounds in Greenwich Park (Plate 23), carefully noting their contents, others at Walton-on-Thames, and with a labourer returned to the mound at Canterbury.

On entering the Church and to provide additional funds to supplement his evidently slender means Douglas decided to sell some of his collection of paintings. In Flanders and Austria he had acquired a more than ordinary knowledge and appreciation of painting. To him Gerard Dou, for example, was much more than a success-

ful painter of market-places and buxom wenches; he understood Dou's technique and saw with an artist's eye the
problem of space, perspective and colour. He himself
drew and painted constantly, maintained an ever-growing
portfolio of work and in Flanders, probably in Ghent, he
had learned the practical business of etching and the
production of aquatints. Art had become a tasteful
enthusiasm second only to antiquity. He is said to have
painted fine portraits in miniature and in oils, but none
are now known. The original illustrations in colour in his
own copy of *Nenia* now in the Grenville Library in the
British Museum (G. 6863) show (e.g. Plates 23-4) to the
full the real excellence of his work. A full-length portrait
of the topographical artist Francis Grose (Plate 18), a
fellow Antiquary, the delicate plate of Coston church
(Plate 19) and a perfect fossil oyster found there printed
in John Nichol's 1795 edition of the *History and Antiquities of the County of Leicester,* and a pencil sketch for
the frontispiece of a book, 'Archaelogical Research unveil-
ing the Treasures of Antiquity', indicate further the
range of his talent. The Grose portrait, with the old man
caught napping caused a little trouble.

The inscription which varies slightly from plate to
plate reads:

> Now, xxxxx like bright Phoebus is sunk into rest,
> Society droops for the loss of his jest,
> Antiquarian debates, unseason'd with mirth,
> To genius and learning will never give birth:
> Then wake brother member and friend from his sleep,
> Lest Apollo should frown and Bacchus should weep.

> This PLATE is cordially dedicated to those MEMBERS of the
> ANTIQUARIAN SOCIETY, who adjourn to the SOMERSET,
> by one of their devoted BRETHREN.

> (Published as the Act directs by W. Stores, No. 3 Piccadilly,
> London, 1785.)

The plate is ornamented further with a representation of
the medieval bronze lamp found at Windsor in 1717 which

has long been the Society's badge and is incorporated in its Common Seal.

Grose who was himself a caricaturist who had depicted the Antiquaries Club in session did not forgive Douglas his lampoon, but esteem was restored when Nichols acknowledged the Coston plate to 'The Revd James Douglas, M.A. [*sic*], F.S.A.'; it had been drawn in 1791 on one of Douglas's visits to Leicestershire and was engraved by Jacob Schnebbelie, the self-taught but officially-appointed draughtsman to the Society of Antiquaries.

Dealing in paintings might be a gentlemanly and indeed an enjoyable way of adding to his income. In January 1783 in London for 10 days on business matters, Douglas wrote to Faussett:

> If you have any thought of adding to your pretty collection of pictures I can procure you an undoubted Peter Nief [we shall use his own variations of artists' names] the sweetest picture I ever saw of the master in most excellent preservation and remarkably cheap—to tell you the truth I have bought it myself and as I would wish you to be the master of a good picture to do honour to your collection, you may have it for what it cost me. I do not collect pictures and I therefore willingly part with it—it is the inside of a Cathedral full of figures and a priest performing mass. I gave four guineas for it, and I believe it on my honour to be worth 30 guineas. The size is 3 feet by 2¾. On my return I shall send you my Teniers [overlined Hemlink] and leave it to your judgment if it be worth the head I call a Vandyke, which should you not think it to be the case, you will do me the favour to accept of it . . .

Douglas used the word 'collect' in a restricted sense best known to himself. All his life he found it hard to forgo what he judged to be a bargain and he was never to be prevented in attempts at dealing. Only a month later when he had firmly decided to enter the Church he was offering Faussett all the pictures he owned. Faussett did buy the Peter Nief, but there was some misunderstanding about the frame being included in the price. Douglas copied it before delivery, hence the delay and misunderstanding—it is 'the sweetest picture my eyes ever beheld . . .

it ingratiates itself so much that I am almost prompted to
revoke its doom!'. He could sell Faussett's head of Edward
VI by Holben [*sic.*], a curiosity it must have been, and it
could come with the Vandyke. If he had but a little money
to spare he had an opportunity of buying some excellent
pictures remarkably cheaply during his stay in London.
In 1685 he was trying hard to identify for Faussett a
most unusual painting—cabbage, carrots and fruit with
ruins in the background, a Flemish master in style
certainly, but a group of ruins painted in this particular
style was unusual. Even the famous Le Brion of Paris,
the first connoisseur in Europe to whom he had recently
sold some pictures to a great amount, very wisely felt
it was utterly impossible to name the artist without
seeing the picture. In London that winter good pictures
were going cheaply. Two small Ruysdaels he bought for
six guineas, and the sumptuous frames alone were worth
the money. He bought also a 'prodigious fine and virgin
picture in a noble frame of Salviati' for 11 guineas which
had sold readily in Christy's Room the year before for
90, and how he wishes he could afford to keep it. Then
in 1790 at Chiddingfold, married and with a young family,
he acquired, as he told Faussett, a most beautiful painting
on copper of the Three Graces by Rotenhumer [Johann
Rottenhammer, noted for his nudes as well as his churches]
but he could not expose it in his own home for the sake
of clerical decorum as the ladies were without their
smerries. And of Gerard Dou, on whom he was something
of an authority:

> If you have actually a Gerard Dou in a tolerable state of
> preservation I know not what it may be worth. The delicacy
> and high finishing of this master will soon declare the truth
> of a real picture. He generally painted to the middle-heads
> and figures looking out of a casement . . . at all events I am
> sure you have made a most miraculous bargain: but [letter
> torn] country and particularly in Kent I am sure there is
> a possibility of picking up some excellent pictures for a trifle.
> The other day I saw an excellent Brugel at a brokers which I
> could have purchased for 5 guineas. A true Brugel if the
> subject be a landscape will have an *owl* in a tree in the fore-
> ground which was his mark.

As he spoke of these 10 painters, chiefly of the Flemish Schools, his remarks reflect a wide practical knowledge of art, of art history and especially of the problems and delights involved in making a picture. As he once told Faussett he had studied pictures in France, Germany, the Netherlands and Switzerland. The fate of the Faussett pictures, many of which he selected, is unfortunately not known. They are not at Liverpool and no Flemish pictures were included in later sales of Mayer's effects. Collateral members of the Faussett family kindly told me some years ago that they did not know what happened to the Heppington pictures.

Douglas knew well the value of pictures, but what would he have made of the buoyancy of present prices when a gentle early pastoral landscape of his favourite Ruysdael reached £69,000 at auction in 1972, and a Gerard Dou, a girl at a window lighting a candle, no less than £27,000.

In several sources, and copied by Thomas Cooper in his account of Douglas in the *Dictionary of National Biography,* it is stated that Douglas produced some excellent amateur portraits of his friends both in oil and miniature, but an extensive search here and in Belgium has not revealed a single example.

5

DISSERTATION

DURING HIS VISITS to Canterbury Douglas had observed closely the curious artificial mound called the Dane John and nearby one or two other smaller mounds of the same conical form known locally as the Dungeon Hills. He remembered that Leland in his 16th century Itinerary had recorded 'Many yeres sins men soute for treasor at a place cauled the Dungen . . . and ther yn digging thei fownd a Corse closed yn leade' but Leland did not identify the mound further. Quite clearly these mounds, if as it seemed, they were burial mounds, would repay the attention of an antiquary and if there was treasure, so much the better. An unusual opportunity came in the hard winter 1783. Part of one of the hills to the south-east of the Dane John planted as an orchard had been 'scarped away' by the heavy frost and in the fall of earth were many fragments of Roman pottery. On further search being made with the assistance of a paid labourer there came to light a pottery urn containing cremated human remains and round it three smaller pottery vessels. This kind of pottery and the accompanying ritual, Douglas noted, was the usual indication of a Roman burial of a person of substance and 'will always appear to discriminate the same from that of other Nations'. He lists the pottery carefully and it is worth while to summarise his notes recorded in the Minutes of the Society of Antiquaries 15 January 1789:

1. a patera 6½ ins wide and 2 ins deep of dark coloured earth:
2. a vessel with a neck to it 6 ins in diameter by 4½ ins high, light red and ordinary composition:
3. very small vessel of oblong cup form (? a lamp) of a very inferior kind of black earth.

At the base of the burial, he noted further, was a stratum of wood ash about 12 inches deep which lay over the 'Native Soil' undisturbed. There were also many fragments of Roman brick, pottery, oyster shells and animal bones. With the help of his labourer he found yet another pot seven inches in height and three inches only in diameter, of conical shape and made of a blackish earth. He also found the bones of a cock, one of which, a leg with its attached spur, he insisted upon exhibiting to the Society of Antiquaries in 1789 because it had not been burned to appease the Manes and it could be compared with the bones of a cock found with other Roman remains at Chesterford. 'We owe a cock to Aesculapius', the dying Socrates had said to Crito, and Douglas recalled the literary context, thought even that food might be provided for the funeral feast if not for the journey across the Styx, but from the Society only the customary 'thanks were ordered to be returned for this curious communication'. What Douglas had discovered was in fact an example of the now well-recognised and characteristic Roman barrows which were built only in certain parts of Britain. They often contained a burial chamber of brick and tile, were usually richly furnished and, as Douglas had said, were the burial places of people of importance. Each might well be expected in Roman Canterbury. This particular mound was destroyed when the railway was built in 1860; indications of another flattened in 1860 could still be seen only a few years ago on the site of St. Mary Bredin School which has now given place to a garage, but only quite rarely can a piece of acute modern literary detection akin to Dr. William Urry's identification of Salt Hill, one of the other lost barrows in the group, be expected to add to our knowledge.

Since his election in 1780 Douglas had read two papers
to the Society of Antiquaries, the first in 1782 on Roman
remains and a house found in constructing the Redoubt
on Chatham Lines which, without evidence, he regarded
as the Headquarters of the *comes litoris Saxonici*, the Commander of the Saxon Shore, and the other in 1783, on
antiquities from barrows opened under his own inspection.
Both were reasonable papers for their time, informative,
well constructed and they had been well received. In the
year following his digging in the Roman barrow at Canterbury he presented a third paper, entitled 'Remarks on
some Singular Celts', which he illustrated by some of his
own excellent drawings and by the exhibition of the
'brass' implements about which he spoke. By a friendly
and not unusual agreement with the Society his paper was
published elsewhere. Together with much additional
material it was printed by John Nichols, a well-known and
enterprising publisher, official printer to the Society of
Antiquaries, as No. 33 in his periodical *Bibliotheca
Topographica Britannica* of 1785 as 'Two Dissertations
on the Brass Instruments called Celts, found near Canterbury, and other Arms of the Antients', the paper being
dedicated to Melville, one of Douglas's personal sponsors
in the Society of Antiquaries and now a Lieutenant-
General. The original draft and sketches still remain in the
Society's library, now bound in MS. 723.

Before we discuss this paper in some detail, Nichols's own
work deserves notice. The original plan, formed in 1780
—and Douglas may well have had some say in it—was the
laudable one of presenting to the public articles on British
topography based on printed books, manuscripts, reprints
of scarce and curious tracts, and it was intended to ask for
original contributions from properly qualified correspondents. As no correspondent would be denied the
privilege of controverting the opinions of another, said
Nichols, so none would be denied the right of appearing
in print without a very fair and impartial reason. The
work was to be produced in parts on a county basis and
would, he hoped, 'withstand every Attack from the Critic

to the Cheesemonger'. The highly-organised publishers of
our modern part-works could not have put it better.
That the periodical was highly successful for ten years
and made eight thick quarto volumes when it came to be
bound was in large part due to the guiding hand of Richard
Gough, the distinguished topographer and Director of the
Society of Antiquaries. Nichols noted with some regret
that while the Society was undoubtedly the proper body
to sponsor such an undertaking, a rather similar plan which
it had put forward in 1754 produced but one reply to its
well-circulated preliminary questionnaire—this, a full and
careful account of Sherborne, still survives. The idea of an
archive of local antiquities, history and natural history,
sometimes with an element of folklore, was not new.
As long ago as 1570 Lambarde had published his *Perambu-
lation of Kent,* the first of the county histories and topo-
graphies. The 17th and 18th centuries had produced
notable historical and topographical works on Cornwall,
Dorset, Herefordshire, Yorkshire, Berkshire and other
counties, while in 1697 Edward Lhwyd, Keeper of the
Ashmolean at Oxford, had laid out a most searching list of
questions in his proposals for a British Dictionary, Historical and Geographical, which was to be published in
1707 as *Archaeologia Britannica.* For the background
there was always the outstanding work of Camden
available for consultation. But to Gough, we think,
must have been due the 56 questions on topography,
antiques and economics and no less than 55 questions
about natural history addressed to the Nobility, Gentlemen, Clergy and Others which opened the first volume
of the *Bibliotheca Topographica Britannica.* So well
was this work received that Nichols was encouraged
to publish in 1812 the first volume of his *Literary
Anecdotes of the Eighteenth Century* and only five
years later the first of a companion series *Illustrations
of the Literary History of the Eighteenth Century.* Many
a present-day scholar has had reason to be grateful for
these works, both of which were to include writings
by James Douglas.

With his constant interest in antiquity and only little less in natural history it is not surprising that the idea of the Bibliotheca should at once appeal to Douglas as a means of publishing his own researches. But not for him as an early contributor to the series was the Editor's grave warning: 'It is to be presumed that persons will be candid enough as well as sufficiently attentive to their own reputation not to obtrude hasty or ill-founded observations on the Publick, for whose sole benefit this Design is proposed'. The two men remained good friends for many years, despite an occasional misunderstanding. The use of the celt, Douglas insisted, deserved a more detailed explanation than had hitherto been attempted, and his paper, even though it did not instruct, might stimulate antiquarian thought on the matter. In explaining the somewhat unusual publication of his paper elsewhere, he courteously assured Fellows of the Society of Antiquaries, it will nevertheless always be his duty to submit to them any future discoveries of importance, a sentiment which had been echoed by many another Fellow in similar circumstances during the Society's long history.

The early part of the Dissertation is concerned with three 'brass instruments'—today we should read bronze to replace his term 'brass'—from his own collection. The first which had not until then been published was an ornate ceremonial shafted axe in the form of a bull found near Canterbury (Plate 20). There were no details of its discovery and it had come to Douglas fourth-hand through his friend Edward Jacob, the Faversham antiquary. This remarkable object which we shall discuss later in this chapter was eventually to pass to the Ashmolean Museum in the University of Oxford, and here we merely note that a comparison of the actual object with Douglas's sepia aquatint bears out once again the excellence of his eye and his artistic skill and patience in depicting objects of antiquity. On the back of the bull was a lachrymatory or a club; the vent was a hole for a substantial shaft secured by a rivet; under the belly were religious, magical or ornamental marks, while the feet of the bull rested on 'the executive part of the instrument'. Was it used in actual funeral rites? He quotes, and correctly, from Tibullus, Horace, Virgil, Varrow, and St. Paul's Epistle to the Hebrews to suggest that it may have been a small hatchet used in sacrifices of minor animals. It is not to be supposed that large animals were always used for 'few families or individuals could have afforded the expence, and we all know that the antients, in matters of superstition, to have been extremely fertile and ingenious in accommodating their religion to their exigencies'. If by reasons of its size, there are objections to the axe being used in this way, then perhaps it was a funeral ensign carried in procession, or even a substitute sacrifice to be buried with the ashes. If the marks on the belly of the bull were magical cyphers, then the instrument was likely to have been dedicated to Pluto. All this supposes, he says, that the instrument was of Roman date. What if it were British, Gaulish or Celtic? There is a passage in Plutarch which suggests that the bull was an ensign of the Celts, and this may well be so. He then passes to a 'Celt' in the form of a wedge' with evident marks of a hammer upon it —we recognise it as a well-known form of socketed hammer of the Late Bronze Age—and a 'Celt in the form of a Gouge'—in fact a socketed gouge of the same date—also found near Canterbury. This was clearly a tool and not a weapon. Looped celts, he thought, could have been used by soldiers 'in works of art', though perhaps he means as arms, and would have then been attached to the belt by the loop. Celts could have been made according to their different uses, for warlike, mechanical or even sepulchral offices. They could have been, he continues, the products of either the Romans or the Britons; he knew that celts had been found with Roman coins (no particulars are given beyond a reference to Dr. William Borlase's *Antiquities of Cornwall* published in 1754, but he could have been quite right though he misunderstood the true archaeological significance), and perhaps therefore they were made under Roman influence but after the departure of the legions. The literary sources known to him did not suggest that 'brass' celts were used before the invention of iron or that they could be assigned to any remote period in history. They had been found with coins of the Lower Empire, he insisted again, and iron in those times was universally used in the wars throughout Britain. Once again he said what he knew from his own knowledge, and this may well have included the reputed discovery of a socketed axe in one of the Canterbury burial mounds. Not yet was he to recognise fully the significance of a secondary burial in a prehistoric or even in a Roman barrow. Discoveries had to be fitted into a familiar classical background. Only after reflection in his later years was he able to judge evidence from an excavation strictly on its own merits. Archaeology in the field, had he known the term, had to be recorded, but it had to be considered against the known classical background.

The second part of the published Dissertation, which was not presented to the Society of Antiquaries, is diffuse, sometimes frankly tedious, but in the end reaches a remarkable conclusion. By now Douglas had acquired news of another axe in the form of a bull which he had been allowed to illustrate. It was in the collection of a London collector-dealer, but had no history, and he takes the opportunity of castigating those gentlemen who 'hoard up antique relics as children collect gegaws, they often expose the more reflecting antiquary whose only view in collecting them is to throw light upon history or place some doubtful custom of an antient people in a more accurate point of light, to the pleasantry of his friends, and the ridicule of the unlettered part of the world'. It was a point of view to be put nearly 200 years later in the forthright language of Sir Mortimer Wheeler: the archaeologist is not digging up *things,* but *people.* Whether the feature on the back of the bulls was to be identified as a club or as a lachrymatory, the instruments appeared to have been used as an offering to the dead. It was most difficult, if not impossible, to be precise in view of the scanty evidence, and everything and every matter for and against a Roman or a British origin should be adequately published. In such a matter 'pedantry and obstinate conceit must always give way to the most candid and liberal exposition . . . truth will otherwise for ever remain concealed from us'. These were brave words from an antiquary in 1784. Douglas then goes on to consider at length an Egyptian sculpture in basalt in the British Museum which represents Osiris and Isis rising under the symbols of an ox and a cow from the human body. The ox, he thinks, represents Osiris, and he enlarges on the symbols on the celts to his own satisfaction, saying that they seem to have been Celtic ensigns, and further that the bull on certain Greek coins was a representation of Bacchus, the Father of All Things. He is on much safer ground, and obviously knows it, when he maintains that all 'celts' whatever their precise form belonged to an early people, though extremely wrong as we now know when, on the still unquoted evidence of a supposed association with Roman coins, he suggests a use down to 'the lowest of the Roman Empire', Swords and celts of 'brass' had been found in Italy, France and Portugal to his own knowledge, and it must be realised by all antiquaries that they were not peculiar to Britain, a view which could no longer be substantiated in whatever quarter it was held. There follow interesting remarks from Douglas's own observations on the relative degree of preservation of iron and 'brass' in varying kinds of soils, and he warns most strongly against the acceptance of a current opinion that the Romans used only weapons of 'brass' because few of iron had been found in their graves. Funeral customs as well as the exact nature of the soil was an important point to be considered. Further, it was not correct to say with Borlase, the Cornish antiquary, that because celts are not represented on the Column of Trajan or the Antonine Column and had not been found in the ruins of Herculaneum, they must have been peculiar to the British. They appear to have been made in many ages by people skilled in casting from moulds, people who had not acquired the art or convenience of forging and beating iron for domestic and military uses. It was even possible that weapons of 'brass' might be made and used by the Romans when the ordinary equipment of the legions was not available for one reason or another.

The end of the discourse is worth quotation. 'Those who will take the pains to consider these brass instruments called Celts, swords, spear-heads, or those in the form of chizels, will find they are all cast in a mould, a process of making arms certainly much more expeditious than forging of tempered iron for warlike uses. The metal seems to have been rendered extremely hard with an addition of *Lapis Calaminaris,* or some other ingredient, and will sharpen to a very keen edge. Were it necessary for that subduing people the Romans to arm a barbarian people with expedition, what process could have been better contrived for all uses, military as well as mechanical, than that of casting implements with a suitable temper, which we know these instruments to have? All nations would certainly give the preference to iron arms, when time, convenience, and skill unite, for the accomplishment of such an operose undertaking'. Dr. Borlase has said that because celts in the form of a chisel had not been discovered on Roman sites, they must have been peculiar to the Britons. 'These kinds of Celts', Douglas continues, 'are not military instruments; consequently are not likely to be found on the Antonine or Trajan pillar. In short, they appear to have been fabricated in all ages, and to have been more particularly the weapons and mechanical instruments of a people who had not the art or convenience of rendering iron malleable for their domestic and military uses; this will be the means of assigning a satisfactory reason why they have not been found in that unhappy city, which flourished at a period when the use of iron was generally known among the Romans; consequently the reason why they do not occur in the world of the afore cited authors, who appear only to have recorded the finest relics of Roman ingenuity and magnificency'. It was an odd argument, to say the very least.

Within a few months the Dissertation was given a carping and ill-natured review in the *Gentleman's Magazine*;

the four columns were anonymous but were later said on little authority to be written by Richard Gough. Such empiricism in science was not new to this country or for that matter outside it. The author who brings out of his treasures things both old and new has treated us with a curious instance of it in the walk of antiquity. If we can understand the preface, continues the reviewer, it seems that the paper met with as civil a repulse as a well-bred Society could give. Had the reviewer been able to read the Society's Minute Book he surely would not have made such a disparaging remark: the Old Lady as Gough well knew as one of her officers, was perfectly capable of administering a rebuke when it was thought necessary. The author's remarks on the owner of the second celt, a man of learning, were but a pretty Canterbury Tale. There continued a dreary attack on Douglas's illustration of the bull as a symbol of a deity and on his theological knowledge of Mosaic doctrine, though two very elegant plates, it was thought, might possibly assist the sales of the book. Comments on the late introduction of iron and other metals to certain nations were acceptable, but there was no reason to assume, the reviewer continued with percipience, that celts were cast by the Romans to arm barbarians. For the rest, he said, the Dissertation was marked by dull puns and a miserable wit. One can only suppose that he himself could make only the one and lacked even the other.

Nearly 30 years later Douglas told Sir Richard Colt Hoare that he had once published two short and undigested papers on celts or the brass arms of the ancients which produced an attack in Mr. Urban's section of the *Gentleman's Magazine,* though it seems that he had no thought of Gough as the attacker. 'I laid on my retaliating lark with no small degree of vengeance', he says, but in fact he replied quickly and in a gentlemanly way to the anonymous review. Where was his crime? At the very worst he can only have made a bad guess; the reviewer begged his main question, opposed no argument, contradicted no assertion. Certainly Douglas had quoted Stukeley

who was an antiquary, but however great his reading
there were some of his opinions in which Douglas had but
little faith, though 'peace be to his ashes'. The eight-
column reply is dull and heavy-handed to be sure, but the
ill-informed and bad-natured review had upset his standard
of antiquarian enquiry, not least his sense of common
justice. More kindly was an account in the contemporary
Monthly Review for December 1786 which said that the
plates were neatly executed, very good representations of
the originals and especially of the coins which the writer
could not help commending as engravings, though he felt
they were totally foreign to the main object of the work.

It is not easy for us to understand the originality, even
the sophistication, of this study. To us the Bronze Age
is well established as one of the three main conventional
stages in the almost world-wide development of prehistoric
man, a stage based on the study of pottery, tools and
weapons. We are familiar enough with the Three Age
System in which it was first suggested by the Danish
prehistorian Christian Thomson in 1819, with Evan's
classical study of bronze implements in 1881, and with
the much more recent work by outstanding scholars in
Britain and on the Continent. It is indeed hard for us to
imagine a time when antiquaries did not share even the
beginnings of such knowledge. Douglas, in his day,
could only experiment in antiquarian practice and thought:
his theories and conclusions are therefore all the more
remarkable. In his later years, as was almost inevitable,
he had some doubts.

The fine ceremonial axe cast in the form of a bull found
near Canterbury (Plate 20 top) passed with much of
Douglas's collection of antiquities to the University of
Oxford in 1829 as the gift of the famous antiquary Sir
Richard Colt Hoare and thus found a home in the
Ashmolean Museum where it was exhibited but its
provenance not recognised. The similar but smaller axe
which he had also illustrated in fine sepia aquatint in his
Dissertation, still a relic of unknown provenance (Plate 20
below), eventually came with the Towneley Collection

to the British Museum where it is now in the reserve collections of the Department of Greek and Roman Antiquities. In 1970 I was privileged to exhibit the Canterbury axe and a photograph of the other at a meeting of the Society of Antiquaries, and noted that there are records of two other such axes from Britain. They were shown in 1868 at Leeds in a National Exhibition of Works of Art, and both were owned by W. H. Forman, a wealthy London and continental collector. The first, about which nothing more is known, was said to have a bone handle in the socket. The other was sold in 1899 by Sotheby's at the sale of the Forman Collection for £50 to W. Talbot Ready, another well-known collector of antiquities, but it did not appear in the sale of Talbot Ready's collection at Paris in 1919 and quite possibly it may still be somewhere in Britain. A label inside the axe which read 'Pr. Vans 1865' suggests a continental provenance or collection. The axe was illustrated in a small number of Sotheby's catalogues, and it was from this source that the well-known German scholars Gustav Körte in 1916 and K. F. Johansen in 1932 obtained their notes. There is yet another axe of the same type in the Museum of the Archaeological Institute of the University of Göttingen, but it, too, lacks a provenance. The Douglas axes were not, of course, known to the later writers.

The four axes have many features in common but differ in detail. Each represents a bull, its horns shorn ready for sacrifice, the Göttingen animal having a rosette on its forehead, the Towneley a groove for a ceremonial girthband (as depicted on many marble sacrificial reliefs and friezes) which may have been enamelled. Each bull has a hollow body for mounting on a horizontal shaft; rivet holes to secure the mounting appear on each and the Towneley axe has in addition a rivet hole for a vertical mount. Three of the axes have grooves at the hinder end of the animal, perhaps for binding the bronze to its shaft. All but the Towneley axe have a Hercules-type club—not the usual sacrificial *malleus*—along the back of the bull, handle towards the tail, and an apparent fault in the casting of the latter axe may be an indication of its intended presence. In each example the blunt unground blade of a sacrificial *securis,* but without its customary shaft, issues from the belly of the bull. The major decoration is a three-leafed or three-pronged feature either in relief or incised and, on the Foreman axe, of 'ansate' wedge-shape in its upper part. The Canterbury axe is further decorated with carefully-made pittings, just possibly a representation of seeds of corn or barley. The significance of the decoration, whether it represents a lotus-plant, corn, a sacrificial instrument or mere ornament is not clear. Some thought of Mithras Tauroctonus where all manner of useful plants issued from the body of the bull may have been in mind, but this can be but unsupported speculation. The Canterbury and the Göttingen axes are remarkably lively pieces of animal modelling and well cast, the Towneley axe being little more than the work of a journeyman. Both the Canterbury and the Towneley axes bear the heavy scratch marks of trimming contemporary with their manufacture. Colour and patination of the three available pieces is satisfactory, and careful expert examination provides no suggestion of anything other than genuine antiquities.

The axes may be priestly insignia used symbolically before a sacrifice but they would have been difficult to see and venerate were they carried on a shoulder-pole in the fashion depicted, for example, on the *Ara Pacis* monument. Were they not rather votive objects dedicated perhaps by priests and then fastened to the wall of a temple or shrine on a horizontal wooden bracket as were many other bronzes and sculptures? A Roman attribution is acceptable enough, as it was to James Douglas, though the ultimate origin of such pieces may have been in an eastern province of the Empire.

It would have pleased him to think that this object from his treasured collection of antiquities would survive the Timeless Oblivion against which he preached so constantly to rest once again almost two centuries later on the President's table of the Society of Antiquaries.

6

FURTHER DISSERTATIONS

AT ROCHESTER, as he walked each day across the old unprotected stone bridge to his church at Strood and with his friends Jacob, Denne, Shrubsole and Wildash toured the nearby countryside, Douglas once again found practical interest in natural history, a reflection of the early days with Ashton Lever at Alkrington Hall. He was already familiar with the chalk downs at Chatham Lines and now saw on his daily peregrinations the nearby chalk banks on the London Road at Strood Hill, where he collected fossils, the chalk bluffs of Frindsbury and the sands and gravels on the banks of the Medway. He saw, too, fossilised bones of what he recognised as an extinct animal, bones found in 1773 in digging foundations for a storehouse in Chatham according to notes taken on the spot by the vicar of St. Margaret's, lately a Minor Canon of Rochester. The bones he secured, drew, and gave to his friend Ashton Lever for his Museum. In addition he saw fossil shells from the local chalk and a fossil tortoise and fruits taken from the clay on the foreshore of the Isle of Sheppey. With his learned friend Dr. Beugo, a skilful physician of Rochester, he had long conversations on the nature and causes of fossilisation and made practical experiments on calcareous and fossil material.

On 12 May 1785, the Reverend James Douglas, Fellow of the Society of Antiquaries, presented to the

Royal Society at its invitation a Dissertation on 'Some animal and testaceous Petrefactions with some Inferences on the Cosmography of our Globe'. The meeting was a full one, and among the 22 guests were several of his Kentish antiquarian friends. By an accepted arrangement of the time the paper was withdrawn the day after reading in order that it could be published at once in book form. The facts that it contained, the author said, he judged proper to circulate to the world. Its contents were startling to say the least, and some of its critics were not slow to suggest that the withdrawal was prompted by the fact that such a paper would not be likely to find official favour with the Royal Society. This cavil seems pointless as the Society was very interested in such matters and its President accepted the dedication of the book which followed.

It was now clear that there was to be no clerical preferment in the strictly orthodox Diocese of Rochester. The perpetual curate of Strood, the Master of Jesus College, Cambridge, secure in his incumbency for the annual acknowledgment of one penny to the Dean and Chapter of Rochester was naturally disinclined to give up his sinecure, still less inclined perhaps to help this curiously-minded assistant.

By the time of the publication of his paper as a quarto volume with six engravings under the title *A Dissertation on the Antiquity of the Earth* at a price of 10s. 6d. later in 1785 (there is a reversal of date in the Dedication), Douglas had moved to London, to a house in Little Stanhope Street, Mayfair, which belonged to his family, the better to 'fag for' preferment in the church, and thence to Conduit Vale at Blackheath, Kent, where he bought a little 'house in the country . . . comfortably situated and everything snug'. It is now named Hyde Vale after a later owner of the Estate. The small brick conduit which supplied water to the Royal Hospital at Greenwich still stands at the head of the Vale overshadowed by a block of modern flats and further down the hill are several pleasant 18th-century houses in one of which the Douglas family almost certainly lived for their short stay at Blackheath.

It was a pleasant enough place, only five miles from London, with splendid mansions, neat boxes and the whimsically ornamented retreats of opulent traders (in the words of a contemporary *Traveller's Companion*) where behind a pleasant grove, stood the row of genteel houses called Chocolate-row, from the house where the Assembly was kept. The small, unfashionable court of Caroline of Brunswick was not to arrive for another four years but Douglas had quickly made no small social acquaintances in the neighbourhood and promised that Mrs. Faussett and his wife could meet in the nearby Chocolate House confident of amusements far abstracted from *disertationes antiquitates*. The family lived in London and Blackheath from March 1784 to September 1785. In October 1785 Douglas was nominated as curate of Chiddingfold on the borders of Surrey and Sussex, by the absentee rector Charles Greene, at a salary of £40 per annum, and four years after his ordination he was priested on 4 March 1787 by the Bishop of Winchester—in whose diocese Chiddingfold was then situated—in the Chapel Royal at St. James's, Westminster. Could it be a coincidence that his wife's family was related to a former Bishop of Winchester? On 17 November of that same year he was presented by Sir William Addington, a Fellow of the Society of Antiquaries, with the rectory of Litchborough, Northamptonshire, which he held in plurality with the curacy at Chiddingfold for 12 years—and was it solely as an encouragement to his studies in antiquity that he was appointed a Chaplain-in-Ordinary to the Prince of Wales in December of that very same year?

What notions were there, we may now ask, about the antiquity of the earth and, so far as it was possible for the question to be posed, about the antiquity of man upon it? The 18th century has been described as an age of reason based on faith, and to some extent there was an alliance between the scientific outlook and religion, though the

vast antiquity of man himself was scarcely discussed. A
full study of the idea of Nature in the thought of the
period and of the main intellectual currents which were
to lead from the 'divinization' of Nature towards the
Romantic Revival has often been made with profound
knowledge, but for our purpose here the question must
be answered quite shortly.

Douglas was well read in his ancient writers—Eusebius,
Diodorus Siculus, Lucian, Herodotus and Strabo. He
knew of Leonardo da Vinci's views on marine fossils
discovered in the Alps, of Sir Thomas Browne's *Urne
Buriall,* of de Buffon's *Histoire naturelle,* and of the
works of Newton, Whitehurst and Toulmin with their
remarks on the origin and early history of the earth.
What he did not know was that about 1690 an enterprising apothecary in looking at a digging for gravel near
the present Gray's Inn Road in London saw the bones
of what he thought was an elephant. 'How the Elephant
came there?' asked John Bagford in a letter in the
second (Hearne's) edition of Leland's *Collectanea* published in 1770. 'I know some will have it to have lain
there ever since the Universal Deluge. For my own part',
he continues, 'I take it to have been brought over with
many others by the Romans in the time of Claudius
[but] not far from the Place where it found, a British
Weapon made of a Flint Lance like unto the Head of a
Spear . . . was also dug up, they having not at that time
the use of Iron or Brass, as the Romans had . . . This
conjecture, perhaps, may seem odd to some'. No doubt
it did, but it marked an outstanding point in the discovery of time. This pear-shaped flint hand-axe, now to
be seen in the British Museum, was the first stone tool
to be recognised as the work of man. Not until 1797,
12 years after Douglas's *Dissertation,* was John Frere
to communicate to the Society of Antiquaries his discovery
of flint weapons at Hoxne in Suffolk and, greatly daring,
suggest that they could be referred 'to a very remote
period indeed—even beyond that of the present world'.
They were in fact hand axes of the Lower Palaeolithic.

The Society gravely thanked its Fellow for his curious and interesting communication; it was printed in due course but aroused no further comment. One or two naturalists had begun to perceive something of the discovery of time. In 1751 a Frenchman realised that there were once volcanoes in the hills of the Auvergne. Nearer home, in 1788, only three years after Douglas's *Dissertation*, James Hutton of Edinburgh, the real founder of modern geological thought, was saying that the earth must be vastly much older than had been previously imagined by those who accepted the Old Testament account as literal truth. This was, of course, the general view. Distaste of hell-fire and a fearsome respect for the Church had long assured a traditional acceptance of the views of Archbishop James Ussher who, 'learned to a miracle', had in 1658 put forward the date of 4004 B.C. as that of the creation of the world. Such is the background in summary. To this cause of the Antiquity of the Earth, Douglas, naturalist and antiquary, now lent all his enquiring faculties.

His *Dissertation,* he says in his opening words, was framed upon many authentic materials and discoveries related to the natural Theory of the Earth, from much careful and serious reading of the works of learned scholars whom, he thought, had been too diffuse in their writings. 'Polemical references only confuse and disgust the reader of taste and discernment. I have therefore concentered a few select facts into a small compass . . . I have therefore only presumed to draw my conclusions from the most obvious effects and which should be presented to the human mind with as much clearness and energy as the writer is master of'. It is a pity that Douglas did not always follow this excellent precept in his own writings, and it is perhaps a little strange that he should choose Porphyry's phrase 'Only men of God are able to speak the truth' to adorn his title-page. His avowed purpose, however, was '. . . a limited approach to first causes, and at a respectable distance to contemplate with a pious wonder the inscrutable works of the Almighty'.

The main part of the Dissertation was put in three Cases, supported by long footnotes on the processes of fossilisation and by a long Appendix in which the author gave accounts of fossil animal bones found at Gibraltar, Thame in Oxfordshire, on the banks of the Ohio and Mississippi Rivers and of various fossils and pebbles found 'in the beds of the Earth'. It closes with critical accounts of de Buffon's system and Toulmin's and Whitehurst's accounts of the antiquity and duration of the world and the original state and formation of the earth.

Douglas considers first the discovery in 1773 of the fossil bones of an extinct animal 12 feet deep in the drift or river-sand at Chatham, and notes that the sand was here covered by a compact undisturbed brick-loam which occurred in the district about 20 feet above the level of the Medway at high water mark and at 100 yards from the strand on the same level. The bones, teeth and tusks were locally thought to be the remains of one of the elephants brought to Britain by the Emperor Claudius, as were those found in Gray's Inn Road, London, which we have already noticed, but Douglas, after comparing the fossils with the bones of a modern hippopotamus in Lever's Museum at Leicester House, in London, was sure that they were relics of that animal. The heavy dark brown aquatint with which he illustrates his remarks, which is unfortunately not suitable for reproduction in this book, suggests rather the remains of a mammoth or even of a rhinoceros, the fossil bones and teeth of which are often found in the river-gravels of the Medway, but the exact palaeontological interpretation does not affect the validity of his argument. We follow his assumption that the bones were those of an extinct animal from a warm climate. They must have been deposited in a water-borne soil; there was no authority in the Pentateuch to say that such animals were impelled by a convulsion in Nature to move from the Nile to the Medway, and the Universal Deluge was not the cause of their appearance at Chatham. Without doubt the bones were deposited by the waters of the Medway at a time when the climate was much warmer than at present; and there was no possibility that the happening had anything at all to do with the submergence of the world in 40 days as set out in the Scriptures. The bones must have lain undisturbed since the remote days when the brickearth was deposited. The animals lived here and could not have floated from the Nile or in the Deluge named in Holy Writ, and the brickearth and sand were not in any way caused by that Deluge. These animals lived, long before written record, in or near the area in which their bones were unearthed. The degree of fossilisation is a measure of relative antiquity but it must be remembered, says Douglas, speaking from his own wide experience in the field, that gravel or sandy soil will often decompose animal substances quickly while chalk and marl preserve bones so long as there is no great infiltration of water. He had often had the opportunity of discovering in different soils human bones 'with the date of their deposit interred near them' and he now continued with a discussion of what might be learned from such cases.

Case I concerned relics from a barrow, one of a group of the 'lower Britons', opened by Douglas in 1779 on Chatham Hill. He took much care to prevent 'adventitious circumstances from the upper coating of the earth', and in a chalky soil found the complete skeleton of a woman accompanied by an ivory armlet and a coin of the Emperor Anthemius 'who flourished A.D. 447' (he meant Anthemius, Emperor of the West, A.D. 467-72, who was killed at the capture of Rome by Ricimer, the king-maker). Both objects are well illustrated. Douglas made chemical tests on the armlet and on the Chatham fossil teeth and said with emphasis that as the ivory had not become in any way fossilised in 1,300 years, the fossil teeth must be immeasurably older, far older, than the ivory.

But since the elephant's tusks and the ivory armlet had both been found in a chalky soil, he proceeded in Case II to cite one of the barrows opened in 1771 on Kingston Down by Bryan Faussett. There were two coins of

widely-separated dates, of Claudius (A.D. 41-54) and of
Carausius (A.D. 287-293), and an East Indian cowry shell
perforated for suspension on a (bronze) ring, perhaps an
amulet of Priapus, he thought, and so anticipated one
modern opinion. The relics are well illustrated. The shell
had remained in the ground for 1,400 years without decay
or fossilisation. If it is compared with the marine fossils
often found in the same stratum of chalk, the *echinus,* the
pectinite, clearly the fossils whatever their ultimate history,
belong to an unknown period of time, to an age vastly
long before that furnished by the coins in the grave.

It would make an endless digression were he to speak
of other similar cases in which fossilisation 'could not
possibly come within the compass of human observation
to fix a period in which the transmutation has been
performed'. Case III is then briefly stated. It concerns a
fossil tortoise which he exhibited to the Royal Society
and a fossil fruit in the possession of its President, Sir
Joseph Banks. Both came from the clay (London Clay)
of the Isle of Sheppey in Kent which had been famous
for the large variety of its tropical fossil plants, fruits and
seeds since 1757—though not until 1810 was Francis Crow,
the Faversham naturalist, to make his Catalogue with some
830 curious drawings. Douglas had a large collection of
Sheppey fossils himself, and he studied also the fossils from
Sheppey in Lever's Museum in Leicester House. The
tortoise (from the illustration it appears to be a turtle,
possibly of the *Lytomala* species) was so large that it
cannot have floated from a tropical land to Sheppey; it
must have lived near the coast in which it was found in
its fossil state, and the fruit (is it not of the stemless
palm, *Nina burtini?*) was also a natural product of the
same place. Fossilised freshwater fish from Sheppey, a
pike in particular, were also to be seen in Douglas's own
collection, and the presence of such a variety of fish
could not be reconciled with the Biblical account of the
Flood. The time allotted in sacred writ for the retreat of
the waters, he continues, was 150 days, and as Moses
does not speak of any natural convulsion which would

have displaced these creatures from their original homes and placed them equably with others already at home in their natural habitats, we must believe that with any reflux of the waters, so most of its inhabitants also retreated. Genesis speaks only of the living creatures of the earth, but the lives of the inhabitants of the sea must also be considered and there is no reason to conclude that the phrase 'All the fountains of the great deep were broke up' meant a convulsion and earth movements equal to those which produced in many parts of the world the phenomenon of fossilisation. The Sheppey clay was of an 'antediluvian period', a period beyond the records of man or scripture when the climate was warmer; in no way could its fossils have resulted from the 40 days of flood; and if the process of fossilisation does still continue, it must take place deep in the bowels of the globe.

But as all men are prone more or less to metaphysical enquiry it is more dangerous, he thinks, for the cause of religion to have the untutored mind puzzled than to set it right in matters capable of explanation. Whether the history of the world is to be regarded according to Mosaic doctrine in its ordinary significance, or rather by the more complicated system which Douglas suggests, the well-regulated mind will have equal cause to venerate the 'great plastic hand of the deity' to whom time was of no account. There follows a detailed description and illustration of a fossil jawbone of an unknown animal found in the rock of Gibraltar—John Hunter, the surgeon, said it was of an extinct species and he, if anyone, should know—and of another found deep in the soil in digging a well at Thame, and both are used with eloquence to support the argument of an antediluvian world inhabited by animals and, '*perhaps,* by human beings'.

The earth, says Douglas, may have been originally in a state of fluidity by water which by the revolution on its axis occasioned consolidation; there may have been subterranean fire and fusion may have reduced some matter to a partially vitrified state; it might have been in contact with a comet; the earth may have cooled and water covered parts of its surface again—'and so we may continue to reason without end'. Fire and water in various forms and degrees have surely been the first cause of all the convolutions on the face of the globe. 'I think myself happy', he ends, 'in having added some further testimony; in hopes that my labours may ultimately tend to restore the minds of a certain description of men, to a sense of physical truths and religious precepts'.

Four conclusions are set forth with precision. The actual animals once lived in those areas of Britain where their fossil remains are now to be found. At a certain and very remote period of time our climate was much warmer than it is at present. The animal remains could not have been removed from far away native climes by an alluvion of 40 days. And fourth, that the soil in certain instances had the power of inducing fossilisation at a period far back beyond the date of any written testimony. This power, he thinks, may still possibly exist by some extraordinary convulsions of matter, remotely concealed from human observation within the bowels of the globe. It is the only time in the book when imagination draws ahead of truth.

The closing words are worth quotation: 'All men are prone more or less to metaphysical enquiry, it is more dangerous for the cause of religion to have the untutored mind puzzled, than to set it right in matters that will bear explanation.

'If we therefore respect the history of the world, the religious and well-regulated mind will have the same cause for venerating the hand of the deity—the power would still be as fully important as that recorded in the first book of Genesis'.

Let us remind ourselves that these are no words of a Joseph Priestly, but the thoughts of a well-read and well-travelled country parson, ex-mercenary soldier and Royal Engineer, a practical excavator for his time although not according to modern concept, a man who moved in recognised antiquarian circles. His views were far more liberal than and far in advance of those of his colleagues; he looked to learn, though he enjoyed a disputation, and altogether he deserves to be regarded, on the merits of this Dissertation, as an outstanding personality in the history of archaeology in Britain.

It was scarcely to be expected that such a *Dissertation* based on scientific ardour supported by an unusual form of religious certainty would be received with approval. Thought about such matters as the antiquity of the earth and man's first appearance upon it was in the main traditional, as we have said, and Douglas's statements could be regarded only as uninformed or, at the worst, as illogical heresy. An anonymous reviewer in *The Monthly Review* of December, 1786—a publication certainly not noted for any liberal view in such matters—was sorry to find that the author had deviated from the true and accepted methods of philosophy by admitting hypotheses instead of demonstrative evidence. This was manifestly untrue. The author was not yet an adept in chemical knowledge; he writes in a very desultory and unmethodical manner, continued the reviewer, and his style betrays haste and inaccuracy. It could be hoped that in time his judgment would control his ideas. The reviewer chose to ignore completely the practical experiments Douglas had first made on fossils and bones, his production of true archaeological evidence and his ideas of life in the valley of the Medway before the Universal Deluge. Another review praised the aquatints with which the book was illustrated, especially those of coins (gentlemanly relics, well understood and much appreciated by collectors of the time) of which the engraving was specially to be commended, but added that the illustrations appeared to be totally foreign to the main subject of the book. They were in fact well integrated with the text, except for a charming little picture of the islands of Cherso and Osero off the Adriatic coast, which adds nothing to the passing mention of the strata of fossil bones found there. More serious was the challenging review of General Sir Robert Melville, one of his sponsors to the Society of Antiquaries,

in the seventh volume of *Archaeologia* published in 1785,
but it received no proper answer.

In August 1785 at Conduit Vale Mrs. Douglas, then
25, was very happy, a fine boy at her side and within a
few days of getting up. Her husband's first and melancholy
duty at Chiddingfold was to bury this son James Bruce
who died aged only 10 months. He is commemorated
by a small inscription in the floor at the east end of the
north aisle which was covered in 1869 during 'restora-
tions' to the fabric. A perusal of the parish registers
suggests that Douglas as Curate or Minister as he variously
signs himself was a faithful and hard-working parish priest,
who over a long period of 13 years took few holidays of
any duration, though in 1787 he was able to spend some
months abroad, visiting Paris, Flanders and Switzerland.
He managed also to travel in Kent, Surrey, Cambridge,
Leicestershire and Wiltshire in search of his beloved
antiquities. In April 1794 he baptised his son, James
Edward Moreton; in May 1798 another son, Richard
William Glode. Faussett had teased him, saying for gentility's sake he ought to keep a cow and two pigs and
wishing therefore, he says in reply, to appear with
gentility in the eye of his friends he had bought the
necessary credentials at a local fair. The parish was a
retired one, though the Arundel coach from Fetter Lane
at six in the morning on three days in the week set down
at the Old Parsonage at one on the same afternoon, as
he told his friends whom he hoped would be encouraged
to visit Chiddingfold. It was but 40 miles from London
Bridge, a pretty village well set in the Weald. For some
years after Douglas wrote the thick woods on the heavy
clay land and the green branch-shaded lanes continued to
be enlivened by countrywomen wearing venerable Red
Riding-hood cloaks charming and unusual enough to find
mention in Mr. Murray's early *Hand-Book*. The Parsonage,
near to the church and now called Glebe House (Plate 21),
is, as it must have been then, a delightful house in a
magnificent situation close by the 38th milestone from
Hyde Park Corner. Much as he would have appreciated

them, Douglas cannot have known the fine Wellingtonias which now ornament its grounds. The Curate kept his eyes and his ears open and, to begin with, chattered to his parishioners: all the more strange is it that he scarcely ever mentions in his writings interesting local matters of antiquity of which he must have had knowledge, the medieval iron and glass industries and the making of walking-sticks. He could not have travelled more than five miles from the Old Parsonage without seeing a hammer-pond and the site of its accompanying forge, or a site used by a Wealden glassmaker, or hearing a place-name which would recall these old industries to his mind.

But there were other matters of antiquity to occupy his attention.

During his sojourn in Kent Douglas had often turned his thoughts to the coastal district known to the Romans as the Saxon Shore and to the defences of Britain, and on 21 November 1782 he explained to the Society of Antiquaries why, in his view, the Roman remains found in the construction of the Redoubt on Chatham Hill were those of an establishment of the *comes litoris Saxonici,* the commander of the Roman shore defences. Now at Chiddingfold he had further thoughts and in 1787 in a paper on the *Urbs Rutupiae* of Ptolemy and the Linden-wick of the Saxons (published by J. Nichols in *Bibliotheca Topographica Britannica* Vol. I, No. 42, part vi, 1787 usually bound in Vol. I, 1780-90, p. 473) he returned to much the same subject. It is a long and tiresomely dull essay, an attempt to prove that the Roman station of Rutupiae was at Canterbury and not at Richborough as generally accepted then and now, and that the London-wic mentioned in Saxon charters and other early documents was either Canterbury or possibly the well-known Roman establishment at Reculver on the north coast of Kent. The essay is little more than a recension of classical authors and sources, led by the mid-second-century *Geography* of Ptolemy whose object Douglas seems to have forgotten was to reform the map of the world, though here and there Douglas shows some appreciation of the principles of historical geography which with his first-hand knowledge of the topography of north-east Kent he might well have applied to better advantage. In the end it is a poor example of book history without geography though it is illustrated by a fine drawing of Richborough Castle from the amphitheatre and the distant Isle of Thanet (Plate 22), pleasing in composition and accurate in detail. His derisive remarks about William Somner of Canterbury, 'who was more a theoretical or speculative than a practical antiquary', on Archdeacon Batteley the author of *Antiquitates Rutupinae,* and on Bede were severe. 'Bede has blundered and his readers have blundered more', and of Batteley 'These kind of *deliria* are extremely pleasing . . . especially when they are seemingly authenticated by a concurrence of materials which an ingenious antiquary can soon wrest to the text of his favourite subject . . . the sanguine antiquary will . . . insensibly be cajoled by a specious appearance of things into an erroneous survey of the plan he is methodising'. This is precisely what Douglas was doing himself in this paper, moving far from Ptolemy's statement that Rutupiae was one of the towns of the Cantii, a tribe who occupied Kent but also land north of the Thames including the site of London. Douglas, usually a practical man in the field, failed to see how Richborough situated on a hill could be supplied with water, an essential for civil or military settlement: the idea of wells seems never to have entered his head. Bede lived in the north too far away to describe the Kentish countryside from personal knowledge. Reculver was part of the port of London; Douglas said that three Roman military roads converged from Dover, Lympne and Richborough on the coast upon Canterbury, the country around which was 'most happily calculated to furnish a people with comfortable abode', and it had 'a remote antiquity as a place of note.' At Richborough there was certainly a blackness of the soil and other manifest signs such as coins, potsherds and other trifling *exuviae*: this was not enough, and *portus* should be translated as meaning *town*. A road from Richborough to Canterbury did not exist, he said, but one cannot altogether blame him for not seeing a feature which was effectively obliterated until recent years.

This strange Dissertation with extracts from and comments upon no less than 11 then accepted authorities, including the Itinerary of Richard of Cirencester, a forged description of Roman Britain by Charles Bertram, a teacher of English at Copenhagen, which was widely accepted by many scholars and not exposed until 1869, gave evidence of Douglas's wide and varied reading in classical and topographical works. It is perhaps understandable that no one thought it worth while to challenge or comment in detail upon this curious and in part nonsensical study of *Urbs Rutupiae*.

7

DISQUISITION

AS HE SAT AT HIS DESK in Rochester making up the pages of his *Travelling Anecdotes* and surveying his collection of relics from the barrows on Chatham Lines and elsewhere, Douglas had thoughts of another book. In June 1782 he tells his friend Faussett that he had very nearly completed a general history of the funeral customs of the ancients, having for the purpose made acquisition of a profusion of materials and spared no labour to accomplish a rational and concise system to ascertain the history of barrows, kist-vaens and cromlechs. He had made about a hundred drawings which he hoped to publish in aquatint. 'My object is not to benefit by the undertaking', he says, 'the getting up of the work will give me pleasure and greatly amuse me in my leisure hours. I shall hope to refund myself in the expence of printing, which will be very great . . . I mean to print my work the size of the Archaeologia for the sake of grouping in a library . . . the great plan I have in view will be to draw a line between all speculative fancies in antiquities and on hypotheses founded on reason and practical observations'. What he really wanted was access to the Faussett Collection 'which as it will ornament my work to a great degree I have not the least doubt of its making it known to the world, and as I shall have an indubitable proof of appreciating their value by an elaborate description of their justly to be admired antique estimation, so I think as you will have an easy opportunity of communicating the discoveries to the world, you will at the same time ensure yourself a channel of making their value known'. Faussett, with his legal training, was not quite so sure. Bearing in mind, no doubt, the difficult terms of the will he reserved access to his father's collections and manuscripts including his Journal *Inventorium Sepulchrale,* which he perhaps had thoughts of publishing himself, but Douglas was soon to visit Heppington making notes and drawings (cf. in Plate 15) with the genial assistance of his host who was himself an accomplished draughtsman.

The Prospectus (see pages 94 and 95), well written and once again in terms which would do some credit to publishers of part-works at the present day, was widely circulated. The book was to contain an account of a hundred graves of the ancient inhabitants of Britain opened under the careful inspection of the author with particulars of the pottery, weapons, decorations of women, of several magical instruments, culinary utensils, some very scarce and unpublished coins, and of a variety of other curious relics deposited with the dead. Gems, bracelets, beads and gold and silver buckles and brooches ornamented with precious stones would add to the variety. It was intended partially to illustrate the history of Britain in the fifth century, and to fix on a more unquestionable criterion for the study of antiquity. There would be added observations on Celtic, British, Roman and Danish barrows discovered in Britain, and some remarks would be directed to antiquaries who wished to engage in this pursuit by which 'they may be enabled to ascertain the truth of many Local Discoveries, which, for the Want of previous Caution, are for ever lost in Error or Uncertainty . . .'. The labours of the antiquary become respected in proportion as they approach to truth, and as they convey information to mankind. 'Posterity will be indebted to them, as long as they continue to justify the traditional writings of early ages, and to correct the wild speculations of modern enthusiasts in the study'. The *tumuli sepulchrales* that are scattered over this country have furnished some of the

On the 1st of MARCH, 1786,

Will be published, the FIRST NUMBER, in Folio,

OF

NENIA BRITANNICA:

OR, AN ACCOUNT OF

SOME HUNDRED SEPULCHRES,

Of the Ancient Inhabitants of BRITAIN.

Opened under a careful Inspection of the AUTHOR;

THE BARROWS CONTAINING

URNS, SWORDS, SPEAR-HEADS, DAGGERS, KNIVES, BATTLE-AXES, SHIELDS, and ARMILLÆ:—Decorations of Women; consisting of GEMS, PENSILE ORNAMENTS, BRACELETS, BEADS, GOLD and SILVER BUCKLES, BROACHES ornamented with Precious Stones; several MAGICAL IMPLEMENTS, CULINARY UTENSILS; some very scarce and unpublished COINS; and a Variety of other curious Relics deposited with the Dead.

TENDING PARTIALLY TO ILLUSTRATE

The HISTORY of BRITAIN in the FIFTH CENTURY; and to fix on a more unquestionable CRITERION for the STUDY of ANTIQUITY:

To which are added,

OBSERVATIONS on the CELTIC, BRITISH, ROMAN, and DANISH BARROWS, discovered in BRITAIN.

ALSO

Some REMARKS submitted to ANTIQUARIES who would wish to engage in this PURSUIT; by which, it is presumed, they may be enabled to ascertain the Truth of many Local Discoveries, which for Want of previous Caution, are for ever lost in Error or Uncertainty.

By the Rev. JAMES DOUGLAS, F. A. S.

Quis autem est, quem non moveat clarissimis monumentis testata consignataque Antiquitas?
Cic. de Div. lib. i.

Printed by J. NICHOLS, Printer to the SOCIETY of ANTIQUARIES; and Sold by G. NICOL, in the Strand, Bookseller to His MAJESTY.

C O N D I T I O N S.

THE Work will be comprized in *Twelve* Numbers, each Number, excepting the laft, will contain a *Sheet and an Half* of Letter-prefs ; and THREE COPPER PLATES, the Size of the Letter Prefs; at FIVE SHILLINGS each Number.

The laft Number will contain the Bulk of the Letter-prefs, at EIGHT SHILLINGS, which, with the former Numbers, will ftrictly fulfill the original Propofals of the Author to his Subfcribers.

A few Copies on Royal Paper.

P L A T E S.

The Engravings are finifhed in *Aqua Tinta*. This Style of Engraving is happily adapted to the Nature of Antique Relics, as it conveys a correct Idea of the Originals.

To avoid Repetitions, and to eftablifh the Nature of the Facts, fome Plates will contain felect Specimens of diftinct Sepulchres. Topographical Plans, Elevations, and Sections of *Tumuli*, will occafionally be added ; and a fyftematical Arrangement of the Relics, claffed under different Heads : by which means, Antiquaries will be enabled to compare their Difcoveries in this Country, with the Facts here eftablifhed ; and thus, by Analogy, to give a fatisfactory Hiftory of them.

The Plates will be coloured from the original Drawings.

N. B. The Author is happy to take this Opportunity of returning Thanks to many of his learned and liberal Correfpondents, who have communicated to him feveral curious Difcoveries, which relate to the Nature of his Work.

** The Subfcribers are requefted to fend for their Numbers when publifhed : for which Purpofe, a Lift of them will be delivered to the Publifher.

most interesting materials for the publication: authentic records of a once refined and formidable people, 'they must ever assert their pre-eminency over the vague and incorrect memorials that have been penned in the ages of superstition and darkness'.

These were wise words well said, and the beginning of a thought however vague that the antiquary was concerned with people as well as with the objects they used in bygone ages. And in writing the now classic words we have already quoted Sir Mortimer Wheeler had in mind the work of his predecessors, such as Douglas, as well as his own unique and long experience in the matter with which he was concerned. To assist his readers Douglas intended to illustrate his work lavishly in aquatint, a style of engraving which 'happily adapted to the Nature of Antique Relics, as it shows a correct Idea of the Originals'. Further, he would add topographical plans, elevations, and sections of tumuli—it was the first time that a British antiquary had realised the outstanding importance of such information— and give a classified systematic arrangement of the various relics so that they could more easily be compared with other discoveries in Britain. Douglas then went on to say that some of these tumuli, in his view, were more particularly confined to a body of the unhappy Britons and Romans who were posted on the sea-coasts by Stilicho to oppose the invasions of the Saxons and the Franks. He had acquired the facility of discriminating between these barrows and the .others so often seen in Britain which had no affinity to them, and for this reason would confine his researches to the fifth century, a period but little known. His account, he hoped, would shed some light on the affairs of Britain during that period. Gentlemen in possession of literary materials or other relative evidence would, he hoped, communicate with him. It was an ambitious plan. Ambition in an antiquary is no bad thing: how well was this author to succeed in presenting antiquarian study in such a novel form? What kind of book would it all make? Before we discuss its progress and contents a few words must be said about the proposals for publication.

Potential subscribers were told that the book in demy folio was to consist of 12 numbers with a frontispiece, each containing a sheet and a half of letter-press and three copper plates the size of the letter-press, at a cost of 5s. per number; the last number, which would contain the bulk of the letter-press, would cost 8s. There were to be some copies on royal paper for collectors with plates coloured from the original drawings which were priced at 8s. 6d., except for the last number which would have to cost 11s. 6d. These magnificent coloured copies of which five seem to have been produced by Douglas and of which the present whereabouts of four is known should not be confused with several copies which were coloured by other hands with no real knowledge of their subjects at much later dates. There are also in existence a very few copies of the plates bound separately. The plates had been accidentally destroyed by fire, Douglas told James Edwards, author of Edward's *Topography* in 1818. Douglas's own copy bound in morocco, with original drawings and 26 extra illustrations never engraved and with MS. additions, 'altogether unique' in the words of the 1842 Grenville Catalogue by Payne and Foss, is now in the Grenville Library (G. 6863) at the British Museum. Of the extra illustrations a view of the barrows in Greenwich Park with grazing deer and the Observatory in the background (Plate 23), of Coldred church, St. Margaret's-at-Cliffe and relics from Boughton Aluph (Plate 24) all in Kent, are delightfully fresh and delicate water-colour drawings. Another of these fine copies coloured by Douglas himself is in the Bibliothèque Royale de Belgique (Réserve précieuse: cote II 3200 D) bought in 1854 at the sale in Amsterdam of the library of Abbé M. A. van Steenwijk. It has the added interest of the signature of the original owner, Captain Richard Gregory of the Coldstream Regiment of Guards. There may be a connection between author and owner for Gregory retired in August 1793, the year *Nenia* was

finished, and his regiment left for the Netherlands campaign in February of that same year, where he may have
served for a short time. The completed book may have
been taken over in his baggage, but equally well he may
have subscribed for the parts as they became due and
had the binding undertaken on the Continent. He became
an Ensign a year before the first number was issued in
1786, and it could be guessed that he might well have met
ex-Captain Douglas socially and perhaps as a fellow
antiquary with a military background. One other original
hand-coloured copy is in Brighton Reference Library, a
relic from the town's old Free Library (F 571-9 D 74)
and another is in the University of Glasgow Library
(S 5 - b 18). This latter copy, bought for the Library from
a dealer, had been known to me since 1936 but I had
not been permitted by its previous owner to see it, and
my indebtedness to the Library is therefore the greater.

It is interesting to see how far the book matched the
high hopes of its author. Like many another book, it was
born in some tribulation and under tiresome difficulties
of production. Much can be learned from his letters
to Faussett reproduced in the latter part of this book.
The general plan was laid down in 1782 during his days
at Rochester. 'I have very nearly completed a general
history of the funeral customs of the ancients', he writes
to Godfrey Faussett at Heppington, 'having for that
purpose made acquisition of a profusion of matterials and
spared no labour to accomplish a rational and concise
system to ascertain the history of barrows—kistvaen,
cromlechs &c. I have made drawings of the most material
part of my small researches, besides of an addition which
I have made to it from various quarters. These drawings
will be published in the *aquatinta* to the amount of near
an hundred'. It had advanced well by the following year
when several plates had been completed, though by then
the proposed price would have to be increased or the
plates would be the ruin of him. In 1784 he was still
working hard at his book as well as at securing some
preferment in his clerical aspirations, and though he felt

he was perhaps a little slow in literary work he gained in point of fullness and accuracy. There was now no doubt that he would have to publish on his own account, take time and run all the risks, being then too proud to solicit subscriptions or to circulate work that would be of no credit to him. A delay of a few months was therefore inevitable. By May 1785 the first plates were finished, and Douglas had printed one or two specimen aquatints in both green and bronze to reproduce the patina of the original metal. By the summer of the same year he had had to alter his plans. 'Was it not for that insatiable thirst in the pursuit of practical enquiry, I should now content myself with the materials I have' he wrote, and this with the literary side and the drawings ought to provide a sufficient store for his work, and when 'please God, a little ready cash comes to hand, which I expect shortly, I shall put to the press'. But it was not so easy. The first number was delayed in publication from March until May 1786, the work being put back by a drunken ingenious artist who cut the head and tail pieces. By September three numbers had been published and by this time the author had readily put his book out to public subscription. In that same year he politely reminded his friend Faussett that he would welcome criticism: what he really wanted was to use further material in the collection of Bryan Faussett to establish 'some literary truths which I think in a great measure depend on the relics which are in your possession' as he tactfully worded his request. Faussett did not approve of some of Douglas's remarks which he felt were disparaging to his father, and he was again unwilling at this time for use to be made of his father's Journal, *Inventorium Sepulchrale,* or of illustrations from the collection. Douglas persisted in his requests. By October 1787 the fourth and fifth numbers had been pub- lished, and on the back of a proof of plate XVI of *Nenia* the author had courteously submitted for approval (Plate 17) he upbraids his correspondent for 'epistolary neglect', saying at the same time that he had himself been for some months in Switzerland conducting a nephew to a foreign

seminary and looking at the relics of Childeric in the
Library of the King of France in Paris where he had
noticed some details not recorded by Chifflet in his official
account of the jewellery of this fifth-century King of the
Merovingian Franks.

Other difficulties presented themselves within the next
six months, and here for the first time we begin to sense
the attitude of despair which from time to time was to
become a marked feature of Douglas's life. He lived, at
Chiddingfold, some long distance from his printers and
found great difficulty in having his work printed with
correctness, 'blunders without end'. His brother, to whom
he was closely attached since his schooldays and who had
often helped financially, had died, and there was much
anxiety with worldly business, 'dead pulls', fag, some
injustice and long bills to pay. He longed for a little milk
of human kindness, some forgiveness and charity, 'all this
like a millstone has kept back the Nenia'. Number 7 was
prepared by July 1789 though his health and particularly
his eyes had been seriously impaired by the *aqua fortis*
which he used in the making of his copper plates, and
he had found by painful experience that no great personal
good had arrived from dabbling in politics as insisted upon
by his family in order to obtain clerical preferment and
promotion which would lead to 'a town residence, the
great emporium to barter knowledge in'. Number 7 was
still with the printers a year later. The printers were
dilatory, proofs took a long time to return corrected.

Matters went from bad to worse. The eighth number did
not go to press until February 1791 and by October 1793
Douglas wrote of the 'confusion, loss, disappointment and
the unspeakable trouble which I have had with booksellers on account of my work which has been shamefully
spoiled and neglected'. He still hoped to have Faussett's
opinion on the general finishing of the book with 'liberal
allowances for the natural errors of an author who had
such a vast field of literature to range in and where
points of sight and belief were so much confused by other
antiquaries and where antiquarian materials were so diffi-

cult to arrange for a proper historical use'. It may be that
the printer then working on the book, John Nichols
(official printer to the Society of Antiquaries), did not
exert himself overmuch and some subscribers certainly
found difficulty in securing their parts, but the real
trouble was that Douglas had insufficient capital to finance
his undertaking. Nichols was an expensive printer and for
that reason was replaced in 1798 at the Society, though
his son and grandson were appointed in later years.
Douglas therefore made over the bound volumes to
Benjamin and John White in the belief that the Whites
were more punctual and regular men in the trade. At
last, in 1793, seven years after the issue of the first number
and some 12 years after the author had started his work
upon it—here let it be remembered that his critic Edward
Hasted spent more than 40 years in producing his
History of Kent—*Nenia Britannica* was published at a cost
of £3 13s. 6d. It seems little short of a wonder that the
book appeared at all; in spite of all the bothers and troubles
it contained 197 pages of text and 36 folio plates. There
was an obsequious dedication to his Patron, George
Augustus Frederick, Prince of Wales, destined 'to reign at
a period, the author is certain Filial Piety wishes far
distant'. Ironically enough the Prince Regent did not come
to the Throne until a year after Douglas's own death.

The title *Nenia Britannica* was chosen only after much
thought. It caused some wry comment in learned circles
for the word *nenia* could properly be used in the sense of
a popular or nursery song as well as in its more frequent
meaning of a funeral dirge which Douglas intended, and
the book was anything but a lullaby. The author quickly
took up the matter with his critics in a long letter to the
Gentleman's Magazine for October 1793, saying that
Festus—and who else but Douglas would think of quoting
the first abridged Latin Lexicon, popular though its
later versions became—proved that Nenia was a goddess
to whom a well-known temple was dedicated. In his choice
of a title the author had also been much influenced by a
conversation he had had with Dr. Johnson shortly before

the latter's death. Douglas, who had called at Bolt Court
to enquire after the Doctor's health on his return from
Derbyshire, wondered about the propriety of the title.
'Why not, Sir', says the Doctor, *'Nenia Britannica* as well
as *Flora Britannica'*. And apart from the shield of this
great literary character, Douglas replied to his critics, any
reasonably well-read Latin scholar ought to remember the
allusions of the Roman historian Festus to the goddess
Nenia. It was much later, as we shall see, that detractors,
envious of Douglas's reputation as an antiquary but aware
of his sometimes unwise efforts to lessen his financial
straits, dubbed the author a 'Ninny'.

In summarising the contents of *Nenia Britannica* we must
remind ourselves that the work was intended to be sold in
parts. Each part was to be illustrated and the text, especially in the later numbers, was dependent upon the supply
of pictures; the original plan by which observations on the
periodical collection of facts were to be left until the
completion of the book was quickly dropped in favour of
a more discursive treatment.

There are some statements in the opening ·Preface
which showed an acute foresight of the application of
modern archaeological method:

> The inscription or the medal are the only facts which can
> obviate error, and produce the substitutes for deficiency of
> antient records: when these are wanting, in vain will the
> human mind be gratified by the most acute investigations;
> incredulity will arise in proportion as the judgement is
> matured.
> By contemplating the relics discovered in our antient
> sepultures, the historian may have an opportunity of com-
> paring them with similar relics found in different places, and
> on which arguments have been grounded by authors who
> have written on the antient inhabitants of Britain. If a medal
> or inscription be found in a sepulchre among other relics, the
> undoubted characteristic of the customs of a people at the
> time of the deposit, and the supscription on the medal or the
> inscription evincing a low period, it will be a self-evident
> position, that similar relics under similar forms of sepulture,
> discovered in other parts of the island, cannot apply to a
> period more remote; hence the most trifling fact will

invalidate many received opinions, and history be reduced
to a more critical analysis . . . No position of this work has
been assumed on mere conjecture, and when deductions
have been made, they have been founded on a scrupulous
comparison of facts . . . the reader may form his own
conclusions, without any apprehension of being involved in
the confusion of self-opinionated theory . . .

These were bold words indeed, and perhaps the earliest
reference to the application of relative dating from a
known to an unknown source, for that clearly is what
Douglas had in mind.

The early sections describe the author's own excavations
of barrows on Chatham Lines, 1779-93, of graves at Ash,
Kent, 1771 and 1783, and Baggrave, Leicestershire. As an
example, the opening pages which describe the first barrow
opened on Chatham Lines may be quoted:

> Fig, 1 [Plate 25] represents an horizontal section of a
> tumulus opened on Chatham Lines, the cist in which the
> body was deposited, the arms &c, the loose excavated chalk
> and the vallum round the tumulus, in its original state before
> the mound was levelled.
>
> The cist was eight feet in length, three feet in breadth, and
> four feet below the level of the native soil, when the upper
> coating was thrown up; the latter about half a foot in
> thickness.
>
> The body in the meridian; head to the south. The bones
> of a male adult, obvious by their size and texture. The
> length and thickness of the fistular bones were such, as to
> admit of the assertion, without occurring to other marks of
> the distinction of the sexes, or to the arms deposited by the
> side of the skeleton. The bones much calcined by age; but,
> on repeated experiments, they are found to contain a great
> proportion of volatile alcali.
>
> No appearance of a coffin.
>
> An iron spear-head and *umbo* of a shield. The spear-head
> fifteen inches long, and the *umbo* four inches in diameter.
>
> The spear-head on the right shoulder; the point in a line
> with the head; the haft containing decayed wood, which, by
> the texture of several similar specimens in my possession,
> appears to be of ash. The metal is reduced to a calx, and
> which by the smallest pressure is liable to be disunited.
>
> The umbo or boss of the shield was found on the center
> of the thigh-bone.

An iron stud with a pin in the centre: uncertain in what position this laid near the body; but by the impression of decayed wood upon it, it appears either to have been driven into the end of the spear at the handle, or into the shield.

A brass [bronze] buckle; near the last bone of the vertebrae, or close to the *os sacrum*.

A bottle of red earth at the feet of the skeleton; twelve inches in height, and four inches in largest diameter.

A thin plate of iron exactly in the center and under the umbo; four inches and a half in length; two rivets at the end, and seems to have received the end of the rivets of the umbo through the wood, as its bracer or stay.

A knife on the right side, with impressions of decayed wood, and very discernible impressions of cloth upon it. The wood appears to have been its case; particularly as the end is fitted for a handle of this material, and which contains a great portion of the same adhering to it.

The face and reverse of an iron stud; four of which were found near the umbo of the shield; similar studs are often seen on the Scotch orbicular shields; the studs of which are generally of brass, the same as the umbo.

An iron sword, on the left side; thirty-five inches and a quarter the whole length; the blade from the handle thirty inches; two inches broad; flat, double edged, and sharp pointed; a great portion of wood covering the blade, which indicates that it was buried in a scabbard; the external covering being leather, and the internal of wood.

The relics from Tumulus II also excavated in 1779 are shown here (Plates 26, 27) as they were drawn by Douglas and as they now appear in the Ashmolean Museum.

There follow notes on the barrow digging on Chartham Downs in 1730 by Dr. Mortimer which we have already considered earlier in this book, and on Bryan Faussett's Kingston grave No. 205 which contained the famous jewelled gold brooch, a description of which shows Douglas's power of close observation:

A GOLD FIBULA, elegantly enchased. The stones within the semi-circles of the outward circles are *garnet* and pale blue *tourquoise*. The stone, like the superior part of a cross is the *turquoise*, and one of the same form alternately enchased between the semi-circles. The vermicular gold chain in the compartment of the second circle is delicately milled with notches, and ENCHASED ON THE GROUND OF THE

FIBULA: the alternate square setting is *garnet*; the four small circles on the third contain in their center a white hemisphere of a shelly substance, with a circular garnet; the triangular enchasement, and the one in form of the head of a cross, *turquoise* stones, and the intermediate garnet; the fourth circle like the second; the fifth like the first; the sixth forms the umbo which protrudes from the ground of the *fibula,* and is a white shelly or *coque de perle* substance, divided into right angles, with a gold enchasing; the next, or seventh, is gold milled in notches; the light circle next to this is plain gold, which rises higher, and receives the central enchased ornament; the small heads of the crosses of a dark tint are *tourquoise*; the rest *garnet,* excepting the central stone of all which is lost . . .

This rich and singular Jewel was doubtless a mark of the distinguished character of the person interred with it. For size and importance, it excels all antique jewels of this nature I have seen in cabinets. When they occur in *tumuli*, the small ones are only found in the proportion of one in 70; and this in clusters of tumuli that exceed an hundred in number, for it generally happens, if the place of interment be extensive, and crouded with barrows, that the contents are more curious and valuable.

Turquoise which a later generation of archaeologists identified as lapis lazuli we now know to be blue glass, and coque de perle which has been variously called shell, bone, ivory or meerschaum we must now recognise as almost any white shell or stone-like material available to the particular jeweller, but Douglas's description of the gold filigree work is as up-to-date as our own.

The book continues with four long, illustrated, systematic inventories called 'Miscellanea Antiqua', of glass-ware, objects found only in the graves of women, jewellery, trinkets and the iron weapons of warriors. Douglas then goes on to describe the opening of ditched barrows in Greenwich Park (Plate 23), by permission of the 'Surveyor General of Royal Domains', discussing with first-hand knowledge the grave cloths of linen and wool and the nature of the well-preserved Roman hair, types of pottery vessels, and coins and their uses and limitations for the dating of burials. A coin of Justinian (527-565) from a grave at Gilton near Ash, for example, could have been

placed there in theory at any time between the earliest
date possible for the coin, that is the accession of
Justinian in 527, and 742 when extra-mural burials were
prohibited outside churchyards. Then again, if the grave
or cemetery was of pagan people, the date would fall
between the accession of Justinian and the conversion of
Kent by St. Augustine in 597, but if of Christians, then
between 597 and the middle of the eighth century. In one
section Douglas suggests that such cemeteries may have
been those of Christians of the sixth or perhaps early
seventh centuries, but elsewhere he thinks that some
might well belong to the early years of the eighth century,
the graves of small local communities some, such as
Silbertswold, Eythorn and Barfreston in East Kent, still
known by their Saxon place-names. From a grave at Ash
there had been recovered a Roman brooch, a circular
stone and a polished flint axe or chisel: the latter could
not be used as evidence of date and could best be regarded
as an amulet, preserved with veneration, from an earlier
epoch. These were indeed novel views, a credit to British
antiquarian study.

Then follows in list form the contents of what Douglas
calls 'the small barrows' which are often found in clusters,
and for the first time in the study of British antiquity
he recognises them not as Roman or Danish but Saxon
burial places, but he is careful to add some warning
notes about the effects of Christian belief on burial and the
contents of graves. As a contrast he then considers
sepulchral remains of the Romans with special reference
to Kingsholm, Gloucestershire, Chesterford, Cambridgeshire, the mound forming part of the Dane John group
at Canterbury, burials at Rochester and Chatham Hill in
Kent, and to the discoveries at Tongres in Flanders which
he knew at first-hand. There follows a short illustrated
account of flint and brass [bronze] tools, placed here one
supposes because the author already possessed the necessary and adequate drawings in his portfolios.

Later sections describe excavations at Boxley, Coldred
St. Margaret's-at-Cliffe and Sibbertswould (Shepherdswell

in Kent and the 'great barrows', Chatham, Chiddingfold, with which are included—largely because the notes were provided by his friend Hayman Rooke and other correspondents—Stanton Moor and other Derbyshire stone circles, Stonehenge, and Tinewald as he called it, in the Isle of Man, a plan of which had been supplied by 'the late Captain Grose' with whom Douglas had long ago made up his quarrel. There is much speculation about the origin and purpose of Stonehenge and whether it was a judicial or astronomical monument or a temple, though not necessarily of Druidic construction. It was not until many years later that Colt Hoare was to say that as Douglas had explained all the mysteries of Stonehenge, no more need be thought about it. He had in fact said in summary that it was built long before the time of the Druids but it may have continued to be used as a meeting place even in Anglo-Saxon times. Colt Hoare's remark was not intended to be wholly serious, but it does imply an appreciation of Douglas's continuous interest in the meaning of the monument and acknowledges his authority.

At the beginning of his book Douglas had set forth his General Aim, and he closes it with an Argument of six pages, a very long Historic Relation and General Conclusion. He ends by saying that 'This sketch is only offered for the investigation of the historian, who will doubtless perceive a vast field of enquiry before him. Sacred and profane history may be cited to prove a concurrence in the interesting research; and what the latter is deficient of, when the question relates to the higher periods of history, the former will incontestably supply, to the satisfaction of the wisest and most learned'.

The closing words were a frank attempt to attract the historians to the basic grammar of a new approach to the study of antiquity, which he had already set out in forthright terms. 'The inscription or the medal are the only facts which can obviate error and produce the substitutes for deficiency of antient records', he had already written, 'and when these are wanting, in vain will the human mind be gratified by the most acute investigations; incredulity will arise in proportion as the judgement is matured'. By observing the relics found in our ancient burial places, the enquiring antiquary and, Douglas emphasises, the historian can compare them with similar relics found in different places and about which arguments have been made by various authors who have taken the trouble to write about the ancient inhabitants of Britain. If a coin or inscription found in a burial indicates a 'low period' it will be a self-evident proposition that similar relics in similar forms of burial in other parts of Britain are not likely to belong to a more remote period. A fact of this sort could invalidate many accepted opinions, and as a result history might have to be reduced to a more critical analysis. Today we realise that Douglas sometimes tended to overstate his case but, as he often pointed out, his deductions were founded on the scrupulous comparison of the facts known to him, and his readers were invited to form their own conclusions 'without any apprehension of being involved in the confusion of self-opinionated theory'. One or two modern writers on fringe archaeology might well take a leaf from his book: 'the assemblage of *facts* can be the only means of producing comparisons which render an argument of force, and conduce to historical truths which depend on such discoveries'. And yet, at times, Douglas was a little too cautious, as in his quite unwarranted stricture of John Twyne's account of the opening of a barrow on Barham Downs by Royal licence of Henry VIII—it is well described in this Canterbury schoolmaster's book *De Rebus Albionicis* which appeared in 1590, nine years after his death—and on himself when he 'raked up a jumble of much absurd nonsense' to substantiate his sensible views on the significance of crystal balls associated with perforated spoons in certain Saxon graves.

In plan Douglas's book was something new. Never before had a zealous and intelligent English antiquary attempted to deal with his subject in such a philosophical way and with such a liberal spirit, never before had anyone formulated a systematic study of relics which could lead

to an interpretation of ancient industry and manners.
It had even greater novelty. Camden, as Sir Thomas
Kendrick reminds us, was the first author to provide an
archaeological illustration in an English book and later
editions of *Britannia* were not lacking in pictures of
antiquarian remains, but it was Douglas who insisted that
the antiquary must look to learn. The plan of the barrow
on Chatham Lines which formed his frontispiece and
the section of graves in the sand-pit at Ash are the earliest
illustrations of English archaeology in the field. His
original drawings and plates are evidence enough of his
dictum that 'drawings must always supercede a verbal
description'. Fortunately he was a skilful draughtsman
well able to follow his own precepts, to appreciate his
subject and its real significance. A sword to him was a
two-edged weapon, a brooch a desirable trinket, and
neither was to be used merely as an artist's exercise. His
drawings show sense and feeling and occasionally, as
may be seen in some of the unpublished examples in his
own copy of *Nenia* now in the Grenville Library in the
British Museum, several of which are reproduced here,
verve and a real distinction. It was to be a long time
before he had an equal in the study of archaeology on a
scientific basis or as an illustrator of archaeological relics.

For his sources Douglas used his own wide experience
in the field, the large collection of relics he had obtained
and carefully recorded, and also material collected by
such well-known antiquaries as Sir Ashton Lever, William
Boys of Sandwich in Kent, Sir William Fagge of Mystole,
Kent, and by the less well-known friends he had made
during his sojourn at Rochester. His wider correspondents
included John Mander of Derbyshire, Major Hayman
Rooke whose interests lay between the field antiquities
of Nottinghamshire, Derbyshire and Yorkshire, most of
which he attributed to the Druids, and the domestic
concerns of the Society of Antiquaries, a friend who
had furnished him with drawings of druidic temples,
barrows, cromlechs, cists and kistvaens for his book, and
the Abbé Van Muyssen of Tongres with whom he kept

in touch for many years after his journeyings in Flanders. Information and drawings from the Abbé Van Muyssen (Plates 29, 30) added much to the value of Douglas's work, and he was able to recall his visit of 1773 and to add a long footnote on the history of Tongres and the health-giving properties of its 'chalybeat' spring water first noted by Pliny, a spring of which, as we have noted, still exists. Van Muyssen was a most unusual character. He would gladly show his considerable collection of antiquities to any interested visitors—'ces Messieurs connaissent, comme il paraît par leur façon de penser que l'homme ne doit pas vivre pour lui seul', he would say, and so much appreciated was Douglas's account of Tongres in *Nenia Britannica* that it was reprinted in full with commendation by the Scientific and Literary Society of Limburg in 1897 (*Bulletin Soc. Scientifique et Litteraire du Limburg*, 18, i (1897), pp. 136-58); and one can but sympathise with the Flemish compositor who had to set it up in English text. Both Douglas and Van Muyssen were far in advance of their contemporaries in realising that relics of antiquity were not mere decorations to a collector's cabinet. Above all he drew heavily on the famous collection made by Bryan Faussett, a collection which he had himself studied in some detail, adding to his knowledge by constant enquiry, not always welcome, from Henry Godfrey Faussett, the son of Bryan, in whose house at Heppington the collection remained. We have already spoken of the friendship between the two men who had a common bond in their devotion to the study of antiquity. And, not perhaps surprisingly, during his residence in London and his many visits there, Douglas studied curiosities and original manuscripts in the British Museum with great profit.

As a background Douglas was familiar with the usual classical authors as might be expected of a Manchester Grammar School boy of his day. Less expected are the little known authors in Latin and Greek, his wide knowledge of Montfaucon's *L'Antiquité expliquée* published in Paris in 1724 and Chifflet's *Anastasis Childerici*, an

account of the tomb of Childeric the First, King of the
Merovingian Franks, published in 1655 at Antwerp and
studied as we have noted by Douglas during a visit to
Paris. He was much at home with our own national
historians and topographers. He was not only well read
in Leland, Camden, Lluyd and Stukeley, but also in the
county historians, William Borlase of Cornwall, Robert
Plot of Oxfordshire and Staffordshire, John Hutchins of
Dorset, Philip Morant of Essex and in Dugdale's *Mona-
sticon* as well as in William Lambarde, Thomas Philipott,
William Gostling and John Twyne, authorities on Kent.
It is evident, too, that he was a careful reader of the
Gentleman's Magazine whose pages provided almost the
only antiquarian forum of his day.

Two manuscripts in his own collection provided material
from Kentish sources. The first was the common-place
book of Heneage Finch, the fifth Earl of Winchilsea
(d. 1726), which he had purchased in 1785, and which
he later described in the *Gentleman's Magazine*, 1802, ii,
718-9, 825. Douglas in common with many authorities
down to the present day writes the family names of
Winchilsea as Winchelsea. Finch's activities as a collector
and lover of antiquity are described by Professor Stuart
Piggott in his book, *William Stukeley* (Oxford, 1950). To
our great regret this manuscript, surely the earliest of
excavation notebooks in Britain, cannot now be traced
despite a wide enquiry. But as a sample of its contents
there is Douglas's reproduction of an original page
(Plate 24) describing and illustrating to scale a spear-head
and three umboes of shields found in 1740 at Boughton
Aluph in Kent, and of pots from a Roman burial discovered at Boxley near Maidstone in the following year.
From these extracts and from his correspondence it is
clear that Lord Winchilsea was an exact and enquiring
antiquary; his field-work, carried out perhaps under the
direction of his friend Stukeley, was a model of what
such activities should be, and to what better inspiration
could the author of *Nenia* turn? The second manuscript,
and it is also now lost, was by the Revd. John Lewis of

Margate, an industrious antiquary known for his histories of the Isle of Thanet (1723) and Faversham Abbey (1727). It contains accounts of excavations of graves in the eastern part of Kent which appear to have been well and concisely written.

Douglas also turned his attention to technical matters. He could take a cast of a coin or brooch and instruct his friends in the process using tea lead or isinglass. He commented upon the identification of cloth and wood from their impression left in the rust of decayed iron-work, the preservative nature of 'copperas' upon leather in certain soils, the influence of certain types of soil on the preservation of cloth, human hair and bones, and discussed the chemical composition of solder used in brooches. Where necessary, he assures his readers, he did not hesitate to perform his own 'analytical experiment'. Not for another century was Charles Roach Smith to make his microscopical examination of traces of wood remaining in the sockets of Anglo-Saxon spear-heads and to prove the shafts were of ash. For many years Douglas had been interested in the nature of discoloura-tions in the soil. At Ash near Richborough 'A darkish stratum of soil in a native sand was always the sign of an interment', an observation that any archaeologist who has excavated in Thanet Sand will at once confirm, and Douglas was the first to notice with understanding and to record the 'marks of a factitious earth in the native sand', that often elusive clue on the proper development of which the value of modern excavation work so often depends. Camden had already called attention to the 'draughts of streets crossing one another' in the corn-field which occupied the interior of the Roman fort at Richborough, and Douglas was equally well aware of the significance of the patterns known to present-day archaeologists as soil-marks and crop-marks. To Douglas, in this particular book, crop-marks had one particu-lar use: luxuriant grass on the top of a burial mound showed that it had already been opened and that it was not worth while to make a further 'ransack'.

Later in his life he was to see what crop-marks could show in detail.

Contemporary antiquarian and literary opinion was scarcely ready to accept a work which depended largely upon a scientific consideration of observed facts relating to relics of antiquity and what was to be called much later history in the open air, and especially as it was put forward by the curate of a remote country parish. For one reason or another it was not noticed in the *Gentleman's Magazine* where new books on history and topography were regularly discussed—it may be that Douglas was having one of his temporary misunderstandings with the editor. An anonymous reviewer in the 1786 volume of the *Monthly Review,* a journal of weight and standing, claimed the first number of *Nenia Britannica* as 'a curious performance to be completed in twelve numbers, each of which will contain three plates, the author's own etching and a written description of what is present', and that was the most to be said for it. The *Critical Review* of August 1793 complained that the completed *Nenia* was but a funeral dirge and the name of the work kept to the subject, to which Douglas quickly retorted that 'however dull and malignant a reviewer be, he should not be either ignorant or unlearned'. It was more than 20 years later in 1835 that Horsfield in his *History of Sussex* was the first to realise the true value of *Nenia Britannica.* 'Up to this time', he writes, 'no genuine attempt had been made to acquire knowledge of our early inhabitants, no extensive plan for a generalisation of known excavations'. Although the whole of Douglas's reasoning may not be perfectly borne out by the discoveries which led to them, he adds, yet nothing is more convincing than the majority of the proofs. Another 21 years was to pass before Charles Roach Smith in his long and detailed introduction to Bryan Faussett's journal *Inventorium Sepulchrale* gave the *Nenia* the commendation it so well deserved. From that time until the present day it has served as a source book for information about Saxon and other antiquities, though apart from two notable instances there has been but little

comment on its sensibility, still less on its deservedly high
place in the early literature of British archaeology. In it
there is mention of some 35 barrows, 15 special beads
and notes on more than 20 coins of special archaeological
interest. His many sites range from Julaber's [Julliberrie's]
Grave, the well-known long barrow at Chilham in East
Kent to the ancient stone monuments of Asia and Etrus-
can tombs with their special pottery. As a final comment,
it may be said that his Index starts with '*Adzes, stone*' and
ends with '*Zones, charmed*'.

8

MINOR PLEASURES

THERE WERE BUT FEW VISITORS to the lovely old
parsonage set picturesquely, as it still is (Plate 21),
facing the village green in the then absolutely retired
parish of Chiddingfold deep in the secluded woodlands
of the Weald. There were times when Douglas became
tired and dispirited with the call of his conscientiously-
performed pastoral duties, with his constant extravagances
in antiquarian publications which, he said, gave endless
trouble and little or no profit, and the preparation of the
promised numbers of *Nenia* became more and more
delayed. A few words of criticism had disturbed him to a
quite unreasonable extent—'I must toss the curs and
mumgrils of critics', he tells Faussett, 'and endure the
bangs and belabourings of blockheads and heavy rogues
who flourish the quill'. There were mounting debts, the
not inconsiderable cost of raising a growing family,
even the maintenance of some social position 'in the little
advantages offered by neighbouring society', and above
all his need for preferment in the church to which end
he made constant approaches to friends and relatives.
He had some thoughts of an excursion to places of
antiquarian interest in Sussex, the tumuli on the Downs,
to Findon and 'a very ancient camp called Cissbury', a
plan indeed of touring it about, than which nothing as
he repeated, can be more delightful and cheering to the

mind as also wonderfully instructive. If Faussett and his
wife could come to Sussex they would be greatly
welcome, brats and all. As some relief to his oppressively
occupied mind he turned to the writing of fiction as he
explains in this letter to Faussett:

Chiddingfold, 5th May, 1790

Dear Faussett,

The above figs. are for the vignette to my 7th no. They
are specimens of Egyptian vitrification which I mean to compare with the green or verditer razed beads found in tumuli
and which are frequently discovered in our most antient. The
beads are of this shape [sketch of a melon-shaped bead].
Some I think you once told me were found in the small
barrows but this I have never remarked, however if so I am
persuaded you will set me rights.

And now my dear sir, by way of expiation for past
trespasses, I desire you will accept of a sorry apology for
not answering your obliging favour wherein was your drawing
of the Mystole pendant. The truth was, I had put aside your
letter and your queries had totally escaped my memory and
as recently I had taken if up to engrave the pendant all my
offences rushed at once into my mind. You ask me whether
the large barrows may not apply to the Saxons and Danes
occasionally and whether I know any such person as *Tumboracos*? I do not believe that any relics were ever found in
the large barrows of this Kingdom to ascertain whether they
were of Saxon or Danish origin. As to the latter on their
subjection of the island they so soon embraced Christianity
that I think it is scarce probable any of the large barrows
can be attributed to them and the smaller ones we are sure
did not. But this disquisition I purpose to postpone to the
last number of my work, when I mean *critically* to comment
on every author that has written on the subject. I certainly
did sign my name *Tumboracos* to the paper in the Gent. Mag.
and wherein I dropped several hints which may have discovered
the author and which I am very certain you could not fail to
apprehend. Mr. Bere has never replied and therefore I think
him a very stupid ungentlemanly fellow.

I cannot help in this letter to express a certain coolness in
your manner which I remarked when I last saw you in town.
I revolved in my mind all manner of things which might have
caused it and could not attribute the same to anything else
but my unhandsome neglect in not answering your last letter.

If herein lies the offence I beg your forgiveness and a renewal of our *auncient* acquaintance.

I rather think the *aqua fortis* which I use copiously in my copper plates has at times injured my health, and by way of relaxation from the dry study of antiquity, I have published two small works of 3 vols. each. It has been a kind of *novel mania* in which I have been engaged, but thank God I hope I am now effectually cured of the delirium—at least I promise you that I am *convalescent*. One of the works is called *Fashionable Infidelity* and the other *The Maid of Kent*. In this latter I have made a Sir Simon Hales the Hero. A very accidental thing I assure you—I had no kind of personal . . . whatever to the Kentish family of that name . . . had printed the first vol. before I had realised that such a family did recently exist in the County. I trust it will not be taken as really so but if it should be, I dare say the similarity of character will not fit. These books I have published with a good intent of introducing a better kind of a thing for the amusement of families than the stupid trash which circulating libraries teem with. But whether I have been successful I must leave to veteran critics—or rather the *blue stocking club,* to decide.

Adieu—my best compliments united with those of Mrs. Douglas to your good Lady and believe me to be with great sincereity, dear Faussett,

Your faithful and obedly,

Jas. Douglas.

A *Tumboracus* letter was printed in the July 1789 number of the *Gentleman's Magazine,* and there may have been others:

> Some few years back, on the opening of a barrow, I was hurried from my repast, in the company of some friends, by three Irish soldiers, who came running out of breath to me with the assurance that they had discovered a perfect skeleton, the enormous size of which they pronounced, before I reached the spot, to have been the carcase of a prodigious giant. Eager to transport myself to the spot, I arrived panting for breath, when to my great mortification, and check to a curious avidity, I found the bones not exceeding the ordinary human stature. Vext from my own disappointment, and the exaggerated account of the Hibernians, I seized a thigh-bone from the grave, and after having made one fellow stand erect to measure it by his own, I belaboured the fellows with it for their natural promptness

to magnify these casual discoveries into the marvellous. It
cured my spleen, and I returned in better humour, though
somewhat disappointed, to my friends.

The excavation can only have been on Chatham Lines,
where Douglas was allowed to employ military labour in
his excavations.

During his years at Chiddingfold Douglas also employed
part of his leisure in a devotion to theological studies. In
1792, the year before the publication of the completed
Nenia, he had written *Twelve Discourses on the Influence
of the Christian Religion in Civil Society.* It was an octavo
volume of 215 pages printed by John Nichols for Cadell
in the Strand, well bound in gilt blue leather with good
marbled edges and end-papers. The author was named
as The Rev. James Douglas, F.A.S. of St. Peter's College,
Cambridge, Chaplain in Ordinary to His Royal Highness
the Prince of Wales. The book was wide in its scope. It
contained discourses on the evidence of Christian religion,
its utility in the world, the local application of scrip-
tural texts, on false judgments and prejudices, charity, the
Lord's Supper, public preaching, our Saviour's prophecy
of death, the credit of Gospel tradition, and on our
Saviour's prophecy on the destruction of Jerusalem. A
short extract from the discourse on public preaching, one
of the best in the book, is of some interest:

> Though we cannot promise ourselves the success of mould-
> ing human nature to a complete conversion to perfect virtue
> and piety, we may still have sufficient encouragement for
> hope, that we may retain some, and confer a salutary service
> on others. Having the instrument of conviction put into our
> hands, it is our indispensable duty to apply every good talent
> as a probe for the evils which human nature is surrounded
> with. Our vigilance, and the abilities which have been imparted
> to us by the great Giver of all good gifts, must be exerted not
> only for the uninformed, but for the remedy against every
> symptom of scriptural or gospel misconstruction: and more
> especially in these days of innovation, when the Established
> Church is on all sides beset with the spirit of false persuasion,
> fantastic principles of religious philosophy, and new visionary
> doctrines imputed to the simple precepts of Christianity; I say,
> it becomes the pastors of the Church to come forward for its

support. The issue must finally be trusted to Almighty God. Our steadfast endeavours will meet with the reward of a good conscience, and the hopes of a heavenly inheritance will be more affirmed in proportion as our calling is most efficacious; and though the folly or obstinacy of ungodly people, or the wilfully ignorant, in the doctrine of Jesus Christ, may occasionally defeat our honest intentions, let us call to mind these words of an Ancient Father [St. Augustine] with which I shall conclude this discourse: 'That they who will not glorify God's mercy in the amendment of their lives here, may glorify his justice in their punishment hereafter'.

The book was very well received, whether or not Douglas wrote it with an eye to the further clerical preferment to a senior office for which he always hoped. 'The writer obviously possesses a very cultivated mind', wrote an anonymous reviewer in the *Gentleman's Magazine* for July of that year, 'his language is sometimes energetic, and always manly. Occasionally he has a fondness for abstruse words and sometimes a want of perspicacity . . . but there is no doubt the book will be read by many with satisfaction and by all with improvement'. It was a far cry from *Travelling Anecdotes,* dinners of the Society of Antiquaries and the ransacking of tumuli.

Of the two novels mentioned to Faussett there appears to be no record, but in 1797 Douglas published *The History of Julia D'Haumont: or the Eventful Connection of the House of Montmelian with that of D'Haumont,* a very heavy boring novel without plot but with descriptions of fortifications and natural history, some scenic description which might have come from recollections of Austria though the story was set in the Dauphiny of Henry the Third, a little proper love and sentiment and a very satisfactory ending for nearly everyone.

> After this singular discovery [of a splendid looted treasure] which was brought to light by the good sense of Rolando, they repaired to the mansion.
> The heart of the Count expanded with goodness, moderation, and the enobled views of enforcing the counsel of the good Rolando.
> The gates of the castle were thrown open to all the inhabitants of the Seigniory.

In a few days the wound of St. Julien [the hero] manifested in his speedy recovery. Julia soon found herself in
the possession of the man her heart fondly cherished from
her earliest youth; and the presence of the Marquis of St.
Julien conspired to heighten, with increased happiness, the
splendid nuptials which soon followed.

Goismorant renewed the ancient festivals of the spot.
Every old custom of the Castle was exhibited, and for
several days mirth, sports, and revelling exhilarated the heart
of the once depressed tenant and retainer.

Suitably to the conditions of the splendid donor, the
liberal largess branches out to every diffusive blessing: the poor
dependant is excited to cheerful industry in his laborious
calling; the energies of human capacity are brought forth;
the dissemination of well-placed rewards induce innumerable
benefits, which finally centre in harmony, cheerfulness and
peace.

Stimulated by this principle, the Count reformed the
languid state of his domain; he lived to see the happy fruits
of his benevolence; the deserted cottage people with a rising
and sturdy generation; the land prolific in culture, the flocks
and herds multiplying around him; the pipe resounding
through the vallies, the peasant joyous in the dance; and the
prayers of all Dauphiny bestowed on the flourishing and
illustrious House of Haumont.

And so to Finis. The two volumes of 30,000 words in
192 pages of duodecimo size bound in marbled boards
with vellum corners and a fine green morocco spine might
well have graced the table of a genteel drawing-room, but
never could have been included with the contemporary
Whims of the Loo Table or even Dr. Buchan's *Instructions
to Sea Bathers,* both of which Douglas might have counted
among 'the stupid trash which our circulating libraries
teem with'. Not even the crystal-enclosed skull of Ourron,
Duke of Savoy and the spar-encrusted dome of the hermit
Roland's cell could really secure a more than casual interest
in Julia and her dusty life. How much Cawthorn of the
British Library in the Strand made from the book can
only be guessed, but it had two printings in one of which
the author is described as the Revd. J. D. of Chiddington,
Sussex, and in the other as the Revd. James Douglas of

Chiddingford, Sussex: as for the author, he could only say, 'I hope they will do no harm in the world; if they amuse, it will be all that I can hope for'.

(As this book was in the press a copy of '*The Maid of Kent* [A Novel], 3 vol., FIRST EDITION, half calf, worn, 8vo 1790' appeared in the sale of the late Sir Thomas Neame's Library at Sotheby & Co. on 4 February 1974. It was sold for £95 to Messrs. Maggs Bros., Ltd., who courteously advise that the sale was on commission on behalf of an American university. The name of the author was not stated in the sale catalogue. The identity of the first owner is a matter for pleasant speculation. Sir Thomas, himself a well-known antiquary and Kentish bibliophile, lived at Faversham where Douglas had good friends.)

9

THE SUSSEX PAD

IT DOES NOT APPEAR that Douglas ever lived for any time at Litchborough during the 12 years he was its rector and he resigned the appointment when, in 1799, on the recommendation of George O'Brien, 3rd Earl of Egremont of Petworth, Sussex, the Lord Chancellor for the Crown presented Douglas to the rectory of Middleton, a very small parish on the coast of the county between Bognor and Littlehampton. This tiny cure, poor and its church already ruinous, he was to retain at least on paper until his death in 1819. There were not then as now gravel-pits and glasshouses to add to its prosperity. Some part of the church was still standing in 1805 according to a correspondent of the *Gentleman's Magazine,* but it had wholly disappeared by the time of the first Ordnance Survey 18 years later. It was in this ruined churchyard where 'the wild blast tears from their tombs the village dead and bones, shells and sea-weed mingle on the shore' that Charlotte Smith, married at 15 and reduced from affluence to abject poverty, wrote her famous sonnet. Did her rector know of her and of her plight?

How did the 3rd Earl, a valuable patron of such noted artists as Benjamin Haydon, Turner, Flaxman, Constable, and Joseph Nollekens come to befriend this 46-year-old parson-antiquary? Douglas had already hinted to a friend that a well-known Sussex nobleman who had never been found to break his word had promised a living in that county. The answer must surely be that the Earl was impressed by Douglas's own drawings and paintings of ancient relics and of landscapes and by his quite outstanding knowledge of painting, especially that of the Flemish school. There may, too, have been some family approach on his behalf, but the Earl was a most remarkable man, himself sometimes rather more than eccentric. Douglas then lived at Petworth 'entirely' out of the world' as he told a bookseller friend, but it is not beyond possibility that here he met Turner for whom the Earl had provided a studio, and saw Constable and Joseph Nollekens, and perhaps advised the Earl on the acquisitions of his remarkable collection of pictures which still grace Petworth House. He did a little topographical drawing himself, chiefly for the books of friends, tended his own now valuable and extensive collection of antiquities and read much in the classics of antiquity. Out of doors he explored burial-mounds on the Sussex Downs and uncovered a bath and part of a mosaic floor in what was to become a famous Roman villa at Bignor, a nearby parish where in addition to Middleton and Petworth he also undertook religious duties. The fact that the land at Bignor belonged to a churchwarden was of importance both then and later when Samuel Lysons, the well-known antiquary, was able to secure nearly all the research for himself.

The gentle jog-trot of the Sussex pad was soon to be interrupted. In 1803 at the instance of a well-meaning friend and fellow-Antiquary, John, 2nd Lord Henniker, its patron, presented Douglas with the vicarage of Kenton, a small isolated parish to the north east of Stowmarket in Suffolk. He had to be in residence and could leave the village only occasionally to gossip in the rather larger neighbouring village of Debenham or for a brief visit to Aldeburgh on the coast where, characteristically, he collected fossils. From the very beginning he did not get on well with his parishioners and neighbours who saw in their countryside with its own distinctive charm and

character—'that sweet and civil county of Suffolk' as
Bishop Joseph Hall described it—little more than a paradise for sportsmen. An inspection of the registers shows
that the vicar did not neglect his duties, but the parishioners had but little time or understanding for a parson
of classical education and tastes who, in his own words,
never in all his travels at home and on the Continent
neglected the contemplation and study of fossil strata.
His few visits included several to the nearby town of
Eye to meet the geologist William Smith—'Strata Smith'
as he was soon to be called—and discuss the relative ages
of rocks by a consideration of their fossils.

There was another and much more disquieting matter:
that of finance. In his letters of this time there is no
reference whatever to national affairs, even to Trafalgar
and the Abolition of Slavery, or to subjects of prime
antiquarian interest. In May 1803 Douglas had assigned
to the Earl of Egremont, his benefactor at Petworth, the
rectory at Middleton together with all its buildings, glebe-
lands and tithes for the sum of £750 and lawful interest
payments. The assignment was secured collaterally by a
policy of insurance on Douglas's life. Its beneficiary was
never to know that half the sum was intended as an
outright gift. The deed, still preserved with many other
Douglas papers under reference MS. 101 in the Petworth
archives, was endorsed only five months later with a
properly drawn and witnessed 'not intending to receive
back' clause ˙and, pathetically, on 8 February 1843
'Cancelled. This should be given to Mr Douglas, if alive'.
By then the Earl had been dead six years and Douglas
almost a quarter of a century. Many letters from Kenton
to his benefactor and his benefactor's agent tell miserable
stories of lack of money. Douglas had again borrowed
heavily from his wealthy brother William at Pendleton.
Could his wife's small remaining capital in government
stocks—her father left her about £1,000 in Consols—be
made over to his daughter who was now of age or
could he perhaps borrow £200 on it. His life insurance
policy in the Equitable Office was surrendered for the

curious sum of £8 8s. 6d. with Lord Egremont's consent. It was not true that he had left the house at Petworth in bad order: some windows needed attention, but they always had. Could his Lordship possibly help by making advances on the poor tithes due from Middleton. Out of some £75 due to be received each year for tithes he had to pay £35 a year for a curate and the Bishop of Chichester had admonished him severely for his neglect of the parish. In any case it was a very small parish with but six houses, a population of 40 souls and a desolate church in process of being engulfed by the sea. Understandably no cleric was interested in such a curacy. There was still one son to be properly educated, the other being at school with financial help from his wife's sister, Lady Glode. Threats of a court action and a further threatened sale of all his effects would mean the end of his career.

These threats and others were staved off by yet further monies from Petworth. He had been reduced, he said, to his last shilling, was in the most possible severe straits and amid a totally alien people. It can be guessed with probability that brother William and Lord Egremont again made substantial gifts of money. In 1813 and in 1819 Douglas was granted official licences of absence from Kenton on the grounds of its small value and that he was the appointed curate of Preston near Brighton. 'Such a set of harpies, they are ready to devour me alive', he wrote before his departure from Kenton. He had been 'Immeasurably foolish', he continues, but then he never really knew how to tie his purse-strings. Ironically enough it is from the devoted manuscript *Collections for a parochial history of Suffolk* made after 1838 by D. E. Davy (British Museum Add. MS. 19097) that many details of his personal life are known. By the spring of 1809 Douglas had succeeded in making his return to Sussex, first to Barnham near Bognor, where he was quite seriously ill with a chest complaint, and by the following year to Arundel as he explains in this fawning letter to John Nichols, the well-known antiquary and topographer, then part editor of the *Gentleman's Magazine*.

Barnham near Arundel, March 19, 1810

Dear Sir,

Having received a letter from my nephew, J. Douglas, of Old-hall, Pendleton, near Manchester, expressing his anxiety of an error in your press, which in your Obituary announced the death of his father, under the name of Alexander instead of William, he has requested me to beg you will have the goodness to correct the same.

I am much obliged by your polite mention of my name. I do assure you that your kind considerations have been always commensurate with that respect I have ever entertained for your own personal worth and your most laborious literary productions, for which I trust your remuneration will be still ample, and in every degree gratifying to your feelings; not always the case in this country, where national favour is more liberally bestowed through part and family interest, than real merit.

On Lady-day I remove to Arundel, where I have taken a house as more convenient for my Churches of Middleton and Tortington. [See below.] I have received an invitation from the Duke of Norfolk, and have dined with his Grace at his Castle; and should you wish for any of the archives of the Howard family in the course of your historical inquiries, I make no doubt of having an opportunity of being an accessory to any assistance you might wish for in this quarter. I have been consulted about the history of this county; the compilation has been offered to me. Much assistance can be had from the manuscripts of the late Sir W. Burrell in the Museum; but the work being under the auspices of a nobleman of the highest consequence, who wishes it to be got up on the most elegant scale, I am afraid the expence will exceed all profit; what say you, my dear Sir? It is likely for an individual, to obtain from the public, a recompence equal to the labour? I am afraid not.

I have serious thoughts of re-publishing Stukeley's Abury and Stonehenge, with notes. The latter I have; the former, with the Stonehenge bound together, some years ago I parted with to White, for some other books, and now I want the Abury. Could you procure me the loan of it? it shall be most faithfully returned on any set time. I want it immediately for an extract, being in correspondence with Sir R. Hoare and Mr. Cunnington, of Heytesbury, who are indefatigable in the work of Antient Wiltshire; a *livraison* of which will be published in April next. I wish to forward this curious and fine publication, with some hints for further eluciations of the history of our celebrated national temple of Stonehenge. The plates of Abury and Stonehenge, with others, I should execute myself, for my own edition. If in any of your literary engagements I can be in any way useful, you may command me, as I shall have leisure on my removal. And if you could propose to me any emolument from any labour of mine, to help me in the education of two fine boys, who are at two expensive schools, I should readily embrace the offer in these times of great national pressure.

With every earnest good wish for the continuance of your health, and the most satisfactory completion of your literary engagements, I have the pleasure to be, with kind regards of Mrs. Douglas, dear Sir, your faithful and much obliged servant,

James Douglas.

Douglas is not listed either as vicar of Tortington or of Arundel, and Francis Steer suggests to me that Douglas was befriended by the Duke of Norfolk and 'helped out' the incumbents of those churches.

He stayed at Arundel for almost two years during which time if John Hawkins's opinion expressed in a letter of 10 July 1812 to Samuel Lysons (included in Francis Steer's edition of *The Letters of John Hawkins and Samuel and Daniel Lysons, 1812-1830,* West Sussex County Council, Chichester, 1966) is to be trusted the Abbé, as he had become slightingly known, 'rendered himself so odious to all classes of people at Arundel that it became absolutely necessary for him to change his residence'. The truth was that the Bishop of Chichester had promised to try to procure for Douglas a living in Sussex but the occupying incumbent was slow to move. It was also true that Douglas was trying with pertinacity to secure the right to excavate the Roman villa at Bignor which Tupper the churchwarden-landowner had promised him, but Tupper, inexorable, lent a deaf ear and thought himself absolved from his promise as Douglas had removed from the neighbourhood. The famous mosaic floors with their portrait-medallions and elaborate formal patterns were being uncovered. Lysons wanted to illustrate them in his

book *Reliquiæ Britannico-Romanæ* (1801-17), then in
progress; he could advise Tupper how to excavate, how to
preserve the site, to control the admission of many
visitors, and, what was of the greatest importance, he
could readily provide the finance which John Hawkins, a
knowledgeable and frequent visitor, assured him was
required. Douglas, for his part, came first to the site, was
an experienced excavator, a most capable artist and
draughtsman, but he had no money. Tupper knew very
well how to do the best for himself, as Francis Steer's
publication of the letters shows, and obviously and
fortunately his interest was in the preservation of the
villa.

The letter to John Nichols already noted mentions
several matters which were to keep Douglas's attention
towards antiquarian matters and the study of antiquity
fully occupied, notably his correspondence with Sir R.
Hoare, usually known as Colt Hoare, and Mr. Cunnington
and a lasting interest in barrows and the problems of
Stonehenge. These letters, and some copies of replies,
covering a period between 1809 and 1814 now preserved
under reference 383/907 in the archives of the Wiltshire
County Record Office at Trowbridge whence they came
from the library of the Hoare family mansion at Stourhead,
also tell much, incidentally, of Douglas's clerical and
personal life as well as of his continuous reading in antiquarian literature, and include occasional pertinent comments on international events and on the activities of the
Prince Regent and his circle at Brighton. A selection is
included in Part II of this book. In many ways they are
of greater value and wider extent than his earlier letters
to Henry Godfrey Faussett.

It is well that we should first remind ourselves of the
characters and achievements of the two main recipients
and then note how they were inspired by Douglas to
think about method of antiquarian research as well as its
practical application, especially at Stonehenge. William
Cunnington, F.S.A. (1754-1810) and Sir Richard Colt
Hoare, F.R.S., F.S.A. (1758-1838) may in pertinent words

once used by Professor Glyn Daniel 'very properly be called the fathers of archaeological excavation in England, just as John Aubrey was the father of field archaeology'. But they were men from widely differing backgrounds. Cunnington was a Northamptonshire wool merchant and draper who had moved to Heytesbury in Wiltshire and there again set up in business using his leisure hours in reading widely, collecting fossils and riding on the Downs to improve his recurring poor health, observing carefully at the same time the many and outstanding earthworks and burial mounds of antiquity. Sir Richard Colt Hoare, the second Baronet, of Stourhead in the same county, son and heir of a wealthy banker, a classical scholar, an artist and patron of artists, had travelled widely on the Continent and made extensive notes which were later to form the basis of notable travel journals. Both men had enquiring minds and a devotion to the study of the past, particularly to the ancient monuments of Wiltshire. They were brought together by local friends with similar antiquarian and classical interests and there ensured a remarkable partnership of excavation (Plate 31) and recording, usually by Cunnington at the cost of Colt Hoare, and subsequent publication from the writings of Colt Hoare, writings which indeed mark the transition from antiquarianism to archaeology in Britain. In the often-quoted passage from the heading to the preface to his first famous work, *The Ancient History of South Wiltshire,* dated from Stourhead in 1810 and published in London in 1812, the author says, 'We speak from facts not theory'. It was largely as the result of Cunnington's hard work, often produced under much pressure, that he could do so. The dedication is indeed to Cunnington in terms of appreciation '. . . who first projected the plan of this history and by your interesting collections and important discoveries encouraged me to pursue it, this work is most gratefully and appropriately dedicated'. Facing the dedication is a portrait of Cunnington by Samuel Woodforde engraved by James Basire (the Younger), official engraver to the Society of Antiquaries.

Something of Romanticism still remained, as it did with James Douglas, but the remarkable Wiltshire partners carefully excavated no less than 380 burial mounds, classified their types, noted the sites of ancient villages and made a bold attempt to set out the differences between the various kinds of ancient camps and earthworks. All, in date, they insisted, had to be attributed to the 'Ancient British'.

There are two other matters for short mention here. On his death in 1810 Colt Hoare bought Cunnington's antiquities and eventually they found their way from the cellars of Stourhead to the Museum of the Wiltshire Archaeological and Natural History Museum at Devizes, where they are now magnificently displayed. On Douglas's death nine years later, Colt Hoare bought a major part of his collection of antiquities and in 1829 presented them to the Ashmolean Museum in the University of Oxford, where they now form part of a notable exhibition. For the full story of Cunnington and Colt Hoare's collaboration and the recognition of Douglas's *Nenia* as a pattern for Colt Hoare's *Ancient Wiltshire,* Kenneth Woodbridge's book, *Landscape and Antiquity* (1970), is not only required but delightful reading, while the Wiltshire Archaeological and Natural History Society's *Guide Catalogue* of the Neolithic and Bronze Age Collections in Devizes Museum by Messrs. F. K. Annable and D. D. A. Simpson published in 1964 has a most useful introduction to Cunnington, Colt Hoare and the Stourhead Collection.

The introduction of Douglas to Cunnington was a formal one, arranged in London through the offices of Aylmer Bourke Lambert (1761-1842) a well-known botanist and zoologist. He was a founder Fellow of the Linnean Society in 1788 and elected F.S.A. in 1791.

> Mr. Douglas with return of Compliments to Mr. Lambert and thinks himself much obliged for the pleasure of an introduction to Mr. Cunnington and will have the honour of paying his respects to Mr. Lambert tomorrow morning at eleven or twelve.
>
> 37 North Baker Street
>   Tuesday After 6 o'clock   [9 May, 1809]

Another letter again written formally in the third person followed the next day saying that Douglas 'had a thousand questions to ask Mr. Cunnington respecting his tumuli researches, but one, the most material, he forgot'. Had Mr. Cunnington ever discovered in the 'higher barrows', or those which he deems aboriginal, razed beads of blue or 'verditer porcelain', examples of which he carefully draws in his letter. In his own collection he has several from Dr. Stukeley's collection, attested to have been found in what the Doctor calls Druidical barrows on Salisbury Plain, near Stonehenge. The same kind of beads were engraved in Gibson's edition of Camden and similar beads were found as amulets with Egyptian mummies, so if Mr. Cunnington could attest this fact 'there might be a probability of approaching to the historic agnation of the higher barrows in question'. The letter closes with excellent drawings of two varieties of the beads which can be recognised as examples of the segmented faience beads worn in Wessex during the Early Bronze Age, beads once thought to be from the Orient but now regarded as of possible European or even local manufacture.

Back home in Bognor and within a fortnight Douglas wrote a much less formal letter to Lambert asking for Cunnington's country address as, with so much leisure time on his hands, he would like to pay Cunnington a visit to discuss their respective tumuli researches provided that the journey would not be more than 40 miles—presumably a day's hard ride—from Bognor. Cleverly he tried to secure Lambert's own interest by describing in detail marine fossil shells recently found at low tide on the Bognor Rocks. This was surely conclusive evidence 'of their induration having taken place at incomputable periods as no examples of recent shells of the same tribe are to be found on this coast'. Bognor Rock is a shelly calcareous sandstone of the London Clay in the Tertiary system: the fossils, at a guess, were lamellibranchs of varieties still found there and of interest to geologists. Lambert perhaps agreed with Douglas's views, unusual though they were in the early years of the 19th century, but the well-intentioned offer of Sussex specimens was merely acknowledged by Lambert's noting at the foot of the letter 'I give up this offer of fossils to you which you might mention if you write. A.B.L.' and sending it to Cunnington. It seems that through Lambert's introduction Douglas and Cunnington met for long conversations in London, and it is a little surprising that the poor curate from Barnham was able to visit London so often, attend meetings of the Society of Antiquaries and stay in fashionable quarters in Villiers Street off the Strand, in North Baker Street and with his sister-in-law Lady Glode in Portman Square.

There followed further letters to Cunnington annotated with small but exact drawings in which Douglas claimed that the porcelain beads had been introduced to Britain by traffic with the natives at remote periods of the most early colonisers, by the Celtic tribes generally known as Phoenicians. But he then goes on to say that the Belgic invasion of the Celtic Pastoral colonisers ought to be excluded if the beads came from barrows containing burials untouched by fire, the latter practice he thought being introduced by the Belgic Gauls as described by Caesar. How, one wonders, would Douglas have reacted to a modern thought: that all the relatively few faience beads found in Britain came in one consignment, even as heirlooms? Stukeley's beads he now seems to exclude —though in later correspondence he was prepared to accept their Wiltshire source—as he bought them from White of Newgate Street, a well-known collector and dealer whose assertions were not always authentic. There follow further offers of fossils from the Sussex chalk and suggestions of a visit to Cunnington by coach as Heytesbury was beyond the reach of his 'one horse chair' from Barnham. The fossils were a 'chamite' (a bivalve mollusc) enclosed in 'martial' (iron) pyrites and an echinus (a sea-urchin) crystallised in a similar mass, and as both were found in chalk the formation of chalk-flints, the fossils and the pyrites must all be of the same date. To us it is elementary enough but again it was a bold view for a country parson to put in writing at the beginning of the 19th century.

Cunnington thought that the 'Egyptian beads' corresponded to the porcelain beads found in his higher barrows; sometimes they were found with skeletons but more often with cremation burials. Inhumation he thought to be the most ancient rite but cremation must have been brought to Britain at a very early period as he had found stone hatchets with burnt bones. He thought burying under tumuli had ceased in Britain before the invasion of Caesar. Douglas would be welcome to see his collection and eat a dinner but as the house was being enlarged he would have to sleep in a Heytesbury inn. In any case Cunnington was unwell and on recovery would be travelling.

Within a few weeks Douglas was again pressing for an invitation. He agreed that burial under the large tumuli which he classed as 'belgic', and in many instances as 'celtic', ceased before Caesar's invasion because he had never found Roman remains under such tumuli. But he knew of a Roman burial found in 1800 at Portslade near Shoreham in Sussex with the usual funerary vessels including 'the red paterae of Saguntum [*sic*] to which from Pliny I have given the name of Samian' and at the same spot a 'british' urn of 'unbaked clay' filled with ashes and placed mouth downwards. From his illustration we can recognise a collared urn of Wessex Bronze Age type and realise that it could never have formed part of the Roman burial. If it be of earlier date, says Douglas, the Romans must have levelled the tumulus 'which I think would be granting rather too much'. The idea of a secondary burial in an already existing barrow though not specifically expressed was not altogether excluded and this thought and the first naming by a British antiquary of the bright red glazed ware which became traditionally though not accurately called samian are two further notable landmarks in our domestic archaeology. Douglas goes on to say that on one of his rides on the very summit of the Downs he had discovered a long barrow of the type called by King [Edward King, author of *Munimenta Antiqua*,

1799-1806] a *ship-barrow* and he proposes to open it.
How far was Heytesbury from the coach-stop at Salisbury,
he wondered, as he anxiously waited for news of an
improvement in Cunnington's health in the hope of being
able to journey to Wiltshire.

Within a short time Cunnington's health had improved
temporarily and arrangements were made for a meeting
to include Aylmer Lambert and Sir Richard Hoare.
Meanwhile the 'ship-barrow' on Rundel Hill, some four
miles from Arundel, possibly at the top of Rewell Hill
as it now is, was being opened, and in a long letter Douglas
told Cunnington of its situation, its contents, and specu-
lated on its age. Nearby was a dyke which ran down to
the sea made, he thought, by 'the second Belgae' and
evidently subsequent to the old British road ascending the
steep hill, a construction of 'the first colonisers'. Two
groups of earthworks including a multilated mound probably a barrow may still be seen on Rewell Hill, but their
date is not determined; the valley which runs down to the
sea, a remarkably fine view, is still to be seen from Dale
Park nearby. There was a contracted human skeleton at
the broad end of the barrow, head towards NNE, lying
on its right side, left arm over breast, on a thin layer of
clay deliberately placed on the natural chalk. It was not
an aged person and by comparing one radius with the
fore-arm of his labourers who was six feet tall—that,
Douglas thought, was the height of the person there buried.
A young man skilled in anatomy who happened to be
present noted certain features which were only to be
seen 'on the sculls of Affricans or the inhabitants near
the southern tropics'. Above the feet of the skeleton and
evidently a careful and methodical deposit, were two pairs
of antlers of stag or red deer. Douglas goes on to quote the
Ossianic poems on the placing of deer horn in the grave
as a symbol of hunting, but suspects Ossian to be a
forgery based on its author's knowledge of authentic
material. Had Douglas but known, the legend of Fingal
and Ossian did exist in his traditional family homeland.
He then went on to say that many long barrows known

to him and described by English authors and one Latin writer were in the form of a ship, keel uppermost. Was this, he said, perhaps an allusion to the maritime expeditions of the builders? But it was necessary ever to be cautious in depending upon theoretical conjectures, though Rundel Hill certainly commanded a most expansive view of the ocean. In characteristic fashion Douglas then continues that he thinks this barrow is one of the oldest in England and rails against 'some modern writers who will hear of nothing beyond Caesar's advent'. There was now ample material for a correct classification of British barrows based on their appearance and contents. He had indeed started work upon such a scheme but did not like the term 'Celtic' applied to our most ancient barrows which it were better to call 'British'. The 'ship-barrow' was not fully explored and he almost forgot to say that on the same day he had opened a nearby circular barrow which contained fragments of an urn of unbaked clay, and that the length of the 'ship-barrow' did not exceed 50 feet. A postscript adds that his seal, which Cunnington may have admired, was a very fine antique of Horatius Cocles, signed by Scopas, mistaken for that of Pompey by good judges.

By the end of August 1809 Douglas had secured his great ambition: not only did he meet Sir Richard Hoare but, as he told Cunnington, he was now staying at Stourhead. Here is his letter of 26 August written in a fine hand from the Hoare family seat:

Dear Sir,

I can only ejaculate! but I will just say that on Monday Mr. Ironmonger and myself will have the pleasure to give you a call and settle the operation of the tumuli research on Salisbury plain.

Everything here exceeds what I have been told of the beauty of the place and the hospitable, polite reception of Sir Richd Hoare will impress me with every grateful consideration and I must add, that you Sir, being in so great a measure instrumental in the reception I have met with, will add considerably to my acknowledgement.

I am, if you are, perfectly decided on meeting you at
Ambresbury on Tuesday.
I am desired to send the kind regards of the Company
here and I am,
                                   Dear Sir
                                   Yours truly
                                   J. Douglas

It was a typical example of the writer at his social best,
even to the practical postscript: 'Can you get me a pair of
black silk stockings which I left at Mr. Lambert's?'

Later in the same year Douglas in a long and closely-
written letter sent Cunnington his views on the origin and
purpose of Stonehenge. He had now visited the monument
and local barrows several times and once at least with the
well-known Wiltshire antiquary Archdeacon Coxe. They
had obviously looked keenly about them and discussed
what they saw, considered many theories and spoke much
of the ideas of early writers. Part of the outcome was semi-
learned nonsense which might well appeal to some present-
day enthusiasts but there were also observations which
have deservedly become part of the history of antiquarian
thought. Unguarded references to astronomy, to Phoenic-
ian origins, to a Temple of the Sun on the site of an earlier
Temple to Mithras find place with the suggestion of a
greater age for 'the stone of adoration' outside the main
stone circle—he meant the isolated Heel Stone—which
may have represented Ceres, the Roman form of Demeter
as a corn-goddess, or her Ancient British equivalent.
Surely, says Douglas, the temple could not have been a
Druidic structure, or it would have been overthrown by
the conquering Romans. He then made two sensible
suggestions. The monument as a whole was a sacred site
with some astronomical significance. A large tumulus
close to the circle ought to be properly excavated
although, as he saw, someone had already been at it,
for information it might yet give about the purpose and
date of the monument. Further, the large recumbent
stone—we know it as the Slaughter Stone—ought to be
raised as it might have been lowered by intention to
cover an important burial. This stone might once have

stood upright, as a representation of the goddess Prosperina, the daughter of Demeter who rising from Hades to return to her mother represents the newly-grown corn. When this stone was lifted by Cunnington in 1801 the tooling and dressing marks first noted by Douglas were clearly seen, and the modern view that it was one of a pair of upright pillars marking an entrance to the monument would have fitted, in part, his own theories though not to the extent of a temple dedicated to Ceres and Proserpina in a 'Celtic' form. This long letter ends by complimenting Cunnington's amiable daughters on their drawings of their father's antiquities—one of them acted as her father's excavation secretary—and wishes he could have stayed longer at Heytesbury to have shown them that 'independant of the eyes there is a mechanical process required to render their labours easy and less irksome'. A camera lucida, perhaps, or a variety of the graphic telescope to be patented later by the famous landscape artist Cornelius Varley by which an image was projected flat on a piece of paper?

In the fine spring of 1810 Douglas was well settled in what he called a commodious house at Arundel, and of his alleged reputation and clerical hopes there we have already spoken. On 24 April he wrote to Cunnington a letter at once ingenious and fantastic, of sense and of non-sense. His commonsense statements about the study of antiquity embody truths which we can still emphasise today, with the reflection that had Douglas always observed them faithfully his work might have out-ranked that of his hero, Stukeley, whom he considered as the Father of British Antiquities, and yet one whose beliefs, he once said in print, suffered from the misfortune of seeing most of our ancient monuments with the magnifying lens of Celtic optics. 'I am always desirous of regulating opinion on fact', he says, 'and never suffer any Theory or Hypothesis to rouse the least sway in a literary stricture. The knowledge of producing the fittest material from antient authorities to assert opinion may be deemed learning; which if not obtruded with affectation must always have weight to elucidate the recondite truths of history. Beyond the knowledge of antient languages, is the knowledge of the materials, of knowing where to apply for the auxiliary in those languages; I mean the critical study of those languages, which is scholarship; the other, is true learning'. Manchester Grammar School might well be proud of its son who, after a detailed commentary on the Triads of ancient Welsh literature and their mythological and antiquarian significance, on Edward Davies's new book about Ancient Britons and Druids, Maurice's obscure *Indian Antiquities,* Pliny and the Welsh *Archaeologia,* saw in Stonehenge a temple to the sun erected for solar and astronomical purposes, at least 1,000 years before the Christian era. He would have much to say in due course about 'the celebrated barrow which contained the *ebony bethyle* covered with *gold plate* . . . I have so much on the subject when I take up my pen', he continues, 'that I am sure you will excuse me for the present'. In a long undated memorandum to Archdeacon Coxe he again returned to the gold-plated breast-plate and the gold-studded dagger case as *Betyles* or charms associated with the mysteries of Mithras, and worship of the sun and so used by primitive British chieftains. These remarkable objects, and many more, were recovered in 1808 by Cunnington from Bush Barrow, Wilsford, near Stonehenge. Both he and Douglas would have been delighted with the modern interpretation of their celebrated relics as the tomb-furnishings of a chieftain of the Wessex Early Bronze Age, including an egg-shaped fossil-headed sceptre, a symbol perhaps of Homeric tradition, further ornamented with carved bone mountings like those from a shaft-grave at Mycenae, though made, it now seems likely, much nearer home.

From a practical point of view he had noted the nature of the earth excavated (presumably by Cunnington) in association with the large prostrate stone and could not agree with Cunnington's view that it had once stood upright. Why was Stonehenge where it was in preference to any other place? There must have been a reason, or why transport some sarsen stones—the local sandstone—

16 miles—his reference is obviously to the great number of sarsen stones on the surface of Marlborough Downs at that distance from Stonehenge. The letter is decorated with a very fine drawing of a chalk fossil, an enchinoid *Micraster,* the 'heart urchin', from Douglas's collection in a presumed allusion to Pliny's odd story of the stone known to the Druids as a snake's egg, to the putting forth of the egg in primitive worship and the oval (horse-shoe trilithons) form of Stonehenge. Here the present-day lunatic-fringe of archaeology could hardly have done better. Douglas would have greatly approved could he but have known that A. W. Rowe, a Kentish doctor, an amateur geologist and antiquary working nearly a century later was to demonstrate progressive evolutionary changes in the genus *Micraster* by which means the relative ages of parts of the great deposits of chalk could be zoned and determined. By the end of this letter his handwriting, usually neat and clear, is bold, sprawling and untidy. His eyesight, as he said, had sometimes been troublesome from the acid he used in etching, but here a friend had arrived and he finished in haste with kindest expressions of friendly concern to all the Cunnington family.

A copy of part of Cunnington's reply to this strange but accomplished letter is among the archives of Trowbridge. In 1801 in the company of Sir Richard Hoare, Mr. Crocker (whether Abraham or his son Philip who made Colt Hoare's drawings [*cf.* Plate 31] we do not know), and an Irish gentleman, Cunnington dug under the prostrate stone (the Slaughter Stone) which without doubt, he thought, was originally upright. The hollow in which it is now laid was caused by frequent diggings to see what lay beneath. The small upright stones within the oval of trilithons were oval or egg-shaped and not circular in plan, and although this did not go against Douglas's hypothesis, he must please remember that there was also a circle of uprights. Douglas's opinions were very consistent, said Cunnington, but he himself did not hold so high an opinion of the Welsh Triads and thought there were no authentic documents prior to the fourth or fifth century. A copy of a paper on Stonehenge which he had written for Sir Richard Hoare was evidently to be enclosed but at this point the draft stops short. So far as one can tell, the Abbé was never to see it. He was certainly not to know that Cunnington had buried under the Slaughter Stone a bottle of port wine, a bottle of which the cork had unfortunately rotted when it was uncovered again in 1920 during excavations by Colonel Hawley.

By the winter of 1810 Cunnington's ill health, his pains, gout and rheumatism, had seriously worsened but despite his indisposition he managed to write to his friend at Arundel, sending a copy of the itinerary of a journey he had made earlier in the year to his birthplace in Nottinghamshire together with notes on the fossil-bearing strata which he was sure the recipient would find interesting. He did, and in a kindly gossiping letter of 26 November Douglas returned to this old interest, reminiscent about his meeting in Suffolk with 'Strata Smith' and about Smith's proposed geological map of England showing the fossil strata of each county, 'a valuable acquisition to geologic researches as founded on a correct survey and establishing *matter of fact data*'; to which he, Douglas, took only one exception concerning the deposition of chalk hills which was not, as Smith seemed to imply, universal. Strangely, there is no mention of John Farey's diagram of a geological section across the Weald published in 1806. Its novelty and scientific value would have appealed to Cunnington; possibly Douglas knew nothing of it. He then goes on to talks of stone circles such as Rollrick (Rollright), Abury (Avebury) and Stonehenge as the temples of various kings or chieftains at various periods, rallying points against invasion or for annual conventions, perhaps. Single detached stones were a key to these structures, the prototypes of the gods to whom the temples were raised, where ceremonies were established at stated periods. To our ears some of his chatter sounds suspiciously modern. His own barrow-digging in the last summer had established a few facts, but revealed no valuable relics. It was a fact that our large

British barrows were built before the fortified posts—the hill-forts—in the Sussex Downs which, as in Wiltshire, can be considered with some probability as Belgic. It was indeed a remarkable forecast of modern archaeological opinion. There followed a piece of informed antiquarian gossip in which Douglas said he had been able to prevent an unnamed antiquary of considerable literary reputation presenting a thesis on Stonehenge as a creation of Aurelius Ambrosius—possibly, it may be guessed, as a communication to the Society of Antiquaries.

The end may be quoted in full:

> With every sincere wish for your restoration to every mental resource or amusement, in your abstract pursuits from worldly transactions of greater moment, in which our social habits are more eminently centred and with my kind regards to Mrs. Cunnington and Miss Cunningtons, I remain sensible to your obliged good wishes,
>
> > Dear Sir,
> > Yours truly,
> > J. Douglas.

On the last day of the year William Cunnington, ancestor of a family which was to give unstinted and distinguished service to archaeology in Wessex almost until the present day, had died. Perhaps, for him, this last pleasant letter had made the afternoon shine.

10

THE LAST DECADE

SOMETHING OF THE PRACTICAL and financial difficulties under which Douglas laboured at Arundel have
already been noticed. There seemed no further prospect
of the history of Sussex about which he had been consulted, and limited by his own lack of money he could
scarcely contemplate a new edition of Stukeley with
additional notes and his own illustrations. There was as
yet no definite news, although a little more hope, of
clerical preferment, and he craved still for more literary
work. Five letters to Colt Hoare written between
18 January 1812 and 11 August 1814 preserved in the
Stourhead Archives in the Wiltshire County Record Office
(383.907) at Trowbridge are among the most interesting
he ever wrote.

The two men had become good friends since Douglas
stayed at Stourhead in 1809, corresponding and apparently
meeting from time to time for antiquarian gossip in
London and on sites of interest near Stonehenge. Colt
Hoare spoke of Douglas's book *Nenia Britannica* in his
own *Ancient Wiltshire* as a very ingenious and elaborate
work, detailed, and written with great perspicuity. But it
dealt only with the remains on the southern coast of
England and chiefly in Kent, a stricture that was not
entirely true. Douglas, said Colt Hoare, dated his barrows
to a much more modern period than those to be found in

Wiltshire. On one page Colt Hoare quotes the time range from Douglas as between 182 and 742 but on a later page more closely as bewteen 582 and 742. These were of course 'literary dates', but Colt Hoare carefully reminded his readers that coins of the Lower Empire had been found in barrows near Chatham in Kent. The Kentish barrows he had never seen and could not therefore compare them at first hand with the examples in Wiltshire, though from Douglas's plans and details the Kentish barrows were of more uniform shape and placed more closely together than those with which he was concerned. On the question of date he might have added that although Douglas could be tiresomely boring with his literary references to dates and what he openly regarded as unproved theories, he could also recognise that Roman coins had sometimes travelled long distances, could perhaps be heirlooms and were often used as personal decorative ornaments and so were not absolute and direct evidence of the date of a barrow deposit. It was nevertheless clear, as Kenneth Woodbridge has pointed out, that Douglas's *Nenia Britannica* was the prototype of Colt Hoare's own book, *Ancient Wiltshire*. It was perhaps a little unfair to say even as a joke to the Revd. Thomas Leman, a well-known antiquary who claimed to have visited every Roman road and station in Britain, that as the Abbé had explained all the mysteries, they need think no more about Stonehenge. Leman who drew specialised maps for Colt Hoare and with Archdeacon Coxe had assisted Hoare in the planning of *Ancient Wiltshire* found it wise to agree with his patron; in any event he had already shown his jealousy of Douglas's work on local Roman roads and settlements by continuing to name him 'Ninny', a poor pun it was even then regarded, on the title of *Nenia Britannica*. Leman had edited a new edition of Richard of Cirencester's 'Itinerary of Roman Britain'; with hindsight we can think it fortunate that neither Leman nor Douglas realised that the work was a complete forgery.

Let Douglas speak for himself. He writes on 18 January 1812 from Arundel to Colt Hoare at *Miller's* Hotel in

Jermyn Street where he was often accustomed to stay
in the winter for his health's sake:

> I am returned from town and have had the honour of an
> audience with the Archbishop: a matter of ceremony with
> no hopes of obtaining any decision until the election takes
> place, when his Grace thinks proper to appoint the meeting
> of the two other nominating trustees [of the British Museum]
> . . . his Grace replied that I had been recommended to his
> notice by the Bishops of Salisbury and Chichester, and bowing
> to His Grace for the honour they had done me and the honor
> of his Grace's reception I drove off just as wise and as uncer-
> tain of success as when I first entered the palace . . . I will only
> say that if Planta [Joseph Planta, Principal Librarian of the
> British Museum] preponderates in the choice I stand no
> chance as he has a friend of his own.

Despite further practical moves by the Bishop of Salisbury
and other friends of influence Douglas, much to his chagrin,
did not secure the greatly coveted appointment as a Curator
to the Museum.

He then went on to discuss reviews of the first number
of Colt Hoare's *Ancient Wiltshire* and the 'illiberal
references' to its dedication to Cunnington 'the most
handsome tribute which could possibly be paid to any man
. . . Had I but lived in town, in the center of these
cerberi, without much gasconade, I flatter myself I
should have hazarded a little *botheration* on that, as
well as some other subjects which related to the ignorant,
though dignified reviewer. Many years ago I published
two short and undigested papers on the Celts or brass
arms of the ancients, which produced an attack in
Mr. Urban [the *Gentleman's Magazine*] and which I had
strong reasons for fixing on my old friend Johnny
Pinkerton [a Scottish historian who claimed that Stonehenge was a Gothic structure]; may God defend him, if
my suspicions were not well founded! A reply was
open to me in the same venerable repository and I laid
on my retaliating lark with no small degree of vengeance,
which certainly procured repose and eased "the stuffed
bosom of that perilous stuff which weighs upon the

heart" '. How well Douglas followed the advice of Macbeth's doctor and ministered to himself we have already seen—the memory still remained after more than 25 years. He continues with some very sensible remarks on practical archaeology, chiefly devoted to the difference between the customs of inhumation and cremation in pre-Roman times. Were not the barrows containing friable British pottery containing ashes encroached upon by the outward circle of Stonehenge and so, surely, they must antedate the edifice? And again where neighbouring barrows opened by Colt Hoare and Cunnington 'produced fragments of the temple, chippings of the stone, this must prove a subsequent interment of the erection'. These practical remarks were indeed to occupy the attention of antiquaries in Wiltshire and elsewhere, as was his suggestion that in Sussex, an area similar to Wiltshire for its barrows, the very early nomadic tribes inhumed their chieftains and distinguished personages. The ideas, theories and above all the practical advice which he gave Cunnington and Colt Hoare in particular played an important part in the development of excavation technique and of a wider, more sensible, study of man's past. He knew nothing of what we have called in modern times the Neolithic Revolution or of the real significance of Long Barrows, but here was an enquiring and logical mind of Douglas at its best. The pity was that the best was now but seldom to be seen.

The letter stops abruptly and is continued a month later 'owing to confinement from cold of myself, Mrs. D. and my son for these several weeks', a malady something worse than a common cold, one thinks, and an ailment to which the writer was already prone and from which he was to suffer more frequently as he grew older, even in the bracing air of Doctor Brighton. Douglas goes on to assure Colt Hoare that he had not put his opinion of the reviews of *Ancient Wiltshire* into print but he would not hesitate to make '*positive assertion*' when he had an opportunity of going to London. There was no news of the British Museum affair and he would be greatly

obliged if it was in his correspondent's power to communicate any hint or information. Meanwhile, though it
not be wise to mention the matter lest it should affect
his chances at the Museum, he had been offered the
Chaplaincy of His Majesty's troops at Brighton with the
additional offer of a parsonage house in the village of
Preston about a mile from Brighton with single duty,
rent-free, a salary which will excuse residence, and permit
his clerical duty with the troops. To this the former officer
of Hussars and the Corps of Engineers obviously looked
forward and it may be said at once that even a brief
reading of the parish registers of Preston shows how
well and with what fine degree and devotion he was,
in due course, to undertake his military chaplaincy. The
letter ends with two paragraphs of antiquarian news.
During his rides on the Downs near Brighton he had
found some curious 'British Tumuli' with dilapidated
kistvaens and cromlechs nearby, several like the examples
in Wiltshire, and he hoped to attack them in the summer.
What he saw, or thought he saw, cannot be certain.
Earthworks, ascribed by him to the Saxons, had already
been noted between 1724 and 1768 by the Revd. William
Clarke, Rector of Buxted, Sussex, and an antiquary on
his rides over the Downs during one of the first sea-side
holidays at Brighton to be recorded. There are many
barrows still remaining but no megalithic structures have
ever been recorded in that area or indeed in Sussex.
It may be guessed that his eye fell upon a few isolated
sarsen stones, as may still be seen locally and are indeed
used in the fabric of the fountain in the Steine Gardens.
And in a few lines Douglas adds that he is in the confidence of the owner of the Bignor Roman pavement who
will allow him to excavate and then he hoped to find an
inscription. A paper about Bignor had already been read
to the Society of Antiquaries by Dr. Meyrick, and James
Dallaway and Samuel and Daniel Lysons, he says, had
had drawings made. Of this particular matter we have
already spoken. Douglas's hopes and expectations were
not to be fulfilled.

Much more fulsome were the terms in which, writing from Preston six months later, Douglas acknowledged the gift of the magnificent third part of *Ancient Wiltshire* (South). Its regular, expeditious and successful publication was valuable in the extreme to the recondite study of our British history and even to the cursory reader the eminently beautiful plates could not fail to afford considerable interest. To its recipient this gift was doubly gratifying, valuable for its antiquarian treasure and coming from a gentleman, for whom he would always entertain the highest regard and respect. The true value would rise beyond the author's expectation, as in fact it did. The editor of *The Quarterly Review* had refused to acknowledge Douglas's long reply to the 'unmannerly, inept and puny critiques' of the first part of Colt Hoare's book—it seems that Colt Hoare may have agreed to this approach though the review of the first two parts had been very reasonable indeed and the only criticism of the author was that his theory was 'inconsistent with observed facts' —and his action could only be explained by the fact that the editor was no antiquary. The Duke of Norfolk and a friend at Cuckfield had bought the work and Douglas was now frequently with gentlemen who 'were beginning to appreciate our curious researches'. Douglas did not say so, but there was a great increase of carriage folk to view the fine mosaic pavements in the Roman villa at Bignor where the Prince Regent was soon to be a visitor with the Earl of Egremont. If Colt Hoare would send a copy of his work to the French Institute it would be highly noticed in view of the prevailing interest in antiquarian researches.

With some friends Douglas had been exploring barrows near Rottingdean, four miles east of Brighton. His friends, he tells Colt Hoare in a letter of 25 June 1812, began on a large flat 'british' [this is Douglas's usual term] barrow excavating from the circumference to the centre without system and without attacking the primary. Skeletons were found and distant from them 'about two urns' of the 'higher british though friable pottery'. These and other facts convinced Douglas on this occasion that cremation and inhumation were in use at the same time. He had either overlooked or forgotten his much earlier ideas of primary and secondary burials in the same barrow, and even though he broke into the 'center' [again Douglas's usual spelling] time did not allow of 'a satisfactory ransack. This I must defer to some other day. We also opened a group of the lower british small bell fashioned barrows: a few only; urns of a similar pottery and shape of the one I sent you; with calcined bones, small iron buckles and fragments of a brass [?arterio] vessel, melted in part by an ardent fire. Similar facts I discovered in a group or groups of the same order, on Lavington Hill on the down beyond Petworth [Douglas may have been referring to the two fine barrows still to be seen between Woolavington Down and Tegleaze Wood and on Bignor Down where six are now visible]. The weather has been against me just at the time I was setting off for the british intrenched hill at Poynings, where I intended breaking into a complete series of the british flat, bell and what Stukeley calls the Druid barrows—a term I do not like—these are situated a short distance from the vallum. I have attacked one of our Cromlechs and the Goldstone but my labours were blank at the time: I have not finished the research'.

The 'Cromlech' called the Goldstone, a Megalith in History to borrow the words of Professor Glyn Daniel, deserves more than passing mention. It gave its name to Goldstone Bottom, an open valley near Hove, and the field in which it stood was known as Goldstone Field in 1617, though the relative volume of the English Place-Name Society prefers to emphasise the name Goldstone Barn on the six-inch map and says that the stone was a mass of breccia deliberately buried early in the 19th century. There is more to its history than that. The area was a recognised centre for military camps and manoeuvres and was remembered particularly for the severe field punishments and executions carried out in 1795 on members of the Oxford Militia stationed at East Blatching ton who had mutinied against the bad quality of their food. Douglas said that his labours were 'blank at the time' and although his research was not finished he would not hesitate to associate the stone with the Druids. Horsfield who illustrated the stone in the first volume of his *History, Antiquities and Topography of Sussex* in 1835 referred to it as possibly the *Gorsed* or sacred stone of the ancient Britons, one of the largest and most remarkable of the Druidical stones on the Downs. It had been removed from its original position about 1834 and with 'unfeeling sacrilege' thrown down into a deep hole dug especially to receive it. North of it were other stones, 'remains of what has been deemed a Drudical circle'. There were others in the fields near Brighton church but whether all these stones of breccia or conglomerate were Druidical or unaccountable freaks of nature must, he presumed, ever remain a secret 'notwithstanding the learned disquisitions of antiquaries and their wondrous derivation of Anglo-Saxon and ancient British names'. This was a sly dig at Douglas and his preoccupation with Druids and their place-names, but he goes on to quote an interesting reference of 1833 by Gideon Mantell, the Sussex geologist, to Douglas's discovery of an urn with human bones and ashes under one of the stones close to Brighton church. A group of these sarsens 'apparently in arc of a circle' is said to appear in a sketch of about 1800 according to Frederick Harrison and J. S. North in their book *Old Brighton, Old Preston, Old Hove* (1937), and other sarsens are known to have been found nearby. They can only have been of natural occurrence like the Goldstone, but the legend of a Druidic enclosure near the church persisted for many years and was even accepted as fact in 1935 by Osbert Sitwell and Margaret Barton in their delightful book, *Brighton.*

Much to the point was the Editor of the 1858 edition of Murray's *Handbook for Kent and Sussex:*

'The down scenery will amply repay wanderers. At the entrance of a valley near Hove, considerably nearer Brighton, *was* a huge mass of breccia, known as "gold-stone at Hove", called Druidical, and possibly sepulchral. (The names gold-rock—guinea-rock—are given to some of the sepulchral stones on Dartmoor.) It was about 6 ft. high, and was a few years since carefully removed and buried in a trench purposely dug for it. Its "dull destroyer" should have been laid by its side. Remains of what has been called a Druidical circle may still be traced at the end of the valley; and similar masses of breccia are scattered here and there about the downs'. Subsequent editions of the Sussex *Handbook* say nothing of it.

Five years earlier the first volume of the *Sussex Archaeological Collections* had made a brief reference to Douglas's words in the report of the first meeting of the Society, and it was wondered, in a general survey of Sussex antiquities, whether the stones were traces of the Druids. Mark Antony Lower in his *History of Sussex* (Vol. 1, 1870), p. 252, was more specific. The Goldstone, he said, was buried about 1833, and 'some archaeologists wish the utilitarian farmer had been buried under it. Without doubt, the stone had been sacred to the Druids'.

It next appears on an excellent coloured post-card published locally about 1910 where it is described as 'The Goldstone (Hove Park). A huge grey-wether supposed to have been a Druidical Altar. Was only rediscovered in 1902'. The picture shows the large vertical stone, five or six smaller lumps of stone carefully arranged round it in a circle, an inscription carved on white stone

GOLDSTONE

DOLMEN

OR

HOLY STONE OF DRUIDS

and the whole group enclosed within a stout iron fence Later, the iron fence was replaced by a carefully kept surrounding of shrubs which still exists, the old inscription moved outside the enclosure and placed by the side of another which records the planting of a tree in the

enclosure in 1929 to mark the 1000th Meeting of the
Ames Lodge of the Ancient Order of Druids, a well-known
and respected Friendly Society, and the Centenary Meeting
of the Royal Arch Chapter No. 38 (Plate 32). It merits but
a dozen words or so in the Sussex Volume VII of the
Victoria County History published in 1940, saying that
it is a large block of sarsen known as the Goldstone, and
the stones surrounding it were brought from elsewhere in
modern times. The area close to the Park is now highly
developed residentially, but where else is there a megalithic folly which has given its name to a neighbourhood,
several roads, a waterworks and a well-known football
ground. It well deserves the care now devoted to its
maintenance.

As one wonders how all this curious field-work was
accomplished in practice there is an almost throw-away
line in which Douglas says he can always get labourers at
command from the 10th Royal Hussars: this was the new
title of the Prince of Wales's own Regiment to which he
had been appointed Chaplain. In a postscript he adds that
he has found the scattered remains of a very large stone
circle on the downs not otherwise identified—and 'all the
entire of your Wiltshire Romanised british villages or
posts. Samian pottery etc., etc. etc.' He recalls the words
of Gildas, that after the advent of the Saxons the towns
and cities of Britain were abandoned and forsaken. The
dwellings of the Britons at this time were out of towns and
cities. This might be about A.D. 500 and the desolate
state may have lasted about 50 years; he adds that he has
some curious matter on this subject, a statement which
we may well believe. If by 'stone' circle Douglas could
possibly have meant one of the now well-known Neolithic
causeway-enclosures or Iron Age hill-forts of the South
Downs, we could applaud his antiquarian foresight. Here
and the more so at Rottingdean the precision of field-
notes such as he had carefully maintained at Chatham
Lines would have been invaluable.

By Midsummer Day of 1812 when the last letter was
being written the Douglas family had settled in the tree-

enclosed vicarage at Preston (Plate 33), a mile out of
Brighton along the London Road and close by the medieval
village church. There seems no doubt that the Earl of
Egremont had helped in securing the incumbency for his
friend and the fact that Douglas was already a Chaplain-
in-Ordinary to the Prince of Wales, a literary man and an
ex-soldier of some past reputation must have stood in
his favour. The town of Brighton was regarded as the
gayest and most fashionable in Britain if not in Europe,
and its atmosphere far removed from that of his more
recent homes at Arundel, Petworth and the remote Wealden
village of Chiddingfold perhaps recalled to Douglas's mind
the earlier and carefree days of Flanders and the lively
Court of Vienna. Not only were there bathing, riding and
picnic parties, dancing in the Assembly Rooms, promenades
on the grass walks of the Steine, the theatre, cricket for
young ladies and racing both at Brighton and Lewes to
attract those of fashion: there was also His Royal Highness.
The Prince Regent, the Prince of Wales, had an especial
affection for Brighton and Brighton loved the Prince of
Pleasure, the First Gentleman in Europe, who with his
entourage and military escort was its magnificent attraction and benefactor. He had completed the first stage of
his Marine Pavilion by 1787; the Riding House and Stables
were added in 1804-8 after the interior had been converted
into a palace of *chinoiserie,* and the end was Nash's
building begun in 1815, the Pavilion as we now know it.
The Prince had married Mrs. Fitzherbert secretly in 1785
and in the following year she took a house near the
Pavilion, and another rather later in the Old Steine, a
house which by a quirk of circumstances was recently the
home of the Y.M.C.A. Often in debt, sometimes in funds,
surrounded by royal, noble and from time to time very
common guests and companions, the First Gentleman
added high spirits and gaiety to the town. He had zest,
enjoyed art of which he had a remarkable knowledge,
sport, duties and pleasures, official and private. Architecture, antiquities and paintings, classical music, some
eccentricities, occupied part of his time. It was such a
royal master, the greatest Royal patron of arts for

many centuries, that Douglas was to serve as Chaplain to his Brighton troops, the 10th Royal Hussars.

Political events and social life at Brighton found brief mention in the third letter, dated 17 August 1813 from Preston Vicarage, but only as a half-hearted excuse for delay in volunteering antiquarian gossip. 'What with our splendid victories, the awful appearance of the approaching crush of warlike conflicts in the North, I find few persons here have a moment to ponder on these retired chamber cogitations, especially on our great bustle for the second arrival of our magnificent Prince'. Wellington's glorious victories at Vittoria and the Battles of the Pyrenees, the continuation of war with the United States, Napoleon's check to the Allies at Dresden and the Luddite Risings in Yorkshire must have made gossip enough in both military mess and Assembly Rooms. Douglas himself prefers to compare and contrast the tumuli and earthworks of the Sussex Downs with those described in Colt Hoare's *Ancient Wiltshire.* Kistvaens on tumuli he classes with 'the first Belgic eruption', but dolmens and stone circles to 'a far more early period'. Did Colt Hoare agree? He was also studying the place-names of Sussex and 'though perfectly aware of the cautious ground I have to treat, lest the decoration of fancy should meander beyond the sober appeal'. It was a sound enough principle, but Douglas as he not uncommonly did at once ignored caution of scholarship in deriving the name of 'our present day watering place which Royalty is preparing to adorn with additional lustre' from Cornish, Welsh and possibly Hebrew sources. Brighthelmstone, otherwise Bryn-el-Towyn, denoted the 'sacred promontory on which the sacred stones are now existing on the hill near the church; and from which the Saxons derived their appellation of Burgh-helef-stein', holy, sacred ground. *Est il vraisemblable?* he asks. Certainly there may well have been local sarsen stones before the area was built over. But modern authority prefers *Beorhthelm's tun* the *Bristelmestune* of Domesday Book, from the old English *tun,* the homestead or village of one Beorhthelm, as the origin of the place-name.

The letter ends with a very polite, polished and indirect request for a further invitation to Stourhead, 'one of the most beautiful places in this Kingdom which the hospitable and polite reception of a Gentleman has so forcibly left on my mind'. More correspondence followed, but no further invitation.

The warm friendship between the two Antiquaries nevertheless continued. Later in 1813 Colt Hoare had sent a kind remembrance, possibly a present, by the hand of his son Henry who while at Brighton had been shipwrecked on an intended excursion to the Isle of Wight. Douglas in a letter dated 5 November says that he had had to stay some time at his family's (Lady Glode's) London house where there was great anxiety by reason of more than one case of serious illness. On his return to Preston he found Mrs. Douglas laid up with a severe indisposition which turned to a fit of gout 'and this owing to the picturesque embellishment of a poor little vicarage garden [see Plate 33] in which my son and his mother presided over the tasteful hand of a gardner, transplanting of trees. This event brought my daughter Mrs. Tucker [she had been married for two years] with my youngest son [Richard, now 15] post haste to see the mother, who thank God is on her legs again and my family now jugged in a very comfortable house in Upper Rock gardens at Brighton, where I reside during the winter months owing to the uncomfortable dampness of our small vicarage house at Preston, beautiful in the fine season but absolutely not tenable in winter'. The damp vicarage among the elms in the London road was demolished many years ago but a dozen or so of the unpretentious bay-windowed terrace houses of the 1790s still remain in the steep Upper Rock Gardens, a reminder of the appearance of this cheaper suburban piece of the eastern sea-side cliff edge of Brighton before the building of Kemp Town.

The letter continues with varied and interesting comments on the current social life in Brighton, but there is no mention of the famous Promenade concerts at the *Castle* and *Old Ship* hotels mainly supported by the Prince or of his rumbustious Festival to mark the overthrow of Napoleon, 'The society here as in other places is divided into *la première, la seconde et la troisième noblesse*; every night balls and supper; my son who is in the Prince's regiment was not home 'till 5 this morning from a party where he met Mr. Hoare to whom I had taken the liberty of introducing him. Tonight there is a regular ball at Mrs. Fitzherbert's where my son is invited with Mr. Hoare; and so on every day in the week, or night rather; the young man is but a recruit and not out of the schools of the regiment which after these bivouacking parties he is obliged to attend most strictly; and on expressing the parental solicitude I am informed it is the proper season-ing for his ensuing spring campaign in the South of France . . . I hope for a better opportunity of seeing your son. So far with your indulgence, a little gossip just to soften the cares of a confused and uncertain state of human affairs'. James Edward Moreton Douglas, his eldest son, was now 19 years old. Had his father already forgotten his own adventures and experiences as an officer cadet at Tongres, at Tournai, in Ghent and at the Court of Vienna nearly 40 years ago?

Cares or no cares and without pausing even to dip pen into ink Douglas turns in his next line to familiar matters of antiquarian study. Colt Hoare had evidently chided him with quoting a wrong reference to Aubrey's *Miscellanies*. '. . . my head must have been in a miscellan-eous jumble', replies Douglas. 'Hearne's Collectanea ought to have come uppermost . . . I regard not the critique of our modern sceptical fogramites at the painstaking etymologist. Can there be a shadow of doubt, but that great light may be thrown on the modern names of places—? where local habitation and name may serve to explain and illustrate the higher periods of our british antiquities'. It was indeed a wise and far-seeing comment, but so fraught with difficulties was this highly specialised and learned branch of knowledge and so cross-grained some of the personalities concerned with it that it was not until 1923 that a Society was formed for the specific

and proper study of English place-names. Douglas's letter
continues with observations on stone cirques, on the
etymology of the words cromlech, dolmen or tolmin and
kistvaen, the importance of their relation to the sun as
the great vivifier and the earth as the great producer. It
all sounds very modern when one considers some present-
day views of the Neolithic earth-mother and the sun-god
of the Bronze Age. Still more in accord with modern
thinking is Douglas's next remark; '. . . notwithstanding
all this, I think with you that the spade and pick-axe are
more likely to evince the assertion of the past than the
most learned commentary'. He hopes that Colt Hoare's
friend in Wales [William Owen, later known as Owen
Pughe, who spent much time in studying the old Welsh
triads] may be led to excavate both the central stone of a
stone circle, which he would perhaps find to be a sepulchral, and a particular cromlech which will as Douglas
thinks prove to be 'templar'.

Douglas was now preparing to meet Colt Hoare at his
headquarters at Marlborough to visit and study in North
Wiltshire, armed with all the literary references applicable
to Stonehenge and the monuments he could find. 'I have
no theory to intrude', he says, 'and the longer I live the
more I think with you that fact alone is our best safeguard: yet I am still convinced that much, very much, is
left undone respecting our earliest memorials of british
antiquities which through the extended race of our first
colonizers may be brought home to a much purer
fountain than has been dreamed of by our antiquaries,
even the best of them; and with all due deference even
without any assistance from their druidical authorities
which are very often too laughable for common sense
to repose upon'. Would that he could have seen Richard
Atkinson's modern work at Stonehenge and ridden to
Fussell's Lodge long barrow, one of his 'lower british'
variety, during its skilled excavation by Paul Ashbee.
The letter ends with congratulations to Colt Hoare on
his opinions of etymology and the derivation of modern
place-names, on his splendid library with its 'Celtic dic-

tionaries &c' so valuable in such researches, with kind remembrances to Archdeacon Coxe, and 'should my residence here be in any way compatible with any commission you wish to forward, I beg you will consider me truly at your service'.

The expedition to north Wiltshire to which both the antiquaries looked forward lasted but 29 days. It was, as Kenneth Woodbridge reminds us in his book *Landscape and Antiquity,* virtually the last of Colt Hoare's field researches in Wiltshire and it may be that one of his frequent attacks of rheumatism or gout·was responsible for his early return to Stourhead. When Douglas wrote from Preston on 11 August 1814—this is the fifth and the last remaining letter of the series preserved in the Wiltshire County Record Office at Trowbridge—his letter addressed to Colt Hoare care of Marlborough Post Office had to be forwarded to Stourhead.

> I have been much mortified in not being able to have visited your highly curious labours. My son was under orders to join his Regiment in North America, and very little more than convalescent from a dangerous inflammatory fever, when he came to me on his route to Hilsea [Hilsea Lines which replaced older earthwork defences of Portsmouth built during the French war] to take leave of us before his departure; when on the second or third day he was attacked with illness and the Inspector of Hospitals in the district was obliged to visit him; from whom he obtained his certificate as at present unfit for actual service. Had not this misfortune happened, my intentions were to have accompanied him to his headquarters at Hilsea and to have crossed the county for Marlborough.

The United States had declared war on Britain in 1812 and the Treaty of Ghent by which it was terminated was to be signed on 24 December 1814, some four months after this letter had been written. The trouble to which the Army was prepared to go in having a medical officer of such relatively high rank examine a young officer-cadet who might possibly be trying to avoid foreign service is an interesting sidelight on the state of Britain's armed forces at that time.

I do not pretend to be an Oedipus (continues Douglas), but under the indulgent auspices of your spade and pick-axe, your plans, your local surveys, &c, &c, I think I should have boldly dared to have entered the Cretean labyrinth of the two mysterious temples; Abury and Stonehenge. I have hoarded up several, indeed a budget of *perhap's* and *conjectures* to approach their awful precincts with all due humility, which after all may be another 'fool's bolt' shot at a venture . . . without your stubborn facts no clue to set honourably out of the labyrinth will be possible.

Douglas then goes on at length to say what ought to be done to elucidate the true history of Abury and Stonehenge. We should set out with facts from the more modern authorities; certain information has been obtained by spade and pick-axe; religious customs can be inferred and where we can show that the 'british' chieftains even by their names were at the head of the priesthood, as was the case with most other nations, the religious and conventional history may be with much safety combined. This was his favourite hobby-horse, and he illustrates his ideas by a detailed double-sized drawing of a gold coin of Dubnovellaunos, the inscription imperfect, from his collection. The coin, he thought, perhaps illustrated in some way the equivalents of Stonehenge or Abury over which this ruler presided: the temple was to the Sun, the upright stone beyond the main circle at Stonehenge to Ceres. It was all very grand, very learned. Little commonsense pervaded much theory and Douglas knew it when he asked Colt Hoare to 'pray excuse a little levity to relieve a very obscure subject'. Fact now stood often behind theory.

There follows a long dissertation on the meaning of local place-names which might apply to Stonehenge. Some of them proved in his view that the 'britons' who used them had lost all knowledge of the builders of Stonehenge, a 'people who existed above 100 years before Caesar's advent'. The remarks would sometimes please our modern place-name experts, but often not. In any case, Douglas was unloading what he called all this 'ramble' to cover his great disappointment at not journeying to Marlborough and not being able to join Colt Hoare in his projected exploration of the stone avenues at Carnac in Brittany. There is then a brief reference to a stone avenue at Hackpen Hill (though obviously not to the 1838 hill-figure of a horse) from the manuscript of Lord Winchilsea which was still in Douglas's possession and, as so often happens, a postscript of value. British villages may be 'elucidated' by the Saxon invasions, that is the Romanised Britons. Such settlements are scattered over the Sussex downs. Are there in Wiltshire groups of small barrows with iron swords, spear-heads and umboes of shields and beads, etc., in the graves of women? There is a small hint that Douglas knew what such barrows really were, but unfortunately the long correspondence with his friends in Wiltshire now comes to an end.

So, too, there are no further comments on the soldier son or on the lively social affairs of the regal court and its seaside watering-place. From the parish registers of Preston—and at this time its nearest ecclesiastical neighbour was the parish church of St. Nicholas in Brighton itself—it can be seen that Douglas employed himself in a full round of parochial duties. There was this difference between Chiddingfold, where he had worked equally hard, and Preston: that whereas at the former he had to be content with more than a fair share of paupers, at Preston he ministered also to troops and to the nearby barracks where among the Hussars, Lancers and Dragoons he must, remembering his own early love of the cavalry, have felt particularly well at ease. Not only did he marry the troopers and baptise their frequent children; his official rank and good offices still combined to procure a team of army labour when he saw fit to make a ransack of downland barrows. As for his own mount, it is said to have been a white pony which he occasionally painted with spots and touches of lemon-colour, brown and other tints. But genius must have some eccentricities, as Mark Anthony Lower said of him in *The Worthies of Sussex* published in 1865, and indeed harmless eccentricities of dress and turn-out were then accounted as marks of distinction. Old inhabitants were later to remember him as a man of simple habits, popular and unaffected manners. Gone were the days when his ardent imagination and brilliant powers of conversation were said to be the admiration of all who knew him and the lively manner in which he put forward his antiquarian speculations commended for a captivating interest. His antiquarian writings now displayed, in an easy and flowing style, a train of thought and reasoning which carried conviction; so wrote Horsfield in his well-known *History of Sussex* published in 1835, only 16 years after Douglas's death.

Nothing more was to be heard of the Howard family papers at Arundel, of the history of Sussex which was was to be on such a lavish scale that as Douglas quickly saw expense would exceed profit, or of the possibilities of a new edition of Stukeley's 1743 book, *Abury, a Temple of the British Druids,* with new plates by Douglas. It was now 1818 and judging from his hand-writing in the parish registers the curate was tired and not in good health. In the summer of that year he was able to ride some three miles to the village of Blatchington near Brighthelmston— now known as West Blatchington, Hove—and it seems particularly fitting that his field work there, the last he was able to undertake, should be linked in both method and humanity to modern archaeology.

From a field in that parish there had often been ploughed up pieces of masonry, bricks and mortar, flue-tiles and pottery which Douglas had no difficulty in recognising as Roman when they were submitted to him for an opinion. The hypocaust tiles 'from a bath or sudatory' were he said quite characteristic. At the time of his visit the field was sown with barley and in the ripening crop his eye quickly noticed lines of stunted growth which probably indicated the burial foundation walls of a Roman villa. This phenomenon Douglas had seen before as a result of his life-long interest in geology and landscape and he recalled Camden's remarks on 'the draughts of streets crossing one another' in the Roman fort at Richborough. It is nevertheless a notable instance of the recognition of the significance of crop-marks, a clue upon which the present-day archaeologist in the field often depends. After the harvest and accompanied by Prince Hoare, a well-known artist and playwright, a relation by marriage to Colt Hoare, who then lived at Brighton, he excavated three rooms of what we should now call a courtyard house and found a variety of Roman pottery, part of a quern or hand-mill, painted wall-plaster, bricks, flue-tiles, two coins of Tetricus scattered he thought from a hoard found previously, but so far as he went there were no tesselated pavements as, for example, at Bignor. There was no delay in publication. In July and September 1818 letters were published in the Lewes Journal section of *The Sussex Advertiser* and in July there was a long letter to Sylvanus Urban—the Editor—printed in the August number of the *Gentleman's Magazine* which was seen by a great number of interested readers and was the primary source from which the site was to be recorded on the official maps of the Ordnance Survey in comparatively recent times. We cannot follow Douglas in his ingenious thinking that his site was the *mansio* of the praefect of the *Portus Adurni* of the *Notitia Dignitatum* which modern opinion places at Portchester in Hampshire and not as he thought near Alderton, the modern Aldrington, but we can nevertheless admire his first-hand knowledge of the discoveries in south-east England.

The story does not end here. Between 1947 and 1949 the site, now Sunning Hill Estate, was being developed as a residential area and excavation by Messrs. N. E. S. Norris and G. P. Burstow, two well-known Sussex archaeologists, showed that during the late Bronze Age it was a small peasant holding whose occupants left, rather unusually, a bronze winged axe and two palstaves as well as their storage pots and cooking-place. Their full report in *Sussex Arch. Collns.,* 89 (1950), 1-56, makes interesting reading. So much for the 'lower british' as Douglas would have called them. People of the prehistoric Iron Age had a small farming settlement close by. The excavators traced Douglas's digging which had been refilled, and showed that his villa was in fact a small villa-type farm house with many corn-drying ovens nearby. The burial of a small child with its feeding-bottle in a corner of the farmyard and the skilled excavation of the pattern of a cast-off boot would have appealed to Douglas's heart and sense. The homely relics found by the excavators bridge the centuries, but an iron spear and the infant's burial take us all into a different world.

It was in July of this same year and from Preston that James Douglas was to write his last piece, an account of the Ancient Barrows on the South Downs. It was published in August as the first paper in Volume I of *The Provincial Magazine* printed by the Sussex Press, Lewes, and in 1819, no doubt in response to a growing local demand from the gentlefolk and cultured middle class for such self-educators, the publication was entitled *The Gleaner's Port-Folio or Provincial Magazine: containing Original Essays, on various subjects, with extracts from the most approved authors, the whole judiciously selected & arranged; with a Copious Index for reference.* No less than eight type-faces set out the title page, the whole range no doubt of the Sussex Press. Every service and every art, as Dr. J. H. Plumb has pertinently reminded us, was then becoming an open invitation to the amateur, and Douglas says in very round terms that his contribution was intended to give instruction and amusement to the general reader particularly as many interesting monuments of antiquity were becoming obliterated from the downland landscape by progress and improvements in agriculture.

Some of his points made from close observation in the field were not to be appreciated fully for many years ahead. Earthworks and barrows attributed by certain Sussex writers to the Romans, Saxons and Danes could not possibly be so; the Roman road called Stone Street, for example, cut through an earlier earthwork entrenchment the course of which avoided barrows 'of the higher order for distinction sake called Celtic' and in which he had found 'british' urns of friable earth. Many earthworks on the Sussex downs were built in pre-Roman times though as discoveries of Roman coins showed those at Cisbury [Cissbury], Chenekbury [Chanctonbury], the poor man's wall commonly called 'the Devil's dyke', and the triple entrenchment called White-hawk hill near the race-course, were occupied in later periods. White-hawk, he suggests, was the first 'Belgic' fortified signal station and of this period of invasion, were Hollingbury, Devil's dyke, Chenekbury [Chanctonbury] to the west and Wool-senbury [Wolstonbury], Ditchling and Caburn to the east. Eack of these sites has in fact been properly excavated by Sussex archaeologists of later and modern times. These places, he says, were also intended as refuges for women, children and cattle and as temporary retreats in times of danger. It was to be noted particularly, and here spoke the former expert in tactics and forti-fication, that all these earlier earthworks were adapted to the natural landscape features and were not as were Roman constructions, rigidly rectangular in plan. They might perhaps have been built three centuries before the invasions of Julius Caesar, if Solinus was correct in his geography and chronology—he gave Tanatus (Thanet) for the first time—or perhaps by other colonists in the century before Caesar in the time of a 'Belgic' ruler.

There are references to the meanings of local place-names, some wildly inaccurate but all of interest to a general reader, and mention of local Roman roads so attributed by Richard of Cirencester whose work was not to be exposed as a forgery until 1869. In a long footnote Douglas tells of his early discoveries at Bignor including part of a pavement and a bath 'which encouraged the further researches of the present possessor to his advantage and to the gratification of the general public'. We have already spoken of the feelings of other people in this matter, but of the influx of visitors there is no doubt. At Hardham on Stone Street he identified what he thought to be a Roman fort where troops would halt

if flooding of the River Arun at Pulborough made passage
impossible and there he discovered Roman pottery and a
large ebony-coloured oaken stake. Modern research has
shown that Hardham was in fact a posting-station, and the
stake evidently came from the Roman crossing over the
Arun marshes.

The paper ends with a suggested classification of
barrows. Those of the 'higher order' are seldom in groups
of more than three or four, many isolated and of large
size: from them come friable hand-made upturned pots
containing cremated human bones, 'brass' spear-heads,
daggers and buckles but no instruments of iron, which
these early people did not use, and no pots of Roman
character. Barrows of the 'lower order' are not usually
found on the same sites as those of earlier date and they
sometimes occur singly or in groups of 40 to, he says,
several hundreds. Burial is by inhumation, there are iron
swords, spears and centres of shields preserved in men's
graves with beads of glass, amber and amethysts and
brooches inlaid with garnets and other gems, together
with gold and silver pendants and buckles in the graves
of women and children. These items can be dated from
the fifth to the latter end of the seventh century when
Christian burial in churchyards began. There were also
other barrows on the Sussex downs in groups of 30 to 50
and more and of a small bell-fashioned shape. They
contained small urns with burnt human bones, small
iron buckles, occasional fragments of melted 'brass'
vessels and sometimes combs of ivory placed separately
in small urns nearby. These, he thinks, belonged to the
rural Romanised Britons of the lower ages who retained
Roman habits after the departure of their troops. And to
the surprise of many a modern reader he claims to have
opened 50 such barrows on Bignor Hill, a group of 15
above Lavington and a group of between 20 and 30 at
Saltdean. The piece ends with a sly dig at an unnamed
author who had published the Rape of Chichester in a
county history of Sussex—it was James Dallaway—and
in it attributed many barrows of the 'higher order' to

the Romans whereas their contents showed clearly that they belonged to a far earlier period.

Again in method and humanity though not in strict technical methods of excavation and record, Douglas was to reach some of the conclusions arrived at by the careful field-work of his brilliant successors in Sussex many generations later. He tried to be clear, simple and human; he showed remarkable classical scholarship and industry, and a deep enthusiasm and what was most important of all, he looked to learn.

In a short time, he said, he hoped to write a more circumstantial and explicit account of several particularly interesting ancient remains in Sussex.

It was not to be. He died in the extreme cold of November 1819, the year of Peterloo and the birth of the Princess Victoria, in his Vicarage House at Preston at the age of sixty-six. A simple tombstone above a vault on the south west side of the churchyard records the date 11 November 1819 (the Parish Register records his burial as on 14 November) and that of his wife Margaret who at the age of 60 outlived him scarcely six months.

11

EPILOGUE

LET THE *SUN* NEWSPAPER of 20 November 1819 speak
his obituary, albeit in the customary overtones of the day:

> He had long been known to the Literary World as the
> Author of a valuable book on British Sepultures, entitled
> Naenia Britannica, and of other Tracts on subjects of ancient
> learning. His writings were not confined to those objects, some
> of his Publications being also of a light and humorous cast.
> The variety of his talents evaded description. His mind was a
> repository of uncounted stores, the richness and overflow of
> which distinguished his conversation at all times from that
> of common man. His attainments were considerable in science
> & in art; his knowledge as a naturalist was very extensive; in
> Classical Learning he delighted, chiefly as it became subservieht
> to his favourite pursuit of research into Antiquity; a pursuit
> not directed by him to trifling minutiae, but in which his
> quest of predominant object was improvement in Religious
> Knowledge. The acquirements of the Naturalist & the Litera-
> ture of the Scholar, were here blended with his professional
> character. His observation was ever active, either to trace
> the Creator in his works through successive ages, or to
> investigate those marks of devotion which, from the earliest
> periods of time, denoted the peculiar homage of the Creature.
> On these topics his intimate friends seldom failed to derive
> delight & instruction from his discourse. His sentiments were
> deeply religious, he worshipped not more in words than in
> heart & spirit, pure and fervent in both. He sought &
> fostered talents, he praised and respected merit, he loved &
> honoured virtue. He was wholly without guile or envy; warmly
> affectionate, & in his judgment of human errors, lenient to

excess. The innocence of his own heart was an unsuspected advocate for the failings of those around him. Mr Douglas was one of those extraordinary men whose example in private life cannot pass by without benefit to those who know them. He was one who would have rewarded promotion by a wider display of piety & learning; have honoured the protection of the Great; but from a want of perseverance in asking, & of confidence in claiming, the return due to merit, he expired in the sixty-seventh year of his age, the Rector of a small Living, and the humble Curate of the village of Preston.

There were some other opinions. Though a man of great archaeological learning, a few people thought that he did not possess any peculiar fitness for the clerical profession, into which he may have been tempted for the sake of learned leisure, and certainly this thought had entered into Douglas's mind many years before his death. But nearly 50 years after his death he was still remembered by many of the older inhabitants of the neighbourhood for his barrow-diggings in which he employed the troops to which he was Chaplain.

A little more was said by T. W. Horsfield in his account of the village of Preston in the *History, Antiquities and Topography of the County of Sussex,* Vol. 1, Lewes (1835), on page 172, after a long account of Douglas's publications quoted from an obituary notice in the *Gentleman's Magazine,* Vol. 89 (1819), page 561, this itself being a publication to which Douglas had made many contributions:

> Mr Douglas was a man whose ardent imagination and brilliant conversational powers were the admiration of all who knew him, and the lively manner in which he introduced his antiquarian speculations gave to them a captivating interest. His writings display, in an easy and flowing style, a train of thought and reasoning which carried conviction to the minds of his readers.

Horsfield's account of the life of Douglas, like most others, contained many errors, but Horsfield was the first to recognise the true value of *Nenia Britannica*. Until Douglas's time no general attempt had been made to acquire real knowledge of our early ancestors from their burial mounds, and although accounts of particular tumuli had been published there was no extensive review of their character and meaning. 'The honour and merit of this is due to Mr Douglas; and although the whole of his reasonings in the Nenia, may not be perfectly borne out by the discoveries which led to them, yet nothing can be more convincing than the majority of proofs he has adduced in favour of his opinions, nor has any subsequent collector been able to equal his exertions; for although Sir Richard Hoare's publications on the same subject contain valuable materials for speculation, yet Sir Richard has not attempted to adduce any result or inference from them'. This was written some 16 years after Douglas's death and three years before Colt Hoare died so that Horsfield knew well what sort of material was available to the serious antiquary. His remarks are well justified.

Horsfield ends by referring to the Douglas collection at one time very large but later much reduced from its former size: its owner, as we know, had a constant and pressing need for ready money. What was left was quickly bought from the impoverished widow by Sir Richard Colt Hoare who in 1829 presented it together, presumably, with the portrait of Douglas by T. Phillips (Plate 1) to the Ashmolean Museum at Oxford. There is in the Ashmolean Museum a manuscript list of 'Various Property left by the late Revd. James Douglas, Author of the Naenia Britannica, now in the care of Mr. P. Hoare'. It is most carefully written in an artistic hand, not a general or legal hand, and several alterations and additions have been made to it at a later time. The words 'now in the care of Mr. P. Hoare' have been enclosed in brackets and 'at Brighton' added. The latter part of the MS. has been roughly cancelled and the word 'NO' written at the end in the same ink as the addition to the title. The most interesting feature perhaps is that it is initialled 'P.H.' apparently in the hand of this later writer. It might just possibly denote Peter Hoare, Colt Hoare's half-brother, but it seems far more likely to be Prince Hoare, the artist-antiquary and one of Douglas's Brighton friends who had helped only the year before his death in the excavation of the Roman villa at West Blatchington.

The list reads:

> *Seven* Pasteboard Boxes, and one small wooden Do, containing inferior fragments and articles, found in barrows opened by Mr Douglas; as exhibited in the Naenia.

> *Three* Boxes fitted up with shelves and drawers (about one foot wide in front) containing various precious articles, in good preservation, found in Barrows, and forming the principal subjects of the beautiful Plates of the Naenia.

> *One* large Box of fragments of Pottery, also dug up from Barrows.

> *Twentysix* Coins, chiefly Roman, of the larger size, and about 120, small, of the Lower Empire.

> *Four* Drawers (Pasteboard) containing Sulphurs and Casts from Medals, said to have 'belonged to the Collection of the late King of France'. [The last ten words have been put in quotation marks and underlined by a later hand, and the succeeding paragraphs have been cancelled by the same later hand.]

> Besides the above Collection, there is a large Box containing various Mss, among which is his Folio Common Place Book, and *Another Box* containing various Papers, Letters &c. Also a *smaller Parcel* of Mss, chiefly Dramatic. This forms the whole of Mr Douglas's *Remains*.

> I have to mention that the *Box* and *smaller parcel* of *Mss* were sometime since purchased by myself, for the sake of sending a little money to Mrs Tucker (Mr Douglas's Daughter and Heiress) as I know she was in Distress. For these I paid her ten Pounds, but I have made no use of them. The other portions of the Collection are those which I valued, as I mentioned to you, at twenty five Pounds; and if it should be thought desirable to retain the whole Collection, I shall very willingly relinquish my purchase at the price I paid for it.

At the end of the list, as we have noted, are the initials 'P.H.', and boldly written and referring to the cancelled paragraphs, the word 'NO'. It is tempting to suppose that the refusal was that of Colt Hoare. And what was 'his'

Folio Common Place Book? Could it possibly have been the famous Folio Common Place Book of Heneage Finch, fifth Earl of Winchilsea, to which we have already referred?

When Colt Hoare presented the Douglas Collection to the Ashmolean in 1829, the Museum was still in a neglected building in Broad Street, and the Latin tabular inscription recording the gift, printed by P. B. Duncan, the then Keeper, in his *Catalogue of the Ashmolean Museum* (1836), p. 128, has long since disappeared. It is curious that the tablet records 'Ex tumulis in agro Sussexensi', whereas by far the greater part of the collection had a Kentish background. Horsfield mentions specifically Colt Hoare's gift of a portrait, but it is not included in Duncan's Catalogue either in the antiquities section or in the list of paintings. There is, however, an excellent portrait in the Ashmolean (Plate 1). In a hard black ink on the stretcher at the back of the frame is inscribed 'This Portrait of the Revd. James Douglas, Author of the Nenia Britannica belongs to his daughter Mrs. Margaret Tucker, 1824' and a tablet on the frame entitles it as a self-portrait. By 1824 Douglas's widow had been dead four years so that the portrait cannot have been included in the collection bought from her by Colt Hoare. Possibly he purchased it later from Mrs. Tucker or from Prince Hoare; and the portrait may not even be in its original frame. Fairly certainly it is not a self-portrait, but in every way it exhibits the characteristics of the work of Thomas Phillips (1770-1845), R.A. 1808, Fellow of the Society of Antiquaries 1819, with its skilled and faithful portraiture, good as to likeness and truthful as to character as the Redgrave brothers described the work of this well-known portrait painter. It has recently been cleaned and now properly titled benevolently observes the Douglas Collection from a wall of the Leeds Room.

Duncan's *Catalogue* contains many interesting items, the relics from the nine or more barrows excavated on Chatham Lines between 1779-82; from Ash, Kent, 1771 and 1783; items from Colchester, Essex; Barham [not Burham as quoted] Downs, Kent; Dorset; the sword-hilt from

Kingsholm, Gloucester, reported by Douglas to the Society of Antiquaries in 1785; the samian patera from Tongres sent as a gift from his friend the Abbé Van Muyssen, all with reference as appropriate to *Nenia Britannica*. Two items of especial interest are nine amber beads from Salisbury Plain which must be those once belonging to Stukeley and mentioned more than once in Douglas's letters to Cunnington and Colt Hoare, and Douglas's own tortoiseshell snuff-box (Plate 35) which had on its lid a small brass of Constantine found in a barrow, a box which was once used as a stamp-box on the desk of a late and eminent Keeper of the Ashmolean. All of the collection is now excellently recorded in detail on a card-index in the Department of Antiquities for the benefit of accredited students.

It should perhaps be said that the fine Roman bronze ceremonial axe from near Canterbury (Plate 20) already noted in our discussion of Douglas's paper on 'The Brass Instruments called Celts' is not particularly indicated by Duncan. Presumably it is either the 'small wedge of brass' No. 258 or, more probably, 'a brass celt' No. 267. The whole collection seems to have included something like 28 items of various kinds.

The list does not include the coins. Mr. Brown kindly confirms that they are included in the large collections of the Coin Room at the Ashmolean, but a list made on internal evidence somewhere about 1830 and presumably at the time of Colt Hoare's gift is in the Bodleian Library as *MS. Num.* d. 3 folio 9-12 under entry 30653 in the *Summary Catalogue of Western Mss.* Included in the 27 registered items are some 140 Greek and Roman coins in various states, a most curious medal, No. 23, which includes *Meretrix Bab—Apocalyps* in its inscription. The fine gold coin of Dubnovellaunos illustrated in Douglas's letter of 11 August 1814 to Colt Hoare does not appear in the list and is not, it seems, in the Ashmolean. In addition to the coins there are about 230 Sulphurs, those included in the Brighton summary of Douglas's collection, said to be cast from the Collection of the late King of

France. This Royal Collection Douglas had visited in
April 1787 principally to see the extremely valuable
relics of Childeric. He was allowed to have two impressions
of the Royal ring and knowing Douglas's powers of persuasion one would not be surprised to know that he had
been able to obtain much more than two impressions of a
single ring.

What can be said in summary of Douglas's place in the
history and development of British archaeology?

To begin with, a list of the places where he had exca-
vated is impressive. In Kent it included Rochester, Chatham
Lines, Canterbury, Barham Downs, St. Margaret's-at-Cliffe,
Ash-by-Sandwich,   Eastry,   Sibertswold (Sheperdswell),
Greenwich Park (Plate 23) and Kit's Coty (Plate 34);
Wimbledon Common, Walton-on-Thames and near Chiddingfold in Surrey; Bignor, Rundell Hill, Rottingdean,
Saltdean, Goldstone, West Blatchington, Hardham, Poynings and Lavington Downs in Sussex; Chesterford, Cambridge; at Manchester; at Baggrave, Leicestershire, and at
Tongres and probably elsewhere in Flanders. In chronology
the sites ranged from the Neolithic of prehistory to the
verge of Christendom. He was familiar with stone circles
and what we should now generally term megaliths,
barrows, cemeteries, prehistoric and Roman earthworks,
with the system of Roman roads, all these especially in the
south east, but he had in addition a first-hand knowledge
of the countryside of his friends in Wessex and in Mercia.

His qualifications, not all of them apparent in *Nenia,*
were many and varied. His observations on the evidence
of coins in relation to chronology were something quite
new in British antiquarian studies. Military duties and his
appreciation of tactics and the construction of fortifications led to an understanding of the influence of topography on human settlement as well as on defence. He
took a great interest in geology, especially in the relation
of various types of soils to patterns of farming and
settlement, in the effect of soils on the preservation of
ancient relics found in them, and in the meaning of soil
and crop-marks. Such matters he discussed often with his

correspondent Hayman Rooke, and emphasised the importance of precise records of find spots as may be seen from
some of his letters included in the latter part of this book.
He was the first antiquary to point out the real anthropo-
logical and chronological differences between the burial
rites of cremation and inhumation, and the import of
secondary burials in burial mounds. In his books Douglas
was particularly well read, in classics both familiar and in
others far less well known and indeed sometimes obscure
—see for example the 12 quoted on page 156 of *Nenia*—
in the works of our national historians, antiquaries and
topographers, in county histories, and in those periodical
works which gave space to antiquarian news and views.
Sometimes, it is true, this devotion to classics led down
what seen to us odd by-ways in the study of magic and
symbolism and in the explanation of place-names, some
of which were boring and with place-names not infrequently uninspired guess-work. His great interest in art
stemmed from his early days on the Continent, particularly
in Flanders, and for his artistic sense and skill it could
well be said that his opportunities of expression were as
good as his never neglected opportunities of observation.
His drawings of antiquities and of landscapes were meticu-
lous and, as we have seen apart perhaps from the efforts
of Stukeley, he was the first antiquary to publish an
acceptable plan and transverse section of an excavation in
Britain. Douglas etched his own plates, could take a mould
of a brooch or a coin, study the remains of a wooden shaft
in an Anglo-Saxon spear-head, analyse solder and other
substances, and with skill examine the texture and pattern
of traces of cloth. His own once large collection and
any others he could persuade the owner to allow him to
view encouraged his researches and added to his practical
knowledge, as did his extensive correspondence—even that
with Hayman Rooke who was always discovering remains
of the Druids in the natural rock-formations of Derbyshire
and Yorkshire—and meetings with brother antiquaries. It
was from all these sources that he drew in making his
classified divisions of *Miscellanea Antiqua*. Nevertheless,

he often looked to knowledge of the present to interpret
the past. Indeed so forward-looking was he in some of his
views, had he lived at the present time we may think that
our highly developed methods of scientific examination,
conservation and dating of antiquities would have received
his constant support and understanding. In particular
instrumental techniques to identify raw materials, their
source and methods of manufacture would have interested
him greatly.

It is a curious trait in Douglas's character that he was
not much interested in ecclesiastical architecture. At
Rochester he once misdescribed the keep of the castle
as Gundulph's Tower, the detached campanile of the
cathedral which was within a stone's throw of his residence
in College Yard. And again, when in a particularly discerning way he compared the design on a gold pendant—
in fact a Saxon bracteate—from Mystole in Kent with the
carving on a capital in Canterbury Cathedral, a building
which he must have known well, he could only say that
it was 'in the alley which leads to the precincts. I think
the place is called the cloysters'. Even the outstanding
features and fittings of his own churches are never mentioned. There is nothing about the fine 13th-century
Purbeck marble font at Kenton, of the interesting Rector's
Pew at Litchborough, or of the truly remarkable wall-
paintings of the murder of Becket and St. Michael with
his scales at Preston.

He could and did admit that he himself had from time
to time made mistakes. Two instances must suffice.
Some years after the publication of his paper on 'The Brass
Instruments called Celts' he did not hesitate to say that
some of his reasoning had been wrong. Further, in 1786,
a special party which included a very curious and know-
ledgable, but unidentified, little Quaker named Jackson
had been formed to open barrows on Wimbledon Common
in Surrey, some of which it was said had already been
opened by a gentleman from London thought to be Mr.
Stukeley. The work went well, and Douglas was truly
surprised at the 'true enthusiasm' of the Quaker who, not

content with the mere digging and careful turning over
of the ground, insisted on the use of a sieve to explore
the contents of the graves. Strangely at times (as for
example at Chiddingfold, *Nenia Britannica,* p. 162) he did
not feel such detailed work to be necessary, but the
memory of the process remained with Douglas as an
example to be followed. Six years later he was writing
to the *Gentleman's Magazine* under his pen-name of
'Tumboracus' emphasising that great attention should be
paid in breaking into undisturbed graves so as not to
disturb the order and stratification, and that the most
minute inspection should be made for coins, fragments of
metal, pottery or indeed any other remains. More than
once he had successfully used careful probing with an
iron crowbar to locate buried remains, and his own digging at Chatham Lines was generally careful.

In the obituary notices Douglas's styles of writing have
been sufficiently described, but it should perhaps be
added that the light touches and humour of the *Travelling
Anecdotes* were seldom to be repeated. One or two
drolleries stay in the reader's mind. His cure for 'antiquarian spleen', described as we have seen under his pen-
name of 'Tumboracus', tricks played on him by 'very
worthy friends', as in persuading him to open the barrow
which covered the burial of a favourite hunter, and the
salting of a grave at Ash in East Kent with an African
trade-bead, and the 'little pleasantry'—what was it, one
cannot but wonder—in the experiment on the sacred
ashes of Edward the First in Westminster Abbey: all
these provide a little light relief in his usually serious
discourses. It is proper to add here that his pastoral duties
were faithfully and lovingly undertaken, except perhaps
at Kenton where he was unhappy and behaved foolishly,
and at Middleton, the tiny parish with its church partly
in ruins. That he could be a 'paper theologian' when
circumstances so dictated is clear from his *Twelve Discourses,* but the 'Ninny' and the 'Abbé' as he was still
nicknamed by some envious acquaintances still remained
a man of many talents.

His barrows he classified by their shape, although the views expressed in *Nenia* were sometimes modified as his experience increased. The small conical barrows he thought of as Anglo-Saxon; 'campaniform' barrows in clusters were dated to the seventh century. Some were clearly Roman, while others, the 'great barrows', he compares with examples from the ancient and vast region of Scythia. Such views of chronology, far removed as they are from those of present-day archaeology, were at least a thoughtful attempt to solve an outstanding problem.

To him classification, interpretation and synthesis were as important as they are to archaeologists of the present day, and indeed some of his observations considered matters which have puzzled his successors in the field. What did the orientation of a grave signify, and why, in some cases, was there nothing to accompany the body while other graves were richly furnished? He was, it seems, the first archaeologist in Britain to realise the difference between urns used to contain cremated remains and those intended for offerings and food-supplies for the dead. The nature of some weapons in graves was clearly Saxon and, he thought, the design of some brooches was Germanic-Gothic in conception, thus anticipating the views of much later specialists, as he did when he suggested that some items in graves showed an Eastern origin and that beads could have been obtained by primitive barter from western Mediterranean countries. More importantly he realised that flint tools, arrow-heads in particular, were of earlier date than those of bronze and iron. He produced a system of relative chronology in its way akin to the famous 'Three Age System' which was to be suggested in 1819, the year of his death, by Christian Thomsen of Copenhagen. Although the Abbé did not know it, he was to help in the beginning of a scientific approach to British archaeology and so indirectly to the broad developments which were soon to follow.

Sometimes of set purpose, but often unwittingly, he did more. In summarising and criticising the works of those who were already trying to recreate the past, in observing and recording facts—buried among long diversions though his pertinent remarks might be—he saw the past in the light of the present and gave to it life and substance. This desire for knowledge was to be a marked feature of the later years of the century in which his life ended, a desire which was to reflect a perfectly natural and universal interest in the past as an interest in life itself. Be he regarded as antiquary or archaeologist he provided an approach to the philosophy of the 19th century and so indirectly to the great Victorian Adventure. But most importantly, as Thurlow Leeds said more than 50 years ago, to James Douglas belongs the credit of being the first man to recognise the remains of the Anglo-Saxons in Britain. There is yet something more. In addition to all this Douglas had ideas of the shape and form of early history and of the field in which such matters should be pursued. He insisted on the comparative study of the antiquities of past civilisations and in general despite his sometimes tedious diversions, he did not confuse the image and the fact of natural existence. What, one wonders, would have been his attitude to 'The New Archaeology', the idea of setting up rules to reconstruct the past, rules and constructions and theories that can be tested in the end by excavation. Occasionally one catches a glimpse of the beginnings of such thoughts in his mind. There is no doubt that he would have had much in common with the thoughts of Professor Alexander Thom, a former Professor of Engineering at Oxford University, who after many years of studying megaliths and stone circles in Britain and in Brittany, believes that the structures are evidence of skilled mathematicians and astronomers in the Stone Age and the Bronze Age, and with Mr. Douglas Heggie's appraisal, from the Institute of Theoretical Astronomy in his own University of Cambridge, that such observations must be given serious consideration. He might even have approved of some of the fantastic remarks of Tom Lethbridge, another Cambridge archaeologist, on the significance of stone circles as 'bio-electronic bearings' for the Sons of God journeying from outer space.

A simple panel of white marble with well-cut lettering erected by a later curate, Charles Townsend, antiquarian, man of arts and letters and sociable friend of Lord Egremont, at Petworth, re-set with others on the interior south-west wall of the nave of St. Peter, Preston (now unfortunately stained by water dripping from the window above) (Plate 36) is his requiem:

M · S

IACOBI · DOVGLAS · A · M

CVIVS · IN · NÆNIA · BRITANNICA ·

QVÆCVNQVE · AD · PRISCORVM · BRITANNIÆ · INCOLARVM·

SEPVLTVRAM · PERTINENT · DOCTISSIME · EXPLICANTVR·

OBIT V · NOVEMB · A·D· MD · CCC·XIX ·ÆT · LXVII

ALIORVM · SEPVULCRA · HAVD · SINE · REVERENTIA · EXTVRBAVIT

IN SVO · PLACIDE · QVIESCAT

In his work entitled *Nenia Britannica* he has most learnedly explained all that relates to the burial of the early inhabitants of Britain. He was a disturber, though not without proper reverence, of other men's sepulchres.

May he, in his own, rest quietly.

PART II

THE LEGIBILITY and sense of Douglas's letters sometimes reflect everyday matters such as the quality of his letter paper, the sharpness of his quills, and occasional lapses in his Latin, a language in which as it happened he was exceptionally well read, and inconsistencies in his spelling of both English and Latin with some curious variations in his French.

His writings were often influenced by the state of his health. His eyesight was not infrequently affected by the fumes from the acid used in etching his plates for books and papers. He was also frequently subject to violent chills and fever, influenza, and severe colds on the chest which confined him to his bed and then to his room so that at times he was scarcely able to write. He suffered in this way at Rochester, at Blackheath, in East Anglia and in Sussex, and there is frequent mention that his family suffered also from persistent colds.

A contemporary apothecary observing these consistent symptoms, noticing a high colour as depicted in the Phillips portrait and the obvious manifestations of a native genius, might have been tempted to suggest that his patient suffered from phthisis or consumption, a disease prevalent enough at the time and still in Bunyan's words, 'the captain of men of death'.

It will be noticed that the majority of the endings of the letters have been set to economise in space. They are printed in order of date, particularly so in order that reference to the extensive collection in the Society of Antiquaries Library may be made the more readily.

12

SELECTION OF LETTERS TO
HENRY GODFREY FAUSSETT OF HEPPINGTON

Canterbury, 1781-94 (from the Society of Antiquaries MS. 723)

Some of these letters were published as a whole or in part by Charles Roach Smith as an Appendix to his edition of Bryan Faussett's Journal, Inventorium Sepulchrale *(1856).*

Dear Sir,

The object of my letter is to request your answer to the following particulars, at the same time apologising for the trouble I have given you, should the proposals be in the least degree foreign to your inclination.

A gentleman high up in the estimation of the antiquarian world and who has himself a great and valuable collection of antiquities, has delegated me to treat for your cabinet should you have any desire to part with it? I am therefore to request of you the sum, which you would set upon it, provided you would listen to a negotiation from me—you will acquiesce with me in supposing that antiquarians do not scruple in making bargains for Rusty [deleted] antique rust, therefore any delicacy on this subject would be ridiculous—however if you have any inclination to listen to proposals, I make no doubt but what I shall be able to introduce your cabinet of *hastie,* umbonae, fibulae &c to a good antiquarian market.

I very much respect your hint as to the Tumulus you pointed out to me, I have explored it much to my satisfaction.

On the receipt of your letter and of your consent, I will enter into particulars, on the sense of which I am sure you will find no scruples.

I have taken a house in the College-Yard Rochester where I shall be extremely happy to see you and your Lady if a *trajet* to this place should enter your mind, or to make use of it as an inn in your road to the Capital.

Mrs. Douglas joins with me in compliments to Mrs. Faucit and I have the honour to be Dr Sir,

> Your faithful and obedient servant J. Douglas.

Chatham 2nd Apl. 1781

Please to direct your letter to the *Office of Ordnance Chatham Lines.* I save postage by this means—my letters are frank'd.   J.D.

> Rochester 23rd Apl. 1781.

Dear Sir,

I have received a letter from my friend in answer to the one I wrote to him specifying your permission of viewing your cabinet. In consequence we propose paying our respects to you on Saturday next, should the day be agreeable to you.

The journey which my friend will make from London is solely for the purpose of seeing your collection for which reason I should be extremely distressed if any thing happens to frustrate the plan—

With respects to you and your Lady from Mrs. D and self, I am, Dr Sir Your very obedt Sert.   J. Douglas.

Roch. 28th May 1781

Dear Sir,

I am extremely sorry to inform you that my friend,
owing to some very particular business can not possibly
leave London before the 4th of next month when without
fail we shall have the pleasure of paying our respects to
you at Heppington—this will be next friday.

It will give both himself and me pain, should the least
inconvenience attend this disappointment.

Having only received my friend Sir Ashton Lever's letter
yesterday, I could not possibly write to you before this
to promise you of our not coming.

I am with the return of compliments from Mrs. D and
self to your lady, Dr Sir, your very obedt & humble
Servt   J. Douglas.

Dr Sir,

I should have no manner of objection of treating with
you concerning your collection of things found in barrows &c. If the value you set on them is compatible with
reason and the scarcity of money in general, indeed I
should say with the poverty of the time. Permit me
now to tell you that I am empowered to negotiate with
you for the purchase but also not to exceed a certain
price; the person is not a very moneyed man, yet if you
conclude the disposing of them he will remit you their
value on the immediate conclusion of the bargain. Whatever transpires with me, I give you my honour shall remain
a secret, but indeed I see no reason why you should have
the least reluctance to make your intention public of disposing of them, since it happens every day that the first
families in the kingdom are selling their collections of pictures, gems, antiquities horses &c., &c.—I believe I could
enumerate many families that do this, not through distress, but merely owing to their fancy changing on other
matters—I find Dr. Jacobs [the Faversham antiquary] has

sold his collection of medals &c which he has been much disappointed in; they fetched a mere trifle indeed.

I apprehend you have no objection to permit your manuscripts that is your father's to go with the things—you know it would be extremely awkward to have the collection without them.

In expectation of your letter signifying your price which I hope you will not be unreasonable in, I have the pleasure in remaining with much sincerity

Dr Sir   Your faithful obedt Servt   James Douglas

College-Yard, Rochester   4th May 1782

Pray present mine and Mrs. D—comts to your Lady. If you ever come this way with Mrs. F—Mr. and Mrs. D will be extremely happy in offering you a bed &c—indeed it will give them both pleasure.

Dr Sir,

I have been greatly indisposed with a violent cold and fever which utterly prevented my answering your obliging letter sooner. I am now confined to my room and can just hold up my head to employ my pen.

It would afford me the greatest pleasure to mention a price on your cabinet, that would be equally satisfactory to your own private valuation and the person willing to purchase. You will agree with me that it is extremely delicate for any gentleman to presume to estimate things of this nature in the possession of another and for this reason. Not knowing the private opinion of the possessor, it might hurt his feelings to undervalue that, which is higher rated —Relics of antiquity independant of their intrinsic value are surely imaginery and how in this case could a fair and competent sum be set upon them. Men will sometimes greatly indulge a partial reigning passion, but you well know Sir, that these are characters which the world would stigmatise with folly and madness—I trust, that those who are willing to treat liberally and reasonably with you for your cabinet—otherwise than this I am sure you also would not require—are not comprehended under the class I have mentioned—I know of no method to decide ultimately on the business in question, but for you to abstract what is *absolutely* the intrinsic value of your antiquities, and then to estimate them at something more enlarged, which I am sure you do not mean should exceed a fair sum. If your estimation will not be conformable with the views of the purchaser you may undoubtedly rely on my honour to keep the same a perfect secret, as shall be, whatever is now transpiring between us, that is if you have any private reasons for its being so.

If you have any *serious* intentions of disposing of your cabinet mention your sum and an opportunity will present itself to you which you perhaps will not so soon meet with again to sell it into private hands. It is you Sir to mention your price—it is impossible that any other person can make you an offer. If your terms will meet with approbation I will have the pleasure to wait upon you and conclude everything to your perfect satisfaction.

I dined with my friend Sir Ashton Lever about ten days since, he desired his compts. to you when I saw you—he is not the person who is now treating with you, as he has dropped all thoughts of laying out a farthing more on the Holophusikon. Mrs. Douglas joins with me in Compts. to Mrs. Fawcet, and believe me to be most sincerely Dr Sir

Your affectionate Humble Sert.   Jas Douglas

P.S. I hope your family have escaped the present reigning influenza—all the families in our quarter have some one or other laid up with it.

Rochester 30th May 1782.

Rochester—18th June 1782

Dear Sir,

I had the pleasure of your favour setting forth your intentions not to part with your collection, unless the

medals were to accompany it. As the person who is willing
to purchase the cabinet (and who by the way is well
acquainted with the particulars) only collects barrow
curiosities he will not therefore accept of coins &c as
the matter thus stands, I apprehend he must abide by your
decision and consequently drop all further thoughts of
having your barrow treasure detached from the medals—
so much of this—now to my own proposal—I have very
nearly completed a general history of the funeral customs
of the antients having for that purpose made acquisition
of a profusion of matterials and spared no labour to
accomplish a rational and concise system to ascertain the
history of barrows—kistvaen—cromlechs &c. I have made
drawings of the most matterial part of my small researches,
besides of an addition which I have made to it from various
quarters—These drawings will be published in the *aqua
tinta* to the amount of near an hundred—the plan is to
diffuse to explain the particulars by letter, but when I
have the pleasure of seeing you, or should you journey to
my part of the world I will communicate the whole to
you and show you my papers &c. my proposal is, to
request the assistance of your collection—which as it will
ornament my work to a great degree, I have not the least
doubt of its making known to the world and as I shall
have an indubitable proof of appreciating their value, by
an elaborate description of their justly to be admired
antique estimation, so I think as you will have an easy
opportunity of communicating the discoveries to the
world, you will at the same time assure yourself a channel
of making their value known.

My object is not, to benefit by the undertaking; the
getting up of the work will give me pleasure, and greatly
amuse me in my leisure hours—I shall hope to refund
myself in the expense of printing, which will be very
great—that is all I flatter myself with and all that I can
possibly expect from a work of this nature—I mean to
print my work the size of the Archaeologia for the sake of
grouping in a library. The communication of any particulars which your long experience in the study of antiquity

must have rendered you well versed in, would prove extremely beneficial to me and will be gratefully received and marked in my work accordingly.

When I have completed some of my *aqua tinta* I shall have the pleasure of transmitting you some of the plates for your opinion of—they only print a *certain number* consequently they will limit the copies of my work to a *certain number.* The great plan I have in view will be to draw a line between all speculative fancies in antiquities and on Hypothesis founded on reason and practical observations.

We recover by degrees of this pestilential malaria in our parts—the garrison at Chatham, has reduced their dead from eight of a night to four.

Mrs. Douglas presents her compliments to your good family and I have the pleasure of subscribing myself most heartily   Dr Sir

Your sincere humble Servt.   Js Douglas

Dr Sir,

It gives me the greatest pleasure to take the earliest opportunity of answering your polite and obliging letter— I am extremely sorry you are not certain of paying a visit in this part of the world. I wish to God you could contrive to run up as far as Rochester, I have a bed at your service and do assure you on the faith of a true Englishman that your company would be highly acceptable to Mrs. D and myself—I do not forget Mrs. Faussett as we expect her of course.

Far be it from my thoughts to entertain any idea of making extracts from your manuscripts—no—nothing I assure you shall escape from me that may in the last degree prove prejudicial to any views you may have to the subject of your Cabinet—What ever your sentiments are on the occasion I shall totally abide by them, nor is it my wish to persuade you to alter them. I am perfectly contented with yr. kind permission to make drawings of those things which I may find serviceable to my plan, which I am labouring upon—but I do not by any means wish to give you trouble to draw them yourself. I propose if a Commanders leave will tally with my intentions to take up my quarters in the town of Canterbury for a few days during the course of this winter, and then my Dr Sir I shall beg leave to employ myself in making some drawings from the delightful antiquities in question.

I have a hoard of tumuli treasures, since I last had the pleasure of seeing you—things which you would admire— they have been taken out of similar barrows to those of Chatham and Barham downs—I have a *speculum* in charming preservation—Some Gold fibulae—part of a necklace Gold ornamented with rubies and *tourquoise* stones, &c. I wish you could see them—some prodigious large beads—I think much larger than those which you have.

Excuse my hasty scrawl—up to my head and ears in ink, paper, books, &c. [A line deleted.] For Godsake wink at this blotting. I am afraid of being too late for the Post. Mrs. D presents her compliments to your worthy Lady, & I remain with much truth Dr Sir,

Your very sincere humble Servt. J. Douglas.

Rochester 19th July, 1782.

Dear Sir,

I have procrastinated my return to Rochester longer than I first intended; when I thought of having the pleasure of penning a few lines to you in the antiquarian line, as well as in an hospitable one, both of which I assure you are impressed on your humble servant. I have therefore wrote from London, where I have been these ten days, and as you may well suppose not inactive in my antiquarian pursuits. I have been introduced to Dr. Hunter, [possibly William Hunter the anatomist, elected F.S.A. 1767] where I saw one of the most splendid collection of early Saxon coins, I suppose in the universe—this suite he means shortly to publish with historical and critical remarks, tending to illustrate that during that dark and intricate passage in our history, the invasion of these barbarous people, the Saxons, where so much doubt and uncertainty perplex the modern historian: as this is precisely the aera on which I labour most earnestly to elucidate, you will not be surprised that I wait impatiently for his work. I have made acquisition of Schedius *de dies Germanis* [?] and Jermandes the Goth from whom I expect some information and my friend Dr. Lort [a well-known Fellow of the Society of Antiquaries] has promised me *Bartolinus* on *Sepulchres*: these books I expect will serve my purpose. I have the promise of any book I please from two excellent libraries, and as I only wait to get an iron out of the fire; the 2d vol. of Trav: Anecdotes, I shall begin to make up my work. The *Nenia Britannia*: for the success of which, as a brother labourer in the vinyard of antiquity, though not quite so pleasantly intoxicating as in the vinyard from whence the Falernian of the antients was reared, I hope to receive your blessing and good wishes . . . [see p. 61]

Please to present my best respects to your lady Mrs. Faucet and believe to be the most sincerely and heartily Dr Sir

       Your affectionate humble Servant   James Douglas.
London
Stratton Street—Piccadilly 8 Jany. 1783.

Dear Fausett,

I have been so much employed in removing from my house in St. Margarets into the town of Rochester that I have not had leisure to answer your obliging letter, or to send the picture sooner. The house I now occupy is so commodious and so much to my mind in point of situation, that I can now sit down and write to my friends with pleasure and alacrity, nay I find myself so comfortable and so well accommodated for business that I feel myself sufficiently bold to enter on the most regular correspondence.

You are now in possession of a painting by the old Hemlink and in most excellent preservation. You may pronounce it a virgin picture—you will see the initial of the name or monogram on the barr of the stool. Peter Neif is the sweetest picture my eyes ever beheld, I must beg the favour you will let me take a copy of it before I send it to you and indeed to be frank with you, it ingratiates itself so much, that I am almost prompted to revoke its doom. I have mentioned the Head of Edwd VI by Holben to a particular friend of mine, who wishes much to have it and has offered me some money for it at a venture, the next time I see him I will beg of him to make it over to you, but as I think it a curiosity and am under promise to show it to him, may I request the favour of you to let it come with your *morceau* of Vandyke, and I will contrive if possible to return it to you. The winter season is now set in, and as is generally the case at this time of year I am a gentleman at large, and what say you, you will mount your palfry and favour me with your company for a few days. I shall be able to dedicate all the time you stay with us entirely for your *propria persona.* I will show you some fine collections of pictures in our neighbourhood. I will show you since I last saw you a great acquisition which I have made to my cabinet of tumuli treasures. I have lately been greatly occupied in making drawings of my collection, arranging matterials and working hard on the anvil of antiquity. My matterials flow in daily from several correspondents; and I find the longer I procrastinate my views of publication the richer I grow (not actually in the splendour of gold by the bye) but in the strength and copiousness of my musty manuscripts.

I thank you much for the drawing which you intend me; I really am much surprised, having such advantages as you have, as well on the side of nature as other wordly conveniences, that you do not stick most devotedly and elaborately to drawing, in which I think you could make a pleasing proficiency, as well to yourself as to your friends.

The *manes* have no reason to lament their *violated treasures.* I have so many bones and skulls so religiously and carefully preserved in my cabinet, that if called upon, I make no doubt I shall be enabled to restore to every one their own. The trinckets I expect they will vouchsafe to leave me for preserving their bones for the hungry worms and the more ravenous jaw of oblivion.

Present mine and Mrs. Douglas's compliments to your lady, Mrs. F &c and believe me to be most sincerely,

> Your affectionate Humble Servant, James Douglas.

P.S. My best respects wait on Sr W. Fagg and his Lady. I have had lately so much on my hands I have not been able to take a copy of his plan [probably of the Mystole excavations in 1730] which I shall now set about at the first opportunity.

Rochester 5th Feby. 1783.

> Rochester—23rd Feby 1783

Dr Sir,

On my return from Lincolnshire (having been some time absent from this quarter) I expected to have been favored with yours, acknowledging the receipt of the case with the Hemskirk. [Egbert van Heemskerk, 1610-80, a Dutch genre painter.] I hope you have received it safe.

This peace will make some revolution in my future condition of life; I have consulted with my friends and I have now effectually decided on entering the Church, for which I am now making the most expeditious preparations. I am afraid I shall not make a long stay in this part of the world, therefore shall find it inconvenient to transfer my pictures. I wish you would take a ride over and spend a few days with me. I do assure you nothing would give me greater pleasure: you shall then judge for yourself, and take what paintings I have on any terms you please. I think you will find some that will please you.

I am quite ashamed that I have detained Sr Wm Fags plan so long, indeed I had not time till lately for copying

it. I beg you will make my respects acceptable to him
and her Ladyship, as also mine and Mrs. Ds to your good
Lady and family. Most heartily wishing you health &c
I am very sincerely Your friend and Humble Servt.

Jas. Douglas

I have not enclosed the plan least on being obliged to
make a parcel of it, it might not come to hand.

Rochester 26th March 1783.

Dear Sir,

I was very much disappointed when I heard you had
paid me a visit in my absence, indeed I was much concerned, but when I inform you that the most important
object of church preferment depended on the exertion of
a moment to get into Orders . . . [See p. 56.]

How did you like Peter Neff—pray is it presumption
in one to wield the brush in the attempts which you may
have observed in my room up stairs? Would to God this
compleat independance was at hand: I should then wade
up to the chin in daub; and bespatter faces with as
much unconcern as some of your signpainters do—You
little know how much I am fond of the art and how
little I can afford the time which is necessary for the
carrying off of it to an eminent degree . . .

Indeed was I to make election I should fix on Canterbury: by the by if you should hear of one or more
curacies that are vacated or about being vacated pray
acquaint me of them—perhaps you may not think it too
much trouble to enquire for the same for me.

Mrs. Douglas joins with me in Compliments to your
Lady and family and believe me to be most heartily and
sincerely Dr Sir
Very much your friend and humble Servant

James Douglas

[P.S.] I beg I may hear soon from you—and that you
will make attonement by your early answer for past

neglect in correspondence—Ha ha! I have no right to chide of all good folks, for I believe I am as lazy as most people. Pray be so obliging as to make an appology for keeping Sir W. Fagg's plan so long in my hands.

Dr Sir,   Write soon

Bis dat qui cito dat

I have put off and put off from day to day the pleasure of writing to you that I hardly know whether I now dare to put a face on so doing—I have not been idle and when I tell you that antiquities have greatly engrossed my time I am sure you will in some respects make a little exercise for their advancement—indeed you are not alone in this predicament, but I assure you I am indebted to many more of my friends in the pen & ink way though they held equal estimation in my mind.

I am greatly happy that you caught Madam Douglas *en chenille,* though very unhappy I was not at home to receive you and your party which I should have rejoiced in so doing. I have been favoured with a call from your Brother [-in-law] & Mr. Fagg who I suppose by this are returned home.

I have lately much encreased and still encreasing my cabinet—I have clandestinly opened a few barrows and am promised in September to complete the range—also I am presented with various fragments of brass armour, similar bosses & spears to ours, &c. &c. taken from a range of tumuli in Leicestershire and which I am promised the ransacking of. My work advances—I must encrease the price—my plates will else be the ruin of me, they are all to be finished in *aqua tinta.* I have several compleated—others in hand—you shall see them soon when I send you my pictures—did I bargain for the frame of the Peter Neef? (or was it meant to go with the picture?)

I can not help thinking how unfortunate I have been in being absent twice when you favoured me with a call

—I wish you had thought of sending me a previous line or two before you set off—and I should have been at home to have received you.

I have enclosed you a little specimen of my own aqua tinta—it is one of your bells I have tinted after the drawing: it was only meant for an essay—since which I have done several large plates—you have my thanks for the drawing of the fibula and the cocks bone.

I forgot to tell you that I have seen in Cambridgeshire near the station of Chesterford according to Stukeley the Camboridum of the Rome: [Great Chesterford was a small walled town with a temple, villas and other constructions, but the Roman name appears to be guesswork] a range of inhumated bodies like to those which your father opened at Crundale—I had labourers on the spot to go through with a days digging but the weather prevented us—I was certain of finding plenty of paterae &c fragments I found there without end—to this place I hope to return—the inhumated bodies with the urns and paterae were explored by a neighbouring farmer who [torn] more transactions of these relics than you or myself if possible.

Heartily wishing you health and presenting mine and Mrs. D's compliments to your good Lady. I remain at the end of a long and hasty letter

Dr Sir   Most affectionately yours   James Douglas

Rochester   8th Augt 1783

Dear Sir

First thanking you for your obliging favour of the drawings &c I beg to inform you that I have postponed writing to you 'till I had broke ground in Greenwich Park, which I did on Thursday and Friday last and opened about twenty barrows, [in *Nenia Britannica*, p. 89 he says about fifty. See also letter of 31 May 1785] some of which [the letter is now torn and sections are illegible] indeed the exterior surface showed the same by the redundancy of the vegetation of the apix of the barrow; but as I had remarked this to be the case with others that had been unexplored, I do not know but what I might have been equally successful. The whole of my labours were not amply though satisfactorily repaid. I found beads and five spear heads; but hear me Faussett and be surprised with me; I now and then in the graves threw up pieces of a dark matter which I thought had the appearance of cloth, and towards the head I thought I observed several times, something like hair—observe that it is an iron gravelly soil very compact, almost (in the native soil that is) compacted to a rock. In one grave which was situated in a footpath, I threw up beads and evident pieces of Cloth—indeed the whole circumference of the grave was sheeted with it—but in no one of the graves were to be found the least remains of bones, not a particle—now judge of my surprise when at the head of this grave I threw up a lump of human-hair agglomerated with cloth—is not this strange—particularly was I struck with it, seeing that gravel, of all soils is the least congenial to the preservation of bodies of any denominations: I forbode to think it possible that this could have been the hair of the person buried, until I had sufficient testimonials of the truth by the various specimens found in different graves.

I have made several enquiries about your Landscape painter and his *carrots*: but the *Cognocenti* cannot hit upon his name. I shall not fail however to try again: the dog is known but I have not as yet met with a person who can recollect his name.

I have received an agreeable packet from my little Tongrian Priest enclosing upwards of fifty coloured drawings of urns, pots &c and a discription joined with them—the bodies were not inhumed—the contents are similar to ours—ashes are [letter torn . . .] posited. I can tell to a nicety when they were interred from the first of Caesars conquest of the Attuaci of the very lowest of the Emp—many and very curious coins have been deposited with them—he has commissioned me to find him a person who will exchange coins with him, as he is forming a collection and is deficient in the suites, colony coins &c.

What do you say. Will you engage with him, I will answer for him that he is a man of honor.

I have likewise received several packets of antiquities from the Revd. Wm. Pearce at Meneage in Cornwall, giving me an account of some druidical remains and some barrows which he has opened. Also from H. Rooke Esqr, Woodhouse place near Mansfield Notts with four elegant descriptive drawings of Druidical temples, barrows &c., kist-vaen or Cromlech's &c.

Would you give us your company at Rochester—*alons donc*—What is the distance—we shall be happy together I am sure—and a change you know is the only true zest of living in this world—dull, dull is that continued rotation of *les mêmes choses*—but I forgot myself. I did not recollect the charms of a family, an agreeable wife and such pretty companions as little children—if therefore you can find resolution to break from these ties and venture the amazing distance of I think thirty miles no one [letter torn] than yourself [letter torn] Mrs. D joins with me [letter torn] to your Lady Mrs. F.

Rochester   25th January 1784

Dear Sir

I expected that ere this some allurement either of pleasure or of business would have brought you to the Capital and that I should have had the pleasure of seeing you at No. 3 Little Stanhope Street where Mrs. D. would also have been happy on receiving Mrs. Faussett: some months have likewise passed since I have heard by letter from you—this silence is indeed too long for persons so nearly connected as we should be by the ties of anti-quarian studies, more dear in the opinion of many persons than that of consanguinity.

I have just returned from the banks of the Thames near Walton, where I have been ransacking more of our tumuli treasures—at a place called Windmill hill, deriving its name from a large barrow on which the Mill was situated, a range of our lower british barrows have for these 50 years past, been occasionally broken into, by removing gravel from a common ground to mend the rodes &c. Spear heads without number have been picked up without any kind of local investigation—a farmer in the neighbourhood of the name of Rosewel, in appearance like some aboriginal having all the usual barbarousness of uninquisitive ignorance had worked at the pit for upwards of 40 years—throwing up bones, spear heads and fragments of other arms &c without observing anything of smaller dimensions than pieces of large *rusty iron*—striking the eye without the least appeal to that reflecting part of man, which God has implanted in the nature of the human race, to exhalt them over the brute creation—therefore by this paucity of argument—the brute Rosewel has carted away *relics* that would have adorned the cabinets even of a Faussett or a Douglas—but what relics! Fibulae—beads—armillae and perhaps many incognitae that would have occasioned the brightest speculation that ever fell from the lips of antiquarians. [Details of these 23 or so round ditched barrows and a probable long barrow are given in *Nenia Britannica*, pp. 93-4. Stukeley had probably dug there many years before, and the Calvinist George Whitefield preached from the summit of one large barrow.]

I have taken an exact drawing of this spot, and have made some remarks, that I think will be of the greatest utility to my Naenia. At some little distance from these tumuli is situated another range as appears by similar discoveries—the place is called Sheperton range—the common of Sheperton—recollect if you please the similarity of names between this place and *Syberts-would*—vulgarly called *Shepherds-would*—would is the Old Saxon for common—sometimes *wood* from *weldern*. I wish I could hit on the etymon of this Shepherd—it is a very common appellation for many places throughout England.

Tomorrow I am invited to see the contents of one or more barrows in the possession of a Lady who was present at the opening of them on her estate—perhaps I may join the particulars to my cabinet which is now very much increased: by the description I suppose them to be of the lower british—spear heads, &c.

If I had a little money to spare: I have lately had opportunities of purchasing some excellent pictures remarkably cheap. I have been so much employed in church duty and fagging so very hard for—what I am not yet permitted to relate—that really I have been obliged to postpone much of my correspondence.

I am now working very hard at my book—though I procrastinate, I find I am in point of fulness and accuracy much the gainer. I mean to publish on my own account—I shall therefore take my own time and run all risks. I am too proud to solicit subscriptions and too proud to circulate a work, that will be of discredit to me. I shall therefore wait a few months longer before I commit my manuscripts to the press.

Pray write to me per return or as soon as convenient and relate what has occurred in the discovery way since I left your region of the world—have you been up in a balloon? Apropos a Mr. Bailey who was on a visit at Sr Hy Oxendens and a gentleman of my acquaintance—told me something of a *gold shield* or *bason* that *was found on Barham Downs*—have you heard any thing of it?

Mrs. D joins me in compliments to your Lady Mrs. F. &c.

I am most heartily, Dr Sir

Yours very sincerely James Douglas

No 3 Little Stanhope Street, May Fair
Septr 19th 1784

When you come to town I expect to see you—mind not a squib visit, just light up the fire of antiquity and then bounce it is out again, by a good day to you

Dr Sir

· It is a considerable time since I had the pleasure of last writing to you, and not receiving an answer, I am

apprehensive the letter did not arrive, or something may
have happened in your family.

I have a complicated store of Tumuli remains come to
hand since I left Kent, and I have been fully employed
in simplifying them for the press. I wish your business
might invite you to town, that we could confer on a study
which we mutually seem to enjoy; I am sure were you to
see the plates I have finished and the advancement of my
work in other respects that you would not pronounce me
wanting of zeal and industry to spur me to the conclusion
of great undertaking, an undertaking which I find more
extensive and serious than I at first apprehended.

I shall forward in a few days to Mr. Boys of Sandwich
a plate of the female barrow which I opened in his
presence at Ash and which I mean to inscribe to him, in
testimony of the civilities which I received from him. And
in return for the many which you have been pleased to
confer on me, I propose to inscribe the plate of the large
fibula, which I shall next begin upon, to you, for which
purpose I shall be obliged to you for an exact account
of the contents of the barrow. I think there were two
or more brass vessels—if you could make a sketch of the
large one, the small one I have drawn, I should be infinitely
obliged to you. I have also to request the favor of the
contents of the barrows with the particulars which were
found with the crystal ball: Of these balls I have some
extraordinary relations which I should be happy to communicate to you.

There is in the British Museum a shell similar to the
one which found in a barrow: this was deposited there
by Sir Wm Hamilton [it may well have been the fine
agate cowry shell, No. 30, in Dr. Ann Birchall's bi-
centenary Hamilton exhibition at the British Museum
in 1972], as much information will depend on the
locality of this discovery, I shall be glad to know what
was found in the barrow which contained yours.

Mr. Rooke a correspondent of mine, and a gentleman
who has opened many barrows in Derbyshire, has transmitted to me an account of the barrows from which

Mr. Manders fibula [the well-known Saxon jewel from White Lowe in the City of Sheffield Museums] was taken by which it appears that they belong to one and the same people; in his last packet I received the drawings of some singular Druid monuments.

I was pleased greatly with the acquisition a few days back of a Manuscript, a kind of Journal, of a Lord Winchelsea [*sic*] who was a great lover of antiquity and whose collection, which was very extensive, was sold some years back. In this manuscript, he has noted several Roman graves which he opened at Crundal and also at Ash—with other similar barrows in various parts.

I have seen two small pictures of Riodale [Ruysdael] which I can buy for six guineas. I think the frames which are sumptous are worth the money. Pictures sell now so cheap that I bought a few weeks past a prodigious fine and virgin picture in a noble frame of *Salviati* for eleven guineas, which to my undoubted knowledge was bought in Christy's room last year by Mr. Shepherd of Harrow for ninety. I wish I could afford to keep it.

Pray let me hear if you are in the land of the living— I should be heartily glad to see you, to provide a bed for you, at least I expect if all is right to have a line very soon from you. In full hopes of being relieved from the consequences which attend on a friendly correspon- dence when a long silence intervenes I remain with much sincerity

Dr Sir,   Your friend and humble servant   Jas Douglas.

No 3 Little Stanhope St.
May fair   20th Decr. 1784

Dear Sir,

Many thanks for your obliging letter, which I should have answered immediately if I had the intelligence necessary to convey to you on the subject of your flemish cabbage, carrots &c painting; I enquired the name of the master from one of our first rate picture dealers who is at a loss, and have waited some days in the hope of getting his name—the ruins in the back ground puzzle the *Cognoscenti,* and they want the sight of the picture to determine —there are many flemish masters who were famous in that way, though none that are recollected to have grouped ruins in their compositions. As soon as I get information, which I shall endeavour at, I will write.

You improve in your drawings, and I thank you much for the vessel Or. I shall readily accept your offer of the drawings of the *rich* barrow with the description of the relics as they were found—and from which I shall make an engraving which I mean to inscribe to the owner. I say a plate but I am apprehensive they will not be contained in two—the large fibula will occupy one.

You are perfectly right in your observations on Lord Winchelsea [*sic*]—he was more properly speaking a collector, his researches at Ash only consisted of opening two or three graves, which seem to have been explored in a very desultory manner: but by his journal it should seem that he had his things of one Mr. Sayer and Col. Lynch of Canterbury. A string of amber and glass beads an Iron Battle Axe and a Sword, two common fibulae and the head of *Pan* in bronze, very small.

I believe you are right in your etymon of Sheparton &c though *ton* should seem a british word.

I am daily acquiring materials and which I have arranged much more distinct and clear than I first apprehended would have been the case.

It gives me pleasure to be able to give you a clear and just description of the crystal balls found in sepulchres, their use &c. They were magical instruments and were usually suspended in the sun's rays in mid day, by a thong of *deers* skin, and the person who had the gift of inspecting the crystal, invoqued certain spirits under particular names and a particular form of conjuration. This custom was handed down as low as Charles the 1st time. You will see a great deal of it in Lilly's life and Dr. Dee on spirits. It is also mentioned in Joachim Camerarius [1500-74] and Paracelsus [a famous Swiss mystic

1493-1591]—I have lately made some very long abstracts from some very curious manuscripts unpublished in the British Museum: which instruct their use and assert most positively that spirits may be invoqued through their means, who will foretell things to come. The chief spirit is called Askaryel—very powerful and of a very *comelie appearance*. The manuscript is coeval with the area of James the first. I could detail very much on their use and of their origin. They seem to have been derived from the antient and patriarchal use of the Urim and *Thummim*, in which the divine effigies made its appearance.

I have lately received fresh communications from Winster where a *cross* almost similar to your silver one was found; and which with other relics show the barrow there to be the same as ours.

The Antiquarian Society is conducted on a very extensive plan and it is now become one of our most fashionable weekly rendésvous's. Instead of old square toes you now behold smooth faces and dainty thin shoes with ponderous buckles on them. Our precedent is My Lord Leicester.

I wish my Dear Sir you would take a trip to town and enquire how these things are—I do not know any one who I should be so heartily glad to see. Mrs. Douglas joins me in respectful remembrances to your lady and the rest of your family. I wish I could convey to you some of my last engravings.

> I am most sincerely and heartily,
> Yours to command &c.   Jas Douglas

London
Little Stanhope Street   4th February 1785

[P.S.] I am sorry to hear the loss of the poor printer: he was an acquisition to the town of Canterbury. The crystal balls were kept in families for the purpose of magical divinations, but everyone had means of invoking the spirits; for which purpose distinguished persons of note made their speculations—persons endowed with the [illegible] sight. This is now believed in Wales and in Scotland.

Dear Sir,

Since I received your obliging packet of the drawings &c I have been employed in removing furniture, *reliquae,* and the other part of my knic knac gentry and family to a little house in the country where, thanks to the fine weather for us who are not occupied in agriculture, we are comfortably situated. As I had adjusted the business which brought me to town and finding the impossibility to make the progress in my work as I could have wished from friendly or rather unfriendly visits, I therefore took the resolution to seat myself as *per* the underwritten address, where I expect to see you in the course of this late spring—I have a spare bed and everything snug and you will please to recollect that more than a year has transpired since you promised to visit me. Remember my Dr Sir, if you please that Mrs. Douglas invites your Lady, and as we are close to Mrs. Aldenhams family and no small acquaintance in the neighbourhood, your lady or ladies may meet with their respective amusements abstracted from *disertationes antiquitatis.*

I have manifold occasions to enquire about your picture. and particularly of the first connoisseur in Europe the famous Le Brion from Paris whose collection was sold at Christies and to whom I have lately sold some pictures to a great amount; he tells me it is impossible, utterly so, to give the name of the master who painted your *Cabbages, turnips, carrots, leeks, onions, parsenips, potatoes, sage, marygold* and all the precious confusion of garden stuff unless he saw the picture—the *ruins* will not sufficiently *typify* . . . [See p. 28.]

I thank you much for your drawings—I have prepared all things for engraving and if I could only commune with you—you little know, the good you would infuse into me for my studies—pray come—pray do—no one will be more rejoiced to see you and yours: the jaunt will be of great service to you and your Lady and confer as I am bound in duty to say a lasting obligation on   Dr Sir

Your most obliged most humble ready & sincere servant

Jas. Douglas

Conduit Vale,   Remember your promise—or as the Ghost
Black Heath   says in *J. Caesar*. I will meet you at
                 Phillippi

Monday 25th April 1785

Dr Sir

I have within this week withdrawn a paper which was read at the royal society—before the council pronounced its fate for their *Transactions* being desirous to publish myself, as the facts which it contains I judged proper to circulate to the world. ['A Dissertation on the Antiquity of the Earth' read 12 May 1785.] Having mentioned the East Indian cowry found in the Kingston tumulus, I should be obliged to you before I sent it to the press, if you would inform me if there were coins found with any one of them and of what Emperors—the plates are finished and I propose publishing in the course of next week, or rather printing. As you are justly entitled to enquire whether this may retard my *Naenia* I beg leave to inform you that you must look at it in the same light as we do the small balloons before the great one ascends, to show the direction which the latter should take.

I am convinced your plans of agriculture and other affairs of this mortal life have prevented your returning to your library: else I should have flattered myself with the pleasure of hearing from you and 'ere this I should have had the pleasure of transmitting to you a plate inscribed to you of the large *fibula* for the Naenia and the other relics found with it. I have variously thought nay pondered on your silence—but I have within my mind finally ascribed it to the Expectation of seeing you soon in Conduit vale Black-Heath with your good Lady, to whom Mrs. D. and self pray our compliments may be acceptable. I have postponed opening the remainder of the *tumuli* in Greenwich park 'till you come. I shall have two great men present on this occasion but no one I really assure you who would give me so much satisfaction than yourself; suffer me to repeat it again how much pleasure your presence would give me on this occasion. If you will give me a line previous to your setting off I shall have time to combine the party. I promise you if you will make me this sacrifice to your good husbandry on your estate at Heppington I will erect an Altar after the roman to your memory and sacrifice many conjectures of our favorite pursuit on it. If I am sometimes a tardy correspondent I am sure you will not find one who is more sincere than Dr Sir,

Your much obliged and faithful Servant   Jas. Douglas
Conduit vale
Black-Heath
31st May 1785

Dear Sir,

I have impatiently waited the pleasure of your promise and in the mean while I have been arduous to compleat a work in which I have introduced some materials in your possession. As I could not venture to trouble you with a drawing of the coins that were found with the cowry, I have made the enclosed plate from the similar *brass* in a series of which I have lately procured. They may be probably more perfect that the actual coins but I have submitted them for your inspection before I publish my work, that I may be able to set a tolerable face on the licence which I have taken—however in return may I request the favor of an emboss from the real coins on your letter which may be done with rubbing pencil on them and from which *fac simile* I have made the enclosed aqua tints, which I have printed either in green to imitate the patina or in bronze colour or in black—your judgement I could wish to take. I am greatly improved as you may see in the aqua tints and have run through a great deal of business with it.

I wish it was in my power to commune with you. I am sure you would perfectly agree with me on the subject of the small tumuli which you and your late learned father have opened. I have discovered something as curious as true concerning their history.

Adieu—pray let me hear soon from you, with Mrs. D's compliments I remain with much sincerity Dr Sir

Your faithful and obdt Servt   Jas Douglas.
Conduit Vale
Black Heath
27th July, 1785

P.S. In looking over Ld. Winchelsea's [*sic*] manuscript I find he mentions the Revd. Mr. Foster of Crundale and has given a curious and very circumstantial detail of several urn burials which the [torn] this clergyman [torn] of your father's. Here he mentions a Mr. Sayer of Canterbury who procured his Lordship various relics from Ash as well as from other places, a dealing collector. I wish you would (for occasion) enquire who this *quiz* was. I have just bought a Chifletius—a clever old buck—but a little wrong about the graphics—he seems to have been lead into that error by Petarius. [Douglas was to write two full folio footnotes in *Nenia Britannica* to set out his views of Chiflet's statements on the jewels of Childeric found at Tournai in 1653.]

Dear Sir,

I am very sorry I put you to so mch trouble about the coins—your drawings are sufficiently correct for my engraving, and give me leave to say, if your leisure would permit you, you would make a great progress in the art; knowing the *germe* of the art already in you.

I am infinitely obliged to you for your sketches &c., was you to role them round a stick they would come very safe by the coach to my direction at this place.

I wish I could have the pleasure of seeing you here—surely you must have business about this time in London—pray call if you go up.

Have you met with no fresh antiquities since I have seen you? I heard yesterday of spear heads and urns being found near the bridge at Walton—in a few days I hope to set off for that place and dig a little: was it not for that insatiable thirst in the pursuit of practical enquiry, I should now content myself with the materials I have, which with the litterary business drawings &c. I think I am now sufficiently well stored for my work, and please God, when a little ready cash comes to hand, which I now expect shortly, I shall put to the press.

I thank you for your polite enquiries after Mrs. Douglas—she is now in a happy state. A fine boy at her side and within a few days of getting up.

My respects wait on your family and with Mrs. Douglas's return of compliments I have the pleasure to be Dr Sir

Your faithful and obedt Servant Jas. Douglas

Conduit vale
Black-Heath
17th August 1785

Dear Sir,

Previous to the publication of the Number of the Nenia Brit. wherein I proposed introducing a plate or more of tumuli relics in your cabinet and to mention your name in terms commensurate with the favors you have been pleased to show the work, I thought it proper to give you a line, and also to request when you send for the first Number of the work which I published the first of this month, it being delayed by a drunken ingenious artist who cut the head and tail pieces, you would ask for two plates which I have engraved of the large fibula, the brass vessels &c, hoping they may meet with your approbation, as to their execution. You know my Dr Sir after all our best endeavours some little imperfections will remain, therefore

I hope you will say with the poet *non ego paucis offendur macculis* or some such words; if great ones occur pray give me a line and also tell me ingeniously what you think of the feature of the first number. You must send for the Royal copy numbers—which shall be delivered to you by my orders, from Mr. Nicol in the Strand.

When I have had the pleasure of your letter, which I shall expect in a few posts, I will send you a more full epistle on the subject of my present pursuit; trusting I may not intrude—the favours I have already received demand my acknowledgement and I shall be happy to make you any return that lies in my power.

I have occasionally seen Mr. Hastead [the Kentish historian] lately. I have not the pleasure of an intimate acquaintance with him; but the little I have had I hope has not inclined him from any circumstance that has unguardedly dropped from me, to behave shy. I sat near him at our Society dinner, and thought him rather so, perhaps he was not so intentionally. I have taken the liberty to mention this circumstance to you, as perhaps in the walk [*sic*] of an antiquary on visiting your neighbourhood I may have given some offence. Tell me if you think so. You said I should be genteel if I kept a cow and two pigs: wishing therefore to appear with gentility in the eye of my friends, I bought my stock or necessary credentials for gentility at a fair a few days back.

Mrs. Douglas desires to join me in compliments to Mrs. Faussett, with Dear Sir

Your faithful and obedt Servant Jas. Douglas

Chidingfold

16th May 1786

P.S. Will you send me word here where I can order the proof plates &c to be sent. Perhaps you have a friend in town who can receive them for you.

Dear Sir,

I have sent for your perusal two sheets of the 4th
Number of my work: as you was so obliging to favour me
with remarks and corrections in your last: you will
therefore confer an addition of favour by returning the
enclosed proofs as soon as possible with your remarks as
to the correctness of the description of the relics in your
cabinet; the drawings of which you have been so kind as
impart to me: and for which I am sure the public will be
thankful. It is morally impossible to inspect our own
compositions with as critical an eye as that of a friend or
even strangers. I am therefore greatly obliged to you for
setting me right in an omission in my last Number: the
sheers in question were doubtless in your Cabinet and
which under *Observations* shall be mentioned accordingly
with your remarks. The other *sheers* be assured I sketched
from those in Sir Wm Fagg's collection: and which at the
time I took them must have been as perfect as the drawing
I made: you was with me and I remember saw them: I have
herewith sent you also the drawing but be this as it may,
the fact is equally substantiated.

Mr. Boys certainly informed me his Crystal Ball came
from Ash. I have his letter by me but he does not seem
to think it came from the same grave as did the other
relics. I am much obliged to you for the drawing of the
touchstone &c. I fear the size in the copper plate will not
exactly answer your sketch: it was drawn from a very
imperfect one. The coin of *Faustina* I have as you may see
taken the liberty to make a little more sharp: it was taken
from a drawing of Mr. Boys: after all it is morally impossible to execute things with the exactest precision human
ability cannot attain the same: non ego paucis offendar
maculis. Your general sketch is very acceptable—and it
will doubtless be of great service: but my Dr Sir I find
the relics of the small *tumuli* are so curious and interesting that with pleasure I could dwell for many more
Numbers upon them, a few more doubtless must transpire:
but as the contents of the large celtic barrows as
well as some relics of the roman interments must also

claim a share in my work, I fear I shall be obliged to take my leave with the greatest reluctance much sooner than I could have wished.

Pray do not spare my proofs but give me your remarks *sans reserve*: see my note on Barham downs and say if you approve of it and the other notes. Notes are now in fashion again since the explanations have been printed to the *Iliad*.

I shall set off for town tomorrow—you will therefore please to direct my packet to me at *Mr. Nichols' Printer Red Lion Passage Fleet Street.* The press will wait for your return. The fibula which you see prefixed to the proof, is to explain some of the matter in the number: the setting is of the same composition as on the ornament to your small *magical vessel*; it is to be printed in black, the red are only my proofs.

You may take off the fibula and the Queens head from the proofs. I believe the Queen is rather handsomer than the original: you must suppose her therefore in her bloom: it would be unfair to give her the aspect which time has now made upon her: and besides I am too gallant a man to treat the ladies so unfavorably. [See *Nenia Britannica*, p. 41.]

I really think you have made a great acquisition in the picture way: what can you desire finer of the Flemish school than a van Harp [??] and as to Gerard Dou: 'twould be such a miracle of an acquisition that I should *even doubt the original if you had it.*

Adieu and believe me to be sincerely obligd to you for your last very obliging letter: and be assured whatever little or great faults may occur in the Nenia—it is not too late to mend them—as *Observations* will include every necessary *erata* and *adenda*.

Pray introduce your Susannah to your drawing soon. I think she would grace that of Sr James's? I beg my compliments may be acceptable to Mrs. Faussett and family & believe me Dr Faussett.

Ever yrs J. Douglas   [1786]

P.S. [written on the outside cover of the letter] I have a prodigious fine picture; about 1½ foot by ¾ of the three graces on Copper—printed inimically by some Italian master—something in the Leonardo da Vinci stile—I am told it is valuable—and a head on wood by Titian—cut out of a larger picture: about ¾ by ½. I have lately been very handsomely offered by one of the most accomplished and manlike spirited Noblemen in this Country the first living in his Gift: he is the greatest patron we have in the church: and strange to tell I am assured he has never been known to break his word. I must beg to repeat: the press is waiting for the proofs—and I shall not leave town until they arrive.

[The letter is endorsed in Faussett's hand 'Mr. Douglas —1786 Proofs of No 4 Pictures even' and Faussett's title on the cover is followed by two roughly-drawn coats of arms of the Faussett family, presumably a mild piece of humour on the part of Douglas.]

Dear Sir   Chidingfold 5th Septr 1786

From the favour of your acquaintance and correspondence on a subject which affords me so much delight, I have long flattered myself with your letter in answer to one which I wrote some time back acquainting you with my intention of publishing the drawings of some of your tumuli relics which you was so polite to transmit to me. Three Numbers of the work are published and I have been in hopes you would have given me a line, whether the general feature of the publication answered the expectation you had entertained of it. I shall take this opportunity to suggest, that it is by no means my wish to intrude further on the goodness respecting the sepulchral facts you are in possession of, were my requests in the least degree intrusive, assuring you at the same time that I have no other view than that of establishing some literary truths which I think in a great measure depend on the relics which are in your possession. I would with pleasure transmit to you proofs of the two plates I have finished of your relics, did I know by what conveyance I should send them; without putting you to too great an expence.

Give me leave to solicit the favour of your letter and believe me to be with much regard

Your ready and sincere servant   Jas Douglas

P.S. I have just received a large packet of tumuli relics, similar to ours, from Gloucester.

Dear Sir,

I hope by this you have received the 2d & 3d numb. of the Nen. As your letter was forwarded to me in Town where I have been for a few days on business with my printer &c I had an opportunity of calling on Mr. Nicol and giving orders for the Numbers in question with good impressions to be forwarded to you.

Be assured the passage you have referred to can by no means apply to a perusal of your fathers manus: it was what I have cautiously avoided. I wished to make the remark as strong as possible and which in a future passage of work will be made more explanatory. If you remember it was your assurance that you had no recollection that *beads* were ever found under the circumstance which Dr. Stukeley had described. Your words and the inspection of your cabinet were my vouchers and I thought I had explained myself accordingly. However be assured, for I have since appealed to a judge for the sense which the sentence may convey and I am acquitted of any hint as to the perusal of a manuscript. I knew you was tender in the permission of the perusal of the man. but do not call to mind your reasons: but if you think any hints of this nature would hinder the disposal of your collection the same shall be studiously avoided: but give me leave to assure you that the publication of your relics whatever you are pleased to transmit to me and which may conform to my arrangements will assuredly add to their value: for every *amateur* will allow that such antient remains are always enhanced in value when they have been engraved and I trust as it is only the assemblage which I count as being sedulous to arrive at truth in these studies, so you will not find it incompatible with your views to transmit an answer to a Query which refers to the position of relics in the Tumuli.

I have received a valuable supply of *tumuli* relics from a range of barrows near Gloucester which I think are rather antecedent to the date of ours. The relics are in many respects similar—but several apply to an older aera perhaps and in their fashion they seem more romanised. The fibulæ partake chiefly of this form [he here illustrates an early form of Roman brooch with solid catch-plate]. The coins are generally as high as the older emperors. Vessels of bronze, &c. An axe of this form [the small illustration depicts a Roman type of axe]. Several specimens of large sheers—daggers—swords and spears: in this as in several other barrow researches, the people who found the relics have construed the bronze vessels into helmets. Unhappily for the cause of critical enquiry they have been thrown up without order. Coffins of lead have been found on the same spot containing bones, but I have not heard that any relics have hitherto been found in them. I suspect this spot has been applied to sepulchral uses by the converted romans and the romanised britons after the departure of the former from the island. I have several coins of the lower empire found there.

My 4th Number will contain two plates of your *rich tumulus*—and a plate with various similar relics from Ash; which I assembled from different places where they have been scattered. Most of them are in my possession. The *plate* exhibits a circular *gold filagree fibula*, the workmanship extremely beautiful, two *amethyst beads*. A large *bronze vessel*. An *Axe*, two coins of Faustina in your possession filed down to weights found to the number of eight piled up: a toutch stone—fragments of scales, a *wooden vessel* plated with brass or copper; a *copper pattera* and a *Glass Cup*. A *crystal ball* I am inclined to think was also found with them, which is now in Mr. Boy's possession. These things were found at the same time: though Mr. B. is rather uncertain in this respect yet as I know the *fibula* undoubtedly was, as also the axe, cup and vessels, which being so analogous to discoveries of this nature has inclined me to groupe them together; the touch stone I think is about this size [a detailed drawing is here included] Pray have you the gold coin of Justinian that was discovered at Ash? I think you have one found with the [cowrie] shell of Clovis. The coin of Just. was found in 1760 you favoured me with the drawing but the inscription is not clear which I should like to have.

I am happy to find you have made such a favourable acquisition in the picture way, and I have no doubt from what you say but they are originals. If you have actually a Gerard Dou in a tolerable state of preservation I know not what it may be worth. The delicacy and high finishing of this master will soon declare the truth of a real picture. He generally painted to the middle-heads and figures looking out of a casement. If I could see your pictures I could speak more to the subject; and as to the picture you describe as a Culprit &c before a flemish tribunal, really it is not in the power of the best conoisseur to judge without seeing it. At all events I am sure you have made a most miraculous bargain, but in the Country and particularly in Kent I am sure there is a possibility of picking up some excellent pictures for a trifle. The other day I saw an excellent Brugel [*sic*] at a Brokers which I could have purchased for 5 Guineas. A true Brugel if the subject be a landscape will have an *owl* in a tree in the foreground which was his mark. Your tribunal picture by your description I should much like to see as I am sure it must be an excellent picture.

Tell me how you like the 2d & 3d numb: of my work. I have reserved the mention of your relics for this number the 4th but really I am at a loss how to conduct myself with propriety. I am sure you will think with me that on a topic of literary matters, truth being the great *desideratum* an author is happy to find it: and if he can procure it by analogy or by comparing one fact with another, all the learned would conspire to assist him in it:

believe me Dr Sir no one will readily attempt such a work
as the one I am engaged in—it is in one sense fortunate that
I execute the plates myself as the expence of publication
would in these works be scarcely ballanced. Trust me I
shall rejoice when I have acquitted myself of the bounden
duty I am under to publish my Nen. and shall be cautious
of a like undertaking unless I have in respect of the
engraving some assistance. It is too much for one person
to perform with satisfaction to himself, and especially
at the distance I am from the press. Favour me with a
line at your leisure and tell me how far you wish to go
in respect to your Cabinet. Mrs. Douglas joins me in
compliments to Mrs. Faussett and believe me to be

                    Yours sincerely,   Jas Douglas
Chidingfold
2d Octr 1786

                              Chidingfold: 11th Octr 1787
                                near Godalming.
          O Pylades! what's life without a friend?
Dear Faussett,
    I am happy to find any excuse to take up my pen to
resume a correspondence with a person whose pursuits
are so congenial to my own, not only in the light of a
brother in *virtu* but as a citizen of the world shall I ever
be led to brag of my esteem. Be honest and soar
above the artful manners of a corrupt generation and
tell me how, or by what trespass, I have merited your
epistolary neglect. Shew me your accusation and let me
defend myself.
    I have been some months about on the Continent,
in Switzerland to conduct a nephew to a foreign seminary:
during my absence I was in hopes my fourth number of
the Nenia would have been published. I hope you have
received it and also the fifth which has been delivered
these several weeks and should have been announced
before in the papers. In this last you will see my com-

mentary on the tomb of Childeric. I have seen the contents of this reputed tomb in the french King's library at Paris and I have observed some particulars which Chifflet did not notice: read it and tell me if any thoughts are your thoughts; and when the chilling blasts of autumn shall drive you from the yellow hoard of Ceres to your snug fire side, in your repository of tumuli treasures, digress from the cares of a country life and return to the lights of mental gratification. You have a favorite place in my ballance of friendship, where I shall set you down as a debtor 'till you think it proper to bring these matters to account.

I here have impressed for your notice an impression of a plate for my next No. which contains miscellaneous relics. Your *cross* and vessels are introduced ‚to ascertain their analogy with similar specimens. See Mr Manders paper in the Arch. There was a glass vessel and cross found in the same barrow. The cross he did not note but a drawing of which I have since been favoured with by Mr. Rooke of Woodhouse place *Notts*. You will oblige me by marking the other relics found with your *cross* which I fear to have given in too large a scale of drawing; also the other relics found with the *cross* from the barrows at Chartham and I trust in this case we shall be able to select some information. The next plate contains some various miscellanies among which is the large *cowry* shell which I esteem a great curiosity: the contents of that barrow will be of great service: were figs 2 and 3 found in the same grave? and what were the other relics. A crystal ball was one.

Figs 4, 5 and 6 [here illustrated] are in the possession of Sir J. Vanhattem at Dinton near Aylsbury *Bucks*. They came out of different graves from a range promiscuously broken into on his estate. I received an invitation to explore the remainder, which I will reserve for a future occasion. [Douglas had been abroad.] The glass vessel *fig 5* is evidently the same manufactory as *fig 2* and of course belonged to the same people, the spears will also show this remark to be obvious.

When my paper admits of larger extent I will digress on either matters with great pleasure.

Living at this distance from the press I find great difficulty in having my work printed with correctness: blunders I am sure you must find without end. I have had frequent opportunities in France, in the Netherlands Germany and Switzerland to delight myself in pictures. Had my purse admitted since the Emperors suppression of the monastries I should have made purchases well worth my notices. You can not be so much absorbed in your plans of improvement and agriculture to turn your thoughts entirely from the fine arts. Business is doubtless essential but we must have our times for relaxation &c. Could you but take a trip into Surrey with your Lady we have every accommodation to make your time pleasant. I would give the best *fibula* in my collection for the pleasure of your confab. I am truly in earnest and see no reason why you could not take a trip this Xmas or before, with your Lady & Child and visit the parsonage at Chidingfold. I can assure you the jaunt would be of service by way of changing the scene.

It is now a considerable time since I have heard from you and it is necessary I should enquire after the health of your family. Little masters and misses, I hope they enjoy the same rosy health I some time past observed in their faces.

Mrs. Douglas and self unite in Compliments to Mrs. Faussett and believe me to remain

With such sincerity your hearty and ready friend

Js Douglas

P.S. Compts to Mr. Sands—whose civilities I should be happy to return if he passes this road.

[Written on a trial pull of what was to become plate XVI of *Nenia Britannica*.]

Dear Faussett,

I have sent you a slight proof of a plate for my succeeding No—I could not venture to publish it before you cast an eye over it and returned me a few notes on the relics which you recognise in it. They are taken from my sketch book; the rapid productions of a few minutes on a cursory survey of your cabinet; and I am reluctant to make out the description from my own notes which I can not well trust to. You will please to believe that that the world will always consider your favours in their just estimation and that you have already made use of my book as the vehicle to make them known.

I shall have a note in this No. on the vessels vulgarly called *Lachrymatories* I use now classic authority for ascribing these vessels to receptacles for tears. Wolfgangius Lazius is the only old author who set this thought current. *Put my tears into your bottle*—will not refer to the customs of the romans in this respect. I rather think they were used for perfumes.

Sometime this spring I have thoughts of giving my wife a treat to Lisle in Flanders, by way of a French jig: and shall certainly if we undertake this excursion take a peep at the *veterumsquae—monumenta vivorum* and shake hands with my living friends in Kent. If I do not go to Flanders this year I have thoughts of going into the North and having a toutch at barrow hunting—to open some of the *celtic tumuli* so called.

I shall bring some of our small barrows down as low as the Danish aera. I am sorry for it, but I cannot help it. Adieu—*Compliments a Madame* s'il vous plait: hope all the brats are well—Mrs. D. in kind remembrance—with my our hearty wishes

Most sincerely yours   Jas Douglas

Chidingfold
7th March 1788

[P.S.] I have had some uncommon share of business on my hands lately, or you would have heard long before this from me. The death of a brother—much anxieties—

wordly business, *hoc aga*—fag—dead pulls, some injustice
and long bills to pay: a little milk of human nature and
some forgiveness and charity—all this like a mill stone has·
kept back the Nenia.

[Written on the reverse of a pull of an aquatint of
various Anglo-Saxon relics, including a bone comb, bronze
work-box, cowry shell, pins, toilet instruments, leather
open strap-work, etc., which appeared on Plate XVIII of
Nenia Britannica.]

Chidingfold near Godalming 9th July 1789

Dear Sir,

A considerable interval of time having elapsed since
I last had the pleasure to take up my pen on the *veteris
aeri monuments* that I have been at a loss to draw a
conclusion from your silence; especially as having transmitted to you a proof or rather rough proof of a plate
in my last No. and to which I received no answer.
Whether I have unintentionally given offence or whether
you have conceived an intrusion on the former favours
relative to your cabinet of antiquities assuredly is a doubt
even now in my breast and to have the same explained
is the chief cause of my present letter. When I reflect
on the obliging letters which you favoured me with I
confess these kinds of doubts have disappeared, but
again when I reflect on the fondness which you have
for the pursuits I am engaged in and finding you still
silent I could not withstand the inclination of having my
apprehensions either realised or effectively done away.
I trust you will now suffer me to make one declaration
before I renew the features of our ancient correspondence,
that in case any false suggestion may have reached your
ear in the character of the author of *Nenia Britannica,*
I may be heard and credited also. Know then, that I
have always in private as well as public expressed my
obligations to you, Sir, for your liberal and unreserved
communication of your materials towards my work—and

as I concluded you had no intention of making the same public yourself so I was the more free to solicit your assistance—and especially so as I was engaged in the cause of critical enquiry more than a display of fancy; and to which great end the correct researches of your late father so particularly tended.

You may now very naturally be inclined to judge my labours in the press have been somewhat too relaxed. I have several excuses. First then—a clerical situation, which had been lately stimulating me to promotion and to a town residence, the grand *emporium* to barter knowledge in; and for the want of which I find many *sneaking* little characters ready to take advantage of an authors absence from his connections. I have also been called upon to dabble in politics, from which no great good arrives I find by experience. The passions are only heated and no conviction is produced, partly inflamed and your own affairs deranged. My health also from the *aqua fortis* I have had some reason to believe has been somewhat impaired—but notwithstanding these interferences, I have been studiously at work on the historic enquiry of the *Nenia* and have also collected a great store of essential materials—sufficient indeed to last me all my life.

But now my Dear Faussett if there should be no misunderstanding and every thing as Sterne says is playing cheerfully round the heart, attend to what I now unfold.

The 7 No. is prepared—the plates finished all but the touches at the last. One plate contains some of your iron *tintinnabula* or bells against the influence of malignant spirits—worn by monks at this day in some countries on the continent for the pious uses of *exorcism*—and perhaps as used by the people who are the subject of this enquiry. Your speculum will also be given with another of a square form which I received from Mr. White of Newgate Street who received it from Mr. Jacob [the Faversham antiquary] and who said it was found on *Barham downs*— did you ever hear of one being discovered there or at Ash? There was a Mr. Hayward an assistant or partner to

Mr. Boys of Sandwich who collected several things from Ash, and who lived at Canterbury.

Pray were there any things of consequence found with the *bell* and the *Speculum*—were they the gegaws of the ladies? I mean to give a drawing of the pendant ornament of Gold with flourishes in Sir Wm Fagg's collection, to whom please to make my respects when you next see him, and assure him I shall be much flattered if he will accept a copy of my work: by the by I have or think I have reproved you for taking a copy from your bookseller and not one from my hands—a *royal copy* which I profferred to you. Let me know your reason for this—was it because you thought me a shabby fellow—because you would not allow me to class myself among the *genteel* authors of the age—but the garretteers who scribble for *pudding* more than for fame *glorious & immortal fame*— the real curse of every poor but well meaning author, who finds himself too proud to [letter torn] name which is generally purchased by the [letter torn] *puffing and living*; I wish for a more accurate drawing to compare it with the drawing which I made of the Saxon Capital at Canterbury—in the alley which leads to the precincts I think the place is called the cloysters.

My acquaintance Mr. Towneley informs me he has been to see your collection as also a very curious and well informed little Quaker of the name of Jackson—who was once with me on an expedition on Wimbledon common to open barrows in a party of some other gentlemen—and the Quaker not content with the mere digging and careful turning over the ground insisted on the necessity of procuring a *sieve* to explore the contents of a grave—with more accuracy—this is true enthusiasm.

Mrs. Douglas unites in best Compliments to Mrs. Faussett and I remain very sincerely yours   J. Douglas

P.S. I shall set off on Monday next for the North, to hunt after barrows—on my return I hope to find your answer. Can you send me an impression of the Gold pendant at Mystole in tea lead or *isinglass*? I now begin to find there is an endless trouble and little or no profit in printing a work on antiquities—but I am tied to the stake and must go through with it—toss the curs and mumgrils of critics and endure the bangs and belabourings of blockheads and heavy rogues who flourish the quill

Dear Faussett.

I sincerely sympathise with you, in your heavy affliction, Mrs. Douglas and myself were both very much affected by the receipt of your melancholly letter and do assure you it was the first announce of your misfortune. . . . [see p. 55.]

My letter in the Gentleman's Magazine should have been answered, respecting the contents as well as history of our large barrows. I wished to enter on a literary argument on the subject as you may well have conjectured by the address.

The mount at Canterbury [the 'Dane John', not one of the group of Roman barrows] I have always considered as in common with similar structures of earth near towns of eminence, to have been raised much antecedent to roman times. I have prepared some materials to treat on them. These mounds are frequently mentioned in Holy writ as raised to take a fortified town by the besiegers; it was an antient mode of attack when military engines were not employed. I would willingly on my conjecture hazard no small sum, that the roman coins on the mount at Canterbury were found on the surface or at a small depth under it, or near the level or base; but under the central part I should just as soon dream of finding the gigantic armour of Goliath as any thing roman. [Douglas realised that the nearby mound into which he had dug in was in fact a Roman barrow.]

I have also an instrument like the one you have sketched found among the roman ruins at Rochester. You may see in looking over your collection of beads one of this form [a sketch of a serrated bead follows]. If you remember it puzzled us both. A similar one I found in a barrow on Chatham lines. It is the like of the large eastern

Cowry or Cypria. It was worn as a female *phallus* on the neck of a child. Mine evidently was, by the size of the bones, and doubtless you will find yours to have been such in the perusal of your minutes.

It gives me pleasure to hear you are amused with my little works of the excursionary kind, I hope they will do no harm in the world. If they amuse it will be all I can hope for.

I find great delay with the press. My 7 No. of the *Nen:* has been with the printer for several weeks past; but it moves very slowly. There will be a great deal of matter in this number—enough for money.

I wish I had recollected when I saw you in town to have mentioned a most beautiful painting on Copper by Rotenhumen [?] of the Graces. Small figures about a foot in length. I sent it to Mr. Hopness the portrait painter in Charles Street St. James's Square. I could not expose it in my home for the sake of clerical decorum—as the ladies were without smerries.

I am very heartily and sincerely   Your   Js Douglas.
Chidingfold,
6th July 1790

Dear Faussett,

I hope your great affliction has from this interval been somewhat lessened and that your health is not materially injured by your heavy loss. I have had you often in my mind as you may naturally suppose from the nature of my engagements, and when this has been the case, I may venture to say with the greatest sincerity that both Mrs. D. and myself have felt a sympathy on the melancholly occasion.

Have you had any time or spirits to peruse my last No. of the Nenia—which I hope has reached you? My plates are finished for the succeeding one, the 8th. and are now forwarded for the press. They contain the *coins*—urns or rather funeral vessels, plans of the groupes of barrows and some few miscellanious relics. This No.

will detail more elaborate matter on the history of the barrows—some corrections of past errors or rather hasty stringing together of remarks from my common-place book; and I rather flatter myself I shall be on the whole, persuasive in making you a *compleat* convert as to their real history. I have said compleat to raise your expectations and also with a view, by speaking boldly and decidedly to be called to order for any human falibility which, if in your power, I hope you will without any ceremony not fail to do—When I say in your power, I mean, if you are in possession of any facts which controvert my assertions or more modestly speaking conjectures, I beg you will not scruple to let me hear from you.

From the trouble, time and expence, with little or no profit, attendant on these kind of publications, I think I may venture to foretell, that you will not set down to arrange your collection for the public as such I trust you will permit me to ask whether you have any desire to introduce any of your remarks; If so I will very readily accept them and faithfully assign them to the writer. I have made this suggestion at this time, because on the ensuing No. to this, I mean to dismiss the matter which relates to the small barrows in clusters, and to proceed to the roman and british, for the completion of which I have some very rich materials. A few months back, I opened an uncommon curious paved barrow of the first rate kind—the contents of an urn, skeleton and some fragments of undefined brass relics—too much corroded even for conjecture—The barrow was curious from its apparent high antiquity and its situation. [On high ground at Gorstead, Chiddingfold, traditionally known as 'Golden-hoard'. The vessel of unbaked clay, probably a beaker or Bronze Age pot, fell to pieces as it was removed. The metal fragments he thought might have been of a clasp or buckle. Most interestingly he noted an underlying hearth of local ironstone belonging to an earlier interment. He recorded it well in *Nenia Britannica*, p. 162, but after noting the name was Gostroud in the parish registers of

1500, Douglas's sense of etymology ran wild as it so often did.]

I think you once told me that you found urns with ashes, in the companiform clusters of barrows, where the bodies, were also interred, but you did not say whether this was evident in any on Barham downs or Siberts-wold-down. Chartham contained some as by Dr. Mortimer's manuscript, but he does not say positively that ashes were found in them. This circumstance is very material as to the dating of their *exact aera*. And if this occurs to your memory or in your notes I shall esteem it a favour if you will acquaint me with the fact.

I shall be extremely happy to hear that you preserve your health and that the anxieties of life have not turned your thoughts entirely from the rust of old times.

I beg when you see Sir Wm and Mr. Fagg you will not fail to present my best remembrances.

        I am with great regard,

                Your sincere friend and Servt. J. Douglas

Chidingfold

19th Feby 1791

Dear Sir,

I thought myself extremely unlucky in not having the pleasure of meeting you while I was in town. Had you left your address I would with pleasure have waited upon you, or we could have made an appointment to have met each other. I have long had thoughts of giving you a letter—but the confusion, loss dissappointment and the unspeak-able trouble which I have had with booksellers on account of my work which has been shamefully spoiled and neglected, have prevented me from writing what I had proposed, and particularly on the subject of a royal paper copy with good impressions which I was desirous of putting into your hands, as also to have had your opinion on the general finishing of the work with your liberal allowances for the natural errors of an author who had such a vast field of literature to range in, and where points of sight were so much confused by other antiquaries; and the materials so difficult to arrange for an historical use.

As to the royal paper copy; it will be out of my power to get one 'till Mr. White has completed the broken numbers; when this is the case and which I am in hopes a few weeks will accomplish, by sending your copy to him I will take care first by giving you a line when it is ready for you, that you shall have one in exchange.

Mr. Nicol's man informed me you was going into Lincolnshire and on your return you would give me a meeting. I would readily wait if you would appoint the time—but could I not prevail on you to take a trip to the Chidingfold Parsonage where your company would afford Mrs. Douglas and particularly myself unspeakable pleasure—especially so as I have a plan to propose to you [regarding?] your collection which I think would meet with your approbation; and in this instance we could confer with a mutual zest on the *res vetusta.* A coach from Fetter lane (the Arundel) at six in the morning Tuesdays Thursdays and Saturdays—would set you down at my house at one o clock and if you please you may return next day to town. At all events I will endeavour to meet you and shall be happy to convince you that I am Dr Faussett

       Your sincere and affectionate   Jas. Douglas
Chidingfold   15 October. 1793

Dear Sir,

Mrs. Douglas and myself were in great hopes your excursion would have permitted your visit to Chidingfold, nothing would have given us greater pleasure and as to myself you know the satisfaction would have been realised as far as the delicious reciprosity of a mutual taste could have admitted. I had much to say to you, many of the *res vetusta* to have shown you which I have accumulated during the several years since my separation from your pleasant and respectable county; a separation

which I shall always regret and which for many reasons
of personal happiness I shall ever hold the remembrance
dear.

I am very sorry you have not got the succeeding part
of the Nenia; I think I told you in my letter that I had
made over the work to Mr. White; but it was the business
of Mr. Nieol to have put your friend in the way of
procuring the remainder. He has your name in the list
of my subscribers and I am certainly at a loss to judge
the reasons why you are deprived of your copy. I shall
be in town in a few weeks and if your friend will leave
his address at Mr. Nicol's I will make a point of waiting
upon him. Nicol did certainly reserve the completion of
the work for the subscribers and whether at the
present moment it is in his hands or those of Mr. White,
it is the same thing. As Mr. White is a more punctual and
regular man in the trade I think your friend, were he to
give himself the trouble to call on him, would procure it
—but I will take the affair upon myself and if you will
give me a line where I can order the continuation to be
sent, it shall be forthcoming.

I am very desirous you should have it, as I have taken
a considerable degree of pains to treat on the distinct
nature of urn burial and body interment, and which you
may compare with your own and your father's opinions
on the subject.

The many places of early Saxon burial are constantly
presenting themselves before me; many in Sussex my
neighbouring county. Were you to give me your company
this spring or summer I really think I should be tempted
to undertake an exploratory excursion with you. Were
you to take a circuitous tour on the Kentish coast and
through Brighton to Chichester I would give you a
meeting. I would meet you at Brighton and take the
coast to a place called Findon celebrated for a very antient
camp called *Cisbury*. The downs are scattered with *tumuli*.
I have a friend at Findon who would be glad to receive
us as also in most of our track thence to my *domicilium*.
This I propose from a supposition that your inclination

leads you to the plan of touring it about, than which nothing can be more delightful and cheering to the mind as also wonderfully instructive. Should you embrace the proposition I will then reserve my thoughts on the subject of the hints I dropped concerning your collection.

So absolutely retired is my parish and the little advantages of neighbouring society, I have serious thoughts of an excursion on the plan I propose; and particularly so as my mind has lately been very oppresively occupied.

I remain with great regard   Dear Mr. Faussett

Your affectionate humble servant   Jas Douglas

Chidingfold

4th Feby 1794.

13

SELECTION OF LETTERS TO
MAJOR HAYMAN ROOKE, 1784, 1787

(Society of Antiquaries Correspondence Files and Rooke Papers, Soc. Ants. MSS.)

H. Rooke, Esqr.   From the Revd. James Douglas

Sir,

I was favoured with your obliging paper enclosing four elegant discriptive drawings of Druidical or antient british remains. I am usually punctual in my correspondence and I should have taken an earlier opportunity of returning you my thanks if Mr. White had delivered the packet before Satur-day last ye 17th Inst.

I compliment you much on the pleasing study which you are engaged in; it will ever furnish a rich store of matterials for the cabinet and for the houers of study: and to gentlemen of independant fortunes it must be tenfold more pleasing.

The Karn and Cromlech on Stack-house Scar Yorkshire is peculiarly acceptable as it confirms me in an opinion which I have long entertained of a British remain in my neighborhood. It is called Kits-Cotys-House [Plate 34] — apparently derived from Catigerne and Horsa who were slain in a battle fought there—*Kits* from *Kists* the British word for chests or tombs: *Cotys* from Categerne and House from Horsa or Horsus: thus by succeeding generations perverted from its original signification. This Kistvaen is situated under Boxley Hill on an eminence near Maidstone in Kent and which you must have seen noticed in the Archael: [Archaeologia] in a field at some small distance where is another of nearly the same dimensions now dilapidated: and which must undoubtedly have been raised coeval with the other. When mathematical certainty or demonstration is not at hand, we can only reason from analogy; and to compare the *Cromleh* on the Stack-house Karn which is evidently composed of a congeries of Stones raised over the dead, to the same kind of remain near Boxley, should we not have a clear deduction to prove their original use? and what gives me farther pleasure is, to find this remark, greatly strengthened, by that practical and sensible antiquary Dr Borlase in His Ant: of Cornw: therefore Sir I think myself much indebted to you for communicating to me these particulars and I shall not fail to make them down accordingly.

The assemblage of rocks I conceive to be appropriated to the religious ceremonies of the Druids; but the Cromlech on the Karn to funeral purposes. It has not I dare say escaped your observation that the Tumulus on Brassington moor with the Kist-vaen on its apix as well as the one of Youl grove moor and Abney moor like to the one on Stack-house Scar, have some remains of religious structures attatched to them; from similar *data* to these, I always draw my inferences.

The Urn which you found on *Cawton-hill* I believe to be British. I have many reasons for thinking that the Romans did not *usually* raise a mound of earth over the dead particularly when they burnt them; especially so in this island.

Having had several opportunities of making local remarks on their burial places I find they were situated and formed differently to those which we see scattered and detatched which seldom contain any relics of consequence and rarely any testimonies of their being roman. [Recent study has proved that Douglas spoke here as he knew, but was wrong in his facts.]

Last week I began on a range of barrows in Greenwich Park and I opened about twenty of them—I think there is about fifty in number, but the frost being so severe, and the days so short, that I desisted from proceeding farther till the spring. I found several had been ransacked before, but I found sufficient matterials for my purpose, consisting of spear-heads, british beads &c. The taste and true zest which you seem to have for the study which I am deeply embarked in, inclined me much to wish for your company on this occasion; a mutual satisfaction I am convinced we should have derived from it: particularly so, as similar barrows to these do not fail to turn out things that are always interesting to an antiquary.

Pray have the beads &c. which you mention in your paper been discovered by you—If so, I could wish for particulars and the drawing of one or more of them.

I have observed that the Cromlechs in various parts of this island are placed towards the Sun in the Equinox —have you made the same observation?

If other matter which relates to the antiquities of this country should occur, when your leisure admits of it, I do not scruple from the offers which have have so obligingly made to me of your services, to solicit without reserve the favour of your remarks.

I am with much truth, Sir,

Your much obliged and faithful Servt.   James Douglas

P.S. The Revd. Wm. Pearce fel: of St. Johns Col: Cambridge has just favoured me with an account of a celtic barrow which he has opened on Crousa downs in Meneage Cornwal, many circumstances relating to it are similar to the one which you opened on Cawton Hill near Chatsworth—evidently belonging to the same people: The Urn is very similar to yours.

I have a house at Rochester where I have lived several years; but as the work which I am engaged in will shortly require me to reside in London, I purpose to leave the church (of Strood) which I have in this neighbourhood, in hopes of getting one in town.

Rochester 24th Jany 1784

Sir,

Your obliging offers to render me service in the plan of my *tumuli* studies, have induced me to request the favor of your enquiring into the state of the barrows on the commons of Winstor near the Kings Manor de Alto Pecco in Derbyshire—one of which was opened and a short paper describing the contents was published in the Arch: of our society, transmitted by Mr Mander of Bakewel in the said county: by your letter of the 2d Jany last, I understand that you made frequent journeys into that county, consequently you might be acquainted with Mr. Mander and have it in your power to inform me if the remainder of the barrows have been explored. If your report should be favorable I have a great inclination to visit that part and open the remainder; and though the season of the year be not so favorable as I could wish I would with readiness set off: I am particularly desirous to undertake this expedition, before I compleat my material for my work, as by this means, I shall, by some accurate investigation, be enabled to fix on some data of the greatest consequence to my plan; which on a convenient opportunity I shall be happy to communicate to you. In a post or two I shall write to Mr. Mander to request some further account of the contents of the barrow in question: but I rather wish to trouble you on this occasion to forward me the desired information, knowing that you are more critical in your enquiries, for without the greatest precision in these pursuits the greatest blunders are continually broached to the world.

I have lately been on a visit in the neighborhood of Walton on Thames and have discovered a range of these burial places for some miles up the river, and almost close to the banks—that is, they are situated on the nearest rising grounds—spear heads—shields—beads &c. &c. —found in them show them to have belonged to the people whose remains I have so frequently ransacked. [See D. C. Whimster, *Archaeology of Surrey,* London 1931, 62, 68, 195.]

A few weeks past I received the contents of a very curious sepulchral deposit of a Roman from the station at Gloucester. A body was found in a leaden coffin—a legionary sword 18 inches long—two fibula one with an inscription—40 coins from Augustus to Tetricus and two remarkably scarce of *Antonina* of the middle bronze—a perfume vessel and the appendage of the sword. [See *Archaeologia* 7, 1785, 376.]

I have compleated the principal part of my work which I am simplifying for the press and I am rapidly advancing with my plates.

When you come to town I shall be extremely happy to see you in little Stanhope Street, May fair No. 3. and show you the produce of my tumuli labours.

I make no doubt, but the fine season of the year has tempted you to renew your very interesting discoveries in druid remains. Hoping to have the pleasure of your early answer I remain with many thanks for the favors which you have conferred on my intended publication.

Sir,

Your most obliged humble Servt.   Jas. Douglas

London,
Little Stanhope Street
May - Fair

8th Octr 1784

P.S. If I do not intrude too much on your time—I should think myself greatly favored with a drawing of the beads which you have discovered in the barrows. There is a difference in the workmanship of the beads of [torn] tumuli and the tumuli of the lower britons.

[The Mander antiquities including a magnificent jewelled gold pendant, are now in Sheffield City Museums. Douglas did not know that the famous White Lowe barrow on Winster Common was levelled under powers given by the Enclosure Acts.]

Sir,

I return you my thanks for your obliging favor of the 20th Inste.—I am sorry your researches were not more interesting, or productive of that decisive informátion which we have a right to flatter ourselves with on the opening of a barrow, yet I can not help thinking, had your time, and conveniency permitted of a further research, but that you would have made some discoveries to your satisfaction. On the sites of barrows which have been removed, either for the repairing of roads, and if of earth, for throwing on land, urns have frequently been taken up; so much of the labour being already bestowed for our discoveries, I confess I should have been tempted had I been with you to have sunk a little into the native soil or under the base on which the barrows were raised; for the cist is often times a few feet under the horizontal level of the plain or neighboring earth. Before you open a barrow I recommend it to you, to view the top of it, and observe whether the grass is more redundant in the centre than on the sides of the cone—, if so, you may persuade yourself, that a previous ransack has been made. Experience has taught me this criterion and it very rarely fails. About H. VIIIth times I have reason to believe that many of our large celtic barrows have been opened, by some people who through a fondness for antiquity or rather through a desire of discovering hidden treasure, made excursions for that purpose.

I am still harping on the barrows in the commons of Winstor inspected by Mr. Mander of Bakewel—if it should be in your power to procure me a plan of this

range, with the names of the Villages or hamlets in the
environs, I should esteem myself greatly obliged—what
expence this may occasion I should be happy to repay. I
am not desirous of having a very accurate plan, but an
explanatory one; the ichnography of the barrows will
answer my purpose, without the perspective view, and if
Mr. Mander could favor me with the drawings of the
glass vessels, the silver bracelet, and the beads found in
the barrow which came under his observation I should
derive great benefit from his transmit—the slightest scratch
of the particulars will serve my purpose, in return if it
could be in my power to serve Mr. Mander in this part
of the world I would not fail to execute his commands.

I thank you much for your polite offers of a bed at
your house on the absence of part of your family—and
if I can possibly visit Notts. this Winter I will not fail
on my road paying my respects to you.

I very much wish for an opportunity of trying my
labour at a Celtic barrow with a Kist-vaen on the top of
it—a fair and critical discovery of urns &c. under it,
would convey much information on the nature of these
memorials—that on Stack house Scar if circumstances
would admit—I should without the least hesitation explore.
A similar discovery would prove a key to our Druid
remains; concerning which I am certain much error is
propogated. If I go into Lancashire—where I am in hopes
of soon seeing a branch of my family—I think I shall
visit Craven.

I thank you for your Druid circle . . . I mean to groupe
with my plates some of your drawings which I find have
not been printed in the Archaeologia . . . and must beg
to be permitted to prefix your name to them. Whatever
else occurs I beg you will communicate and believe me
to be with a grateful sense for favors conferred, Sir,

      Your most obedt Servt   Jas. Douglas.

Little Stanhope Street
May-Fair 31st Octr 1784

Sir,

Little
Stanhope St 〉London Nov 16th 1774

Having day after day been in hopes of finishing some papers which I was at work on, and being under engagements to transmit the same to a friend, I am now happy in having it in my power to answer your very obliging favor of so long back as the 3d Inst—which has conveyed to me the result of your druidical and tumuli researches.

I am sorry to learn the fate of Winstor common, [see note after letter dated 8 Oct. 1784] where I was in hopes a groupe of rich barrows would have presented themselves to your observation. I say rich, for I know these kind of barrows are always productive of many curious relics. If the common was laid down in paster [*sic*] or meadow, I am still inclined to think you may trace out the cists of the bodies by the superior redundancy of herbage. When the barrows were levelled for cultivation, I do not think it likely the peasants would have ransacked them.

I should have been glad to have known if the site of these barrows was on a rising ground to the S.W. near a rivulet or stream, which I conjecture to have been the case: I am satisfied by the specimen of the fibula vis: the drawing in the Arch, found in one of them that they were of lower british structure towards the close of the fifth cent: an: 478, and I am confirmed in this by their being concentered in a groupe. The village of Elton, which is doubtless, by its etymon, of remote antiquity, is to far distant from the barrows, to suppose that the common was a burial place of a british establishment there. The large tumulus of Bleaklow tower and the other of a mile's distance, are Celtic, very antient and they must be considered as distinct from those of Winster.

I am concerned to think whenever a celt is found, that the precise locality is not attended to; were this to be the case many great absurdities would be put aside, which are now adopted on the use of these instruments. This instrument was no promiscuous deposit in the quarry,

and had a discerning eye attended to its situation, it is
not unlikely but some sepulchral signs would have appeared
near it; your drawing is verry correct and it appears to
be of a form that is rather unusual to these instruments,
a prodigious quantity of which I have had opportunities
of inspecting. Col. Vallancy favored the Society a few
evenings back with the drawing of one that was found in
Portugal: were you to attend to some reasons which I
could give on the subject you would conclude with me
that they are of roman manufactory, and one that I
have in the form of a bull with a lachrymatory on the
back puts it beyond a doubt. see and the *sketch* [latter
words in the margin]. In the course of the meeting last
year I sent the society a paper on the subject. [The
sketch is of the Roman bronze ceremonial axe described
in Chapter 5.]

The barrow which you opened within the vallum of
the circle of stones, I should apprehend to be of subsequent
era to the circle, but very antient and most likely british.
The fact is a curious one and may serve to throw light
on these circles which we generally ascribe to the Druids.
Your critical observation on the exact distances of these
remains is very pertinent and it is fair to conclude, that
the stone circles and barrows were of coeval date. I do
not with submission think with you that the circle of
stones were erected for funeral purposes, but rather for
religious ceremonies.—The religion of the Druids was
very similar to the magical institutions of the Persian
magi, as well as to the Greek rites: hence the enchanted
circle sacred to their mysteries, which has through all
ages and among most nations been supposed to have the
power of confirming the good genii who presided on these
occasions and of repelling the evil ones who might intrude
on their pious [original letter torn away].

If we deduce any argument on the nature of d[ruidical]
superstition in this island from Claus Wormius [torn away]
be led into error, I have long found much dissimilitude in
the Northern customs to the british: circles of stones I
have not the least doubt, were appropriated to religious as

well as civil purposes, and in my opinion never to tumul-
tuary sites unless they surrounded a barrow; as I have
often seen and heard of. Many barrows have trenches
round them and they obviate those of stones, by screening
the remains of the dead from the intrusion of evil genii,
and which circles were probably rendered sacred by the
magical incantations or spells of the priests.

The village of Birchover is not near enough to Winster
to serve my purpose if there is a running stream near
Winster, in a valley, I am right, and that will answer the
end required. These are my data like the principles of the
rule of three to work out some latent truths. What
other matter may occur I shall think myself much obliged
by your kind communication of it—for this and other
favors, Sir, I remain greatly indebted.

Your faithful humble Servt.   James Douglas

Sir,

I am happy to return your thanks for your obliging
communication of the Mining Low. It is a great acquisition
to my materials on the remote history of our british
sepulchres. In a short time I hope to say something more
as large and decisive on the subject; It is first necessary
to finish the detail which leads to them, after which I
shall covet with great avidity the further facts which
from time to time you are pleased to convey to me. To
explore by an excursionary and practical survey the parts
of this kingdom which exhibit these kinds of remains is
not in the ability of one man; to perform which, many
requisites are also necessary. I must doubtless therefore
be indebted to some literary correspondent for some
assistance and in this respect I am greatly obliged to you
and shall be proud on any occasion to show a sense of
obligation.

I conceive these vast structures of earth to have been
templa—relics of the antient fire worshipers: of the first
colonizers of the island. The Kist-vens were probably

of a subsequent deposit or erection. In sacred History we find sepulchres of the priests and distinguished orders of the people were admitted near the Adytum or holy spot of worship: and I am particularly inclined to think Mining-low was a mount of worship from the research made a few years back [in 1776] into Silbury-Mount by Mr. Drax and the late Duke of Northumberland: who employing miners from Cornwall for the purpose of exploring it, sunk into the very heart of it to its base without making any sepulchral discovery. [The excavation of this, the largest man-made mound in Europe, sponsored by BBC2 under the direction of Professor Richard Atkinson in 1963-9, also used professional miners, but from Wales. Its story proved to be complicated.] Dr. Stukeley indeed found a piece of iron like the bit of a bridle which he believed to have been the remains of a relic devoted to some sepulchral office of a british king. All was british with the Dr.—but this relic was only found on the surface or near it. The stone coffin found in one of the Bartlow barrows, in Essex, laid near the side, not at the bottom. There is no fact therefore to judge from, to ascertain that these vast conferies of earth were sepulchral, unless they contained internal proofs. [The Bartlow Hills are in fact the finest Roman barrows in Britain: see R. F. Jessup in the Bibliography.]

It would be presuming I fear too much on your goodness, or I should request at your leisure a perspective elevation with some little of the adjoining scenery, of the Mining-low. It would be a great acquisition, particularly so, as your pencil has the power of so much freedom and truth.

I have a strong *presentiment* that Derbyshire from its mountainous, and in some respects uncultivated state, contains many extraordinary fine undiscribed and unexplored remains of very antient places of sepulchre.

I hope you have recd the 4 first Nos. of my work. The 4th will be published in a few days.

When you have leisure to communicate, I shall esteem yr favours highly. Yr research is precisely the *desiderata* of my enquiries.

I have the honour to be with great [torn]
Sir,
              Your faithful & obliged Servt   Jas. Douglas
Chidingfold
near Godalming 12th Jany 1787

Sir,

I am infinitely obliged to you for your favour of the 7th *Ulto* and should have returned an earlier answer had I not entertained hopes of seeing you in person much about this period. Having been presented to a living in Northamptonshire I had thoughts on taking possession to pursue my route through your part of the world into Lancashire, but the unfavourable season of the year and being detained at home longer than I intended, have made me drop all thoughts of proceeding farther than Northamptonshire.

[It would seem that Douglas never lived for long in his Rectory at Litchborough, Northants which he held 1787-99.]

My next No will contain miscellaneous relics of the smaller tumuli and a more general enquiry into their history. I hope soon to enter on the history of our early sepuchral remains; but which I have chiefly reserved for the conclusion of my work. I am apprehensive I shall be found to differ very much on the general received opinion of those remains which are call druidical and which in the course of my reading and observation I have hitherto found no reason for ascribing to these people.

Our circular monuments of unhewn stone and other mishapen and distorted piles of stone, barrows &c. are evidently similar to the remains of this nature in Norway weeden and Denmark recorded also by Saxo Grammaticus 1140-1206], whose narations I have been long led to consider as fabulous and which *Torfaeus* [Thormodur Torfason (1636-1719)] in his *Regium Danæ* has sufficiently attested. The Scandenavians have no authentic history till the 11th Centy. Our antiquaries must therefore be too credulous to receive their *data* from Saxo's authority, who seems hitherto to have misled most writers on the enquiry into the history of our reputed Druidical antiquities. The analogy of these remains in Britain to the Sweedish Danish &c. is too great to admit of any doubt but the same race of people must have been their first compilers. As the Druids seem not to have frequented the aforesaid countries, we cannot therefore attribute these remains to that people. I have taken the liberty to suggest this link for your future consideration. These remains I point at are to be considered of Scythian origin and which enumerable facts will trace upwards to the Northern regions and successively by a chain of undisputed authority to eastern climes, their primeval origin.

I hold myself greatly indebted to you for your obliging transmits of *tumuli* remains and trust, when other acquisitions of this nature are in your power to command you will do me the honour to present me with them.

I can not help entertaining an unshaken belief that a careful survey of the uncultivated districts in your part of the world and especially in Derbyshire must produce many ranges of the smaller *tumuli*, which when examined with proper care, do never fail to repay very amply any enquisitive antiquary for his trouble.

I have the pleasure to subscribe myself with much esteem and with many thanks for your contributions.   Sir,

Your most obedt humble Servt   J. Douglas

Chidingfold 6th Novr. 1787

[Douglas was glad to acknowledge and add to Rooke's opinions, *e.g. Nenia Britannica,* 1793, pp. 36, 68, 165.]

14

SELECTION OF LETTERS TO THE
3rd LORD EGREMONT AND HIS AGENT 1803-1806

(Petworth House MS. 101.)

Kenton Debenham 5th Decr 1803

Sir,

I have received a letter from Mr. Ellis of Hatton Garden, employed by Lord Winterton to sue me for the remainder of the money on the late judgement which was executed against me, with a threat of execution should the money not be paid before the 11th Instant. In consequence I have written to Mr. Ellis some time now elapsed and have offered to surrender for the payment my income of Middleton; as it is totally out of my power to procure the money immediately. I shall esteem it a favour if you will ask Mr. Johnson what the sum is, as I have never been able to get the statement, nor was the same specified in the letter of Mr Ellis; and I will empower you to settle this cruel and unpleasant business with his Lordship from my Middleton income, if you will have the goodness to relieve my great anxiety by doing me this service; at the same time expressing my fears lest I am intruding on your time and trouble by any unwarantable liberty. My distance is so great and the expence of a journey so very inconvenient to me at this time, that I know not how to turn myself without some assistance and should his Lordship's threat be acted upon, doubtless my situation must be dreadful in the extreme. As you are pretty well acquainted with my· actual situation I am sure you can alledge nothing but truth on my side, with the most perfect integrity of doing every thing, that is just and right in my power and that I have not pleaded inability from any sinister motive. Mr. Daintry assured me that Lord Winterton had agreed, in a conference with Mr. Johnson, to accept £20 yearly instalment. I think the sum left unpaid on the sale of my effects was about £80 and it was my intention to have fulfilled the same on Lady day ensuing.

It should appear by this decision of Lady Winterton, for his Lordship is out of the question, that some great resentment influences her conduct, but for what cause I am a perfect stranger. Mr. Johnson most indisputably assured me, however such a thing may be denied, that after the judgement was entered up, no further steps would have taken place. Had my property been sold as it ought, it would have more than have paid my debt; but such has been their malice through the whole business that they have sought every method how to distress me most, and to ruin me; for my property was litterally given away and sold to the first bidder.

I hope his Lordship [Lord Egremont] and family are well. Intreating the favour of your immediate answer I am with compliments of my Wife, Sir,

> Your humble servant.   James Douglas.

Mr Tyler.

[It would seem that Douglas had left in bad repair not only his church at Middleton but also the house in which he lived at Petworth which was probably the property of the Earl of Winterton, Baron Turnour of Shillinglee Park, Sussex. The chancel of the church was repaired at Douglas's cost, but the Petworth house obviously needed attention.]

Kenton Debenham 16th Jany 1804.

Sir,

I had entertained the hope of receiving a line from you on the business of Lord Winterton's claim, which I trust is settled with that degree of humanity, which strictly speaking I am sure you would not fail to recommend.

Being in town on business for a few days, I was in hopes it would have been in my power to have seen you at Petworth to have requested your advice and assistance in a matter, which no other person but those who are acquainted with my affairs could serve me in; but circumstances have obliged me to return home and I have taken the liberty to trespass on your time by a letter. The circumstance is this: Mrs Douglas had left her by her father 1,259£ capital stock in the 3 per cent govern. Cons: *for her use during her life, and then to her children in such portions as she should direct*; and the Revd. Mr. Cane of Southwell Notts, was left trustee for the same; he is dead, as also his wife and of course his trust devolved to their executors who are strangers to us, and we have had much difficulty in getting the dividends paid; they would have no objection to be rid of the trust; the question I have to propose is; my daughter being of age, if the property with sanction of my wife could ·not be made over to my daughter, and thereby empowered to make use of the capital.

My reason is this, being obliged from various circumstances, to realise for my immediate use 200£ I mean not to injure my children; for by keeping on foot the assurance on my life for £350 I shall more than replace it; on the other hand Sir, if you could yourself, or procure me the assistance of some monied man to advance the *two hundred pounds,* I will make over through Mrs Douglas the interest of the capital, which is, £36.18.0d. annually. The power of Attorney to receive the dividends, is now lodged in my name, with an order from the executors, in the hands of Messrs. Loyd Jones Hulme & Co. Bankers, Lothbury.

The sale of my little crops or produce of my farm is so low, I shall get nothing by it this year, if I save myself, and my expences for repairs which were unavoidable, have exceeded my expectations; and the people being so clamorous for money on all sides throughout this part of the world, that I am obliged to take some immediate method, or I shall lose my credit, which will render it impossible for me to live in this wretched place.

May I also be permitted to state, that if you have released a portion of my Middleton living, from the grasp of Lord Winterton, whether such a portion would not be sufficient to raise the £200 and as good a security?

I must apologize for the liberty I have taken to trouble you, but the reiterated conflicts of this kind render my life miserable and I am obliged to use some effort to restore myself and family to some degree of peace. May I beg an early answer? and with the compliments of Mrs D——

I remain, Sir,

           Your obedt humble Servant   James Douglas

[To Lord Egremont at Petworth.]

                                        Kenton 29th Septr 1805.

Dear Sir,

If it should be in any way convenient to you, to favour me with a remittance of my Middleton half yearly payment it will be doing me service; as my tithes at this place are not due 'till Novr I should otherwise find difficulty in answering a few demands at this time of the year.

An acquaintance of mine in this part of the world having seen an advertisement in the Lewes journal respecting Bignor park, is desirous of becoming a purchaser; if it should be on sale and if in your power to give me any information you will much oblige me.

On old Michaelmas day I have some payments to make and should esteem it a favour if you could oblige me with your remittance in time for this purpose.

I beg you will remember me to Mr. Palmer [tenant and church warden at Middleton] when you see or send to him and should be happy to hear my friends in Petworth and the neighbourhood are well.

    Mrs Douglas desires her Compliments and I am, Dr Sir,

        Your obedt humble Servant   J. Douglas

[To W. Tyler.]

                        Kenton 19th April 1806

Dear Sir,

I have been in a state of great anxiety respecting a letter which I wrote to you about a fortnight since, stating my inability to pay my half yearly king's taxes, parish rates &c without assistance from my Middleton payment.

My anxieties have also increased, under the apprehension lest any thing might have happened materially to prevent the same; and it has been only through the possibility of your absence from home that I have been able to quiet my mind on the subject; and especially as I have heard nothing from the Chancellor I can not help being very uneasy.

    I am, Dr Sir,

        Your obedient humble Servant   J. Douglas

[To W. Tyler.]

                      Kenton 26th May 1806

Dear Sir,

I acknowledge by this post the receipt of £8.4.10½ being the balance of my account with Lord Winterton and I hereby am happy to return you my thanks for your kindness in undertaking to settle this disagreeable concern for me; and I shall be for ever mindful of the great obligations which will be due to that goodness which has enabled me to surmount the difficulty and to acquit me

of a debt which I always held myself in honour bound
to pay, but which I must ever consider as having been
enforced with great cruelty.

Mrs Douglas desires her compliments and I am   Dear Sir
            Your very obliged humble Servt   J. Douglas
[To W. Tyler.]

                                    Kenton Debenham 3d Decembr
                                                        1806
My Lord,

After having used every possible means in my power
as far as my remote distance would admit to procure
duty for the church of Middleton, I have received the
enclosed letter from the Bishop of Chichester, which I
answered immediately and I am entertaining the hope,
that your Lordship will not think me too troublesome in
soliciting your protection in a case wherein, almost the
existence of my self and family depend. I have been
twenty four years in the church, and I can venture
with truth to say, that I have always endeavoured to the
best of my power to discharge my obligations. Having
lived near five years in the neighbourhood of Your Lordship, in the constant service of several churches, I should
hope you might in some respects bear testimony to my
dilligence, and having served my own church of Middleton
a great part of that period, in all seasons of the year,
many miles from Petworth.

On receiving the resignation of Mr Grant at Michaelmas,
the gentleman who did the duty of Middleton, I wrote
to the Bishop requesting his Lordship to procure me a
person: knowing the Bishop was desirous of interfering
in the nomination, as he had heretofore done with
Middleton. The answer I received was, that Middleton,
being so much in the angle of the country, the clergy
hesitated, unless the stipend was increased. I also wrote
to Mr Grant, to ask his further assistance, which was

continued some weeks longer, and to Mr Taylor to request him to make application for the duty being served. I also wrote to Mr Turner, who after some delay answered my letter, saying he had made application, enclosing a letter from Mr Grant who had continued the duty some little longer, and saying I should soon hear further from him on the subject, which I have not; and I can assure your Lordship that I was totally unconscious that my Church was not served until I received the very severe letter of the Bishop; conceiving that if the duty had been improperly omitted, Mr Palmer the churchwarden of the place, who had every reason to show me a kindness, would have given me immediate notice.

My great distance from Sussex, the expence and little likelyhood of getting my church here served, render ·me incapable of taking a journey to Middleton; but if cited by the Bishop, however inconvenient or painful, I must set off; unless it can be in your Lordship's power, to interfere in my behalf; and I have also to assure your Lordship that if I was conscious in any degree of negligence or indifference to my interest or my duty, I should feel that I had no pretence for troubling any friend or your Lordship to render me a service; and indeed my Lord as to friends or acquaintances, I have scarcely any left excepting my little family, being almost entirely secluded from the world and all connections with it. Having lived fourteen years at Chiddingfold near five at Petworth and four years in this place your Lordship will naturally believe, that I am forgotten by many, and have but very few claims to make my necessities known.

The small stipend from Middleton, I have been but a little time in full possession of, and which with much patient frugality has but rarely enabled me to exist; and the prospect of seeing myself deprived of this little, is almost as much as my mind can support.

I have considered myself as very unfortunate, in not having been permitted to accept of the exchange which your Lordship kindly proposed to me; the emolument of which would have made myself and family comfortable, which is not now the case; but I have been informed by Mr Buckle the Rector of Worlingworth, whose sister purchased that living for him from the late Lord Henniker, that the present Lord Henniker and the Duchess of Chandos, being joint patrons of this living, most probably had previously engaged it; and which he considered as the reason of his Lordship's refusal.

I am conscious that I owe to your Lordship every grateful consideration and most anxiously do I hope that you will not my Lord find your goodness to me, in any degree misapplied.

I am with proper respect,   My Lord

Your Lordship's most humble and obedt Servant

James Douglas.

The Earl of Egremont.

15

SELECTION OF LETTERS
TO WILLIAM CUNNINGTON, 1809-10

(Wiltshire County and Diocesan Archives, Trowbridge. Colt Hoare
Papers 383.907.)

Bognor Sussex. 21st May 1809

[To A. B. Lambert.]

Sir,

I ventured on the freedom of knocking at your door
before I left town, to request the address of Mr. Cunnington, who I was informed had returned into the country,
whose residence I am still unacquainted with. —

Having several particulars to impart to him respecting
our *tumuli* researches, I should think myself much
obliged with your information, where I am to address
him. Having also much leisure, I should feel much
gratified to pay him a visit, if his abode is not more
than forty miles from this place.

Within these few days I have found some uncommon
fine specimens of extraneous fossils at this place; of
the concha veneris and other chamites; imbedded in very
hard Shistose; when fractured presenting micacious par-
ticles, the shells entirely permeated with the schistose.
This stone has been fractured and raised from the
bed of the sea at low water mark, from the Bognor rocks
for building and other purposes. They furnish a good
geological evidence, that Mr. Kirwan is right, in his

assertion that most of our petrifications are produced by cristallization at the bottom of the sea; but also a conclusive evidence of their induration having taken place at incomputable periods; as no exemplars of recent shells of the same tribe are to be found on this coast. Any of these specimens are at your service or indeed any of the fossils which I am in possession of, when you please to command their transport to you.

With many thanks for your polite introduction to Mr Cunnington and presenting my respects to Mrs. Lambert I have the pleasure to be with much consideration, Sir,

Your very obedt humble St.   J. Douglas.

[Footnote to Cunnington.]

I give up his offer of fossils to you which you might mention if you write.   A.B.L.

[A. B. Lambert (1761-1842) to whom this letter was sent at Boyton, Wilts, was a well-known natural historian and geologist who advised Colt Hoare on tree-planting and other ground improvements.]

Sir,

I am much obliged by Mr Lambert's transmit of my note to you and I return you my best thanks for your kind answer to my questions respecting the beads found in the higher tumuli. I have sent you a rough tint of the porcelain beads and other relics of the same kind of vitrification, of Egyptian manufactory; which may be compared with the rayed beads you have found in the most antient barrows. 1. 2. 3. 4 and 5 are Egyptian; 6. 7 are british; and as my notes attest discovered in barrows on Salisbury plain. [Several of the items illustrated here had appeared as the heading on p. 75 of *Nenia Britannica.*] You will doubtless therefore be able to establish the analogy, and I am persuaded you will think with me, that these beads must have been introduced into Britain by traffic with the natives, at remote periods of the most early colonisers; the celtic tribes; which I think might safely date before the second captivity of the Syrians and Sidonians by Nebuchadnezzar; which people, under the general name of phœnicians, had, as history warrants the conclusion, traded with the inhabitants of Britain. The Belgic invasion of the celtic pastoral colonisers, I think might be excluded from the claim especially if you have it in your power to prove that the beads in question were discovered in barrows which contained the bones untouched by fire; which ceremony I have reason to think was introduced by the belgic gauls who Cæsar is explicit in describing, as having burnt their dead.

The other beads asserted to have been found on Salisbury plain from the collection of Dr. Stukeley, I did not think of any use to make a drawing of; as I had always my doubts of the fact. I purchased them of Mr. White of Newgate Street, long deceased, a well known collector and dealer in curiosities; whose assertions I have been given to understand were not always authentic.

You shall certainly have any of the fossils in my collection which may be thought worthy of your acceptance; and I shall not fail taking the first opportunity of waiting upon Mr. Holloway whose acquaintance I shall be happy to cultivate and to render him any service in my power.

Should you be at home and disengaged, as your distance is beyond the reach of my single horse chair, I will get into the coach for Heytesbury; which I had thoughts of doing the beginning of next week; but I am at present confined with a cold on my chest, and can not fix the time; previous to which I will trouble you with a short letter, lest unforseen business might call you from home.

I have recently met with a good specimen of a small charmite enclosed in martial pyrites; and I have also another specimen of an echinus encrusted or more properly crystallized in a similar mass; both found in chalk; facts which ascertain the formation of flint and pyrites to be of the same date.

With thanks for your obliging attention and kind invitation to see your collection of tumuli researches, I am, sincerely wishing your health may be reestablished.   Sir,

Your much obliged and faithful humble servant,

James Douglas.

Barnham, near Bognor
Sussex, 5th June 1809

Copy of a letter to Mr. Douglas [from William Cunnington]

Heytesbury June 14 1809

Sir,

I am extremely obliged by your letter with drawings of the beads and other articles of Egyptian manufacture —all of which correspond with the Porcelain Beads &c found in our higher Barrows. Our Porcelain Beads are sometimes found with Skeletons, but more frequently where burning has been practiced. Interring the body itself was certainly the most ancient rite—but cremation must have been brought into this Country at a very early period—we have found stone hatchets &c with burnt bones. I am of opinion that burying under tumuli had (in this Island) ceased before the invasion of Cæsar.

I have much more to say when I have the pleasure of seeing you, but I am just now I may say unfortunately situated as since I wrote you last I have suddenly engaged in enlarging my small House & have now the Masons at one end and the middle—thus circumstanced I can only ask you to see my collection & to eat a dinner with me— we have a good Inn in this Town where you can sleep. I shall be at home from the 23rd Inst. to the 1st July— after that period I shall be from home some time if my health is rather better. I thank you for the offer of fossils & am respectfully, Sir,

Your most humble Servant,

Barnham near Bognor 7th July 1809

Dear Sir,

Had not some ecclesiastical business prevented me I had proposed myself the great pleasure of visiting you on or about the 26th Ulto. This pleasure I have therefore postponed 'till your return to Heytesbury, as you informed me it was your intention to leave home on or after the 1st of this month; therefore when you may think it convenient to receive me, allow me to request the favour of a line and I flatter myself no obstruction will intervene to deprive me of a gratification the hope of which I have so long cherished.

I think with you that burying under the large Tumuli which I class as belgic, and in many instances as celtic, might have ceased before the invasion of Cæsar; because in no one instance in them have I ever discovered roman remains, such as pottery, utensils, coins or military instruments of these people, which I think would have been the case had any intercourse taken place with the romans by the britons; but I have an instance before me, on the inspection of a roman burial place discovered at Portslade near Shoreham in this county An: 1800 perfect and correct in its nature, from the urn being surrounded with the usual funeral vessels and the red pateræ of Saguntum to which from Pliny I have given the same of Samian, of a british urn being found in the same spot invested with its cineritious contents, but certainly with no tumulus over it, which might have been scarped off for the succeeding deposit. The urn was of this form, which I conceive can leave no doubt of its identity. At all events, it is a proof that the urn of unbaked clay was a contemporary date also with roman times; unless we assign a reason as I have stated for its anterior date, by supposing the romans to have levelled the tumulus for their funeral obseqy which I think would be granting rather too much. [Despite Douglas's caution, this is a very early appreciation of the meaning of secondary burial.]

In one of my rides on the South downs I have discovered at an almost inaccessable height one of the long barrows, which Mr. King [Edward King in *Munimenta Antiqua*, 1799-1805] calls a *ship barrow*. It is at a very considerable distance from any other barrow and is overlooking a british road deeply excavated for it ascent to the Hill. It appears to me of the highest antiquity, very perfect with not the least appearance of its ever having been broken into. I therefore purpose in a short time to undertake the opening of it.

You did not inform me, what distance Heytesbury is from Salisbury, which you will allow me to ask the favour of, when your leisure or convenience may admit of your writing.

With every sincere wish for the preservation of your health I am anxiously waiting to hear from you in the hope of soon being able to perform my journey to Heytesbury, and I am, Dear Sir,

Your much obliged and very faithful Servant,

James Douglas.

Barnham, Bognor, 11th Augt 1809
Dear Sir,

I thought your obliging communication demanded on my side a similar return and I have taken up my pen to give you a description of the *ship* barrow, which I had long determined to explore, and which I began upon on the 5th Inst.

This barrow is situated on the apix of a very steep hill called Rundel, near Dale Park, the seat of Sr. G. Thomas, about four miles from Arundel. The ascent is by a very antient british road, deeply excavated, winding round the declivity. At sixty paces from the barrow, a deep intrenchment crosses the road at right angles and stops at the steep declivity of the hill, where the scarpe is of itself sufficiently repulsive of approach. This intrenchment, on which are large yew trecs. at least one thousand years old, runs in a line to the sea almost tangent to the arm of it, in the low grounds on the west side of Little-

Hampton. It is thrown up like our *graafs* or dykes, or what are called boundary lines; evidently subsequent to the road. As the barrow was situated on the very summit above the road, I had every reason to believe the barrow was nearly coeval with the road and my expectation seems to be confirmed; having no hesitation to affix the graaf to the second Belgæ and the road to the first colonizers.

According to your intimation I found a skeleton; at the broadest end about the S.S.W. direction. The scull N.N.E. On its right side. The left *femur* over the right; the left *radius,* over the breast. At a right angle, about a foot above the feet, two pair of large antlers of the stag or red deer, parallel to each other. Each pair, one foot apart; the coronets or root ends in the same direction; evincing a careful and methodical deposit. The translator of Ossian says, '*the antient scots opened a grave, six or eight feet deep*; the bottom was lined *with fine clay and on this they laid the body: with the horn of a deer the symbol of hunting'.* I mention this, as a singular coincidence and I have found this fact in one other instance. I always suspected Ossian to be a forgery; but I have contended that McPhaerson [*sic*] must have had authentic materials to build his poem upon; and in this instance, I perceived a yellow mould under the bones, which convinces me, as the material was chalk and therefore the mould easily defined, that the body was laid upon a thin sheeting of clay: the coincidence is remarkable, as the horns in his description were placed in an elevated situation above the feet, precisely like those discovered in this barrow. All the northern nations appear to have had this custom (see the Edda) Keysler &c &c.

There was something remarkable in the Os frontis of this skeleton, which I should have disregarded, had not a young man, skilled in anatomy, been present; who assured me that it presented a singular dissimilarity to the usual osteological identities; inasmuch as the *sagital suture,* passed in a straight line to the *nasal suture*; only perceived on the sculls of Affricans or the inhabitants

near the southern tropics. By the radius, measured with
a labourer who was six feet in height, the bones
corresponded with a man of this admeasurement. By
the thickness of the fistular bones, the person could
not have been aged.

I have been ever cautious in depending on the deliria
or theoretical conjectures of many writers on antiquity;
but from repeated observations, I have had great reason
to believe, that many of our long barrows, presenting the
form of a ship keel upwards, might have received such
form intentionally from the very antient inhabitants of
this island; perhaps in allusion to their maritime expeditions. Near the road between Dorchester and Bridport, is
a vast barrow called Shipton-hill. See Hutchin's [the
Dorset historian]. Wormius speaks of such a one. Regios
tumulus ad magnitudinem et figuram *carince maxime
navis* ex us quas possidebant fabricatos volunt. Mon:
Danic: p. 42. Dr. Salmon describes a barrow of this form.
Survey of England, p. 618. Mr. Vine mentions one,
Gent: Mag: vol. XXXVII, p. 384. I could cite several
others, perhaps unnoticed.

Rundel hill, commands a most expansive view of the
ocean, the Isle of Wight, with the intermediate campagnia
round Chichester. This barrow on the top, I conceive to
be one of the oldest in the kingdom. In the numerous
barrows which you have opened in Wiltshire, you have
perhaps met with similar instances of the horns of deer;
and as analogy after all is a very safe guide, I think we may
gather some appropriate conclusion from this discovery,
to venture at a closer approach to the first colonization
of this kingdom, than some of our modern writers are
aware of; who will hear of nothing beyond Cæsar's
advent. I have often thought, that we are in possession of
ample materials for a correct classification of our british
barrows and which, had not other avocations intervened,
I certainly should have arranged having already began
it to a certain degree.

I look forward with pleasure to the happiness of meeting your friends Sr. R. Hoare and Mr. Lambert on the

20th to whom I beg you will present my respects and, with every good wish to yourself I am, Dear Sir,

Your faithful and obedient Servant, James Douglas.

P.S. I have not finally explored the Rundel hill ship barrow, which I mean to do the first opportunity. I forgot to say at a short distance from it I opened a circular one, the same day; evidently ustrinal, from the fragments of the unbaked urn. I do not like the name of *Celtic* being applied to our most antient barrows. I think *british better,* and the classification varied to the description: contents &c. &c.

You will perceive I have not been particular in my transmit, to avoid tediousness; otherwise I ought to have mentioned the length *of the ship barrow,* which did not exceed fifty feet.

My seal is a very fine antique of *Horatius Cocles* by Scopas; mistaken for that of Pompey by good judges. The name of Scopas is upon it; which therefore can not apply to his time.

Barnham near Bognor. 7th Novr 1809

My dear Sir,

I have availed myself of the convenience of a packet to Mr. Lambert to fulfil my engagement respecting the Sussex fossils which I promised and which I am informed by letter from my friend, Mr. Haron of Cuckfield are to meet me with this gentleman at Chichester on friday the 10th Inst. therefore as I have not yet seen them I am writing from home to be in readiness with the transmits to forward them from thence. The fossil specimens in question are from a congeries of bufonites [toadstone] and the bones of fish from a thin and very superficial strata in the neighbourhood of Cuckfield used as materials for mending the road; the further particulars you shall hereafter receive.

I should be much gratified in hearing that Sir Rd. Hoare had made further discoveries in the neighbourhood of Stone-henge or yourself being nearer to it. You must not be surprized that a similarity of pursuit and an eager propensity in a study which has afforded me every pleasing resource to my retired habits and which for many years has occupied my mind, should, on the inspection of your valuable cabinet and the amiable manner with which you received my visit excite me to further energy and stimulate my curiosity.

It is now I think upwards of six weeks since I answered a letter from Mr. Archdn: Coxe respecting a pamphlet sent for my address to Dr. Latham of Romsey, who I believe has been waiting to forward my packet to Mr. Lambert and therefore my receipt of Mr. Coxe's letter may have been detained. I feel rather anxious, lest this gentleman may not have received it, perhaps owing to the absence of the Bishop of Salisbury who having franked his letter, I took the liberty of making an *envelope* of Mr. Coxe's to his Lordship. In my letter in answer to a query, I said something about Stone-henge which I should be happy to communicate to you, but I feel diffident of advancing any new matter, being conscious that yourself and Sir Rich. Hoare must have obtained every relative argument on its history; however, I have ventured to hazard an opinion that the *Bethyle,* or Stone of Adoration, situated without the cespetitious or grass circle, was the primary erection, to which the temple was dedicated; the stone in the first place to the pure worship of the Deity and the temple afterwards to the Mithraic, or fire worship; and therefore considered justly by Stukeley as a temple to the Sun especially as the adytum is certainly open to the eastern quarter. Sammes [Aylett Sammes, author of *Britannia Antiqua Restaurata,* 1676] who wrote before Stukeley, is right in his conjecture of its being of Phœnician origin erected to their celebrated Hercules, whose rites were symbolic of the Sun and therefore the deity represented as looking through chinks or crevises with this motto OMNIA VIDENS. Both greek and roman authority assert the existence of his pillars at Cades; doubtless a structure of unhewn stone; and his representation of leaning on a club is only a vulgar perversion of his real history by the ignorant greek writers, who had assimilated the mythology of all nations to theirs, and by their national vanity, confounded and perplexed the real history of their progenitors. Holinshed in his chronicle of Scotland has this curious entry in the life of King Mamius; I shall here transcribe it for your perusal as an argument to prove that the writers of the Scottish history from whom he quotes, always considered these cirques of unhewn stones of a far remoter period, than the succeeding writers in Charles's days. 'Mamius King of Scotland, upon a religious devotion towarde the Goddes, having an assured belief, that without their favour all worldly policies were but vain, devysed sundrie partes of his dominions to be appoynted out, and compassed about with *great huge stones round lyke a ring,* but towards the South was one *Mightie Stone farre greater than all the rest, pitched up in manner of an aulter,* whereon (*at which*) their priests might make their sacrifices in honour of their Goddes. In witness of the King there remayneth unto this day certaine of those greate stones standing round, ring-wide (vid: Rolrick stones) which places are called by the common people the old Chapels of the Goddes. A man would marvel by what shift, policy or strength such mightie stones were raised in that manner.' N.B. This king according to Harrison and Boetius florished about 300 years before Christ. If not tired with my antiquary gossip, I shall venture another remark . . . Had Stone-henge been of Druid origin or even afterwards consecrated to their rights, the romans under Claudius and the succeeding emperors, who abolished their rites and supprest their convocations, would most assuredly have overthrown the temple of Stone-henge. The absurd idea that has been started of its being erected after their times, from its not being mentioned in the writings of Tacitus or Dio, maybe satisfactorily answered with this remark; that these errections or similar cirques of the Eastern colonizers were common in all the northern regions which they over-run; (nor do I think they were dilapidated before the Christian era;) and which the romans held sacred to the gods of those nations whom they conquered.

In my letter to Mr. Coxe I mentioned the prostrate stone just opposite the *Bethyle* and close within the outward circle. This puzzled Stukeley, who ascribed it to an altar stone. I think this probable, but not an altar stone to the temple, but to the single Obeliscal Stone or *Bethyle*; at all events from the methodical position of it, it is worthy of being raised; for if it had been originally erect; there might be a possibility of its being laid prostrate for some sepulchral purpose; and therefore some funeral relics might be found under it.

My fortunate visit to Stone-henge in the company of Mr. Coxe has afforded me considerable field of enquiry beyond the written descriptions which I have perused. I believe all that has been said on the subject of this most interesting remains of british antiquity; and one particular fact I trust, it has enabled me to produce on the discrimination of the various modes of antient interment, considered by antiquaries as a *desideratum.* I mean that of *ustrinal,* and the *body entire.* The former I shall venture to ascribe to the fire worshipper or what I call the Mithraic or Chanaanitic order and the latter to the patriarchial or worshipper of the one God and mother earth.

I am very anxious to know what success you have had in the King barrow, which you began upon. I ascended it with Mr. Coxe and picked up several animal bones, fragments, from the interiour mould, but no shard could I perceive in the soil, which inclined me to believe they were not of ustrinal connection. The large barrow close to the temple ought to be opened. It is very interesting, the apex has been rather broken into; but no primary interment I am convinced was ever discovered.

Pray let me have the pleasure of soon hearing from you; which I sincerely hope will give me better tidings of your health, which you much complained of on my leaving Wiltshire. I beg to present my best regards to Mrs. Cunnington and compliments to your amiable daughters, to whom I strongly recommend their perseverance in the use of the pencil. Their skill will improve daily and had I been so fortunate as to have prolonged my stay a little longer in your neighbourhood I think I could have facilitated their progress, in qualifying them to have made some pleasing drawings of your curious relics: independant of the eye there is a mechanical process required to render their labours easy and less irksome.

I believe some apology is necessary for my long epistle; but the suavity of your manners and open generous conference, have drawn it from me, therefore I shall lay my culpability to your account.

My Dear Sir,

I am truly Yours,

James Douglas.

I hope soon to be settled more to my satisfaction than my present temporary abode, as the Bishop of Chichester has kindly procured me a Church and parsonage in this County, which allowing for the convenience of the removal of the present minister I hope soon to occupy, before the winter is advanced: when I flatter myself with the pleasure of unpacking a case of my barrow relics and some fossils to select some things for you from duplicates; but they are now nailed up with iron hoops on the outside of the case. There is only one impression of bone on a specimen of the Cuckfield specimens; hereafter I may obtain a better one.

Arundel 24th April 1810

My dear Sir,

I have now settled myself in a commodious house at Arundel and can with pleasure take up my pen to gossip with you on our favourite pursuits; sincerely hoping your indisposition will give way to this fine season of the year,

to enable you to resume your interesting researches on
the downs.

I have been studying the welsh triads, comparing notes
with my analogies (as I could always wish to deem them)
for an approach to our earliest stone erections; of course
your famous Stone-henge does not a little interest me. I am
still of opinion that the druids were not the original erectors of the temple, for so it must indisputably be deemed,
although they had incorporated their mythology with the
more pure, but far more antient british rites; this is ably
detailed in *the mythology and rites of the British druids,* by
Davies, whose work you have doubtless seen, and who, in
his translation of the Welsh bard *Aneurin* in his *Gododin* or
Stone-henge, has conveyed a prodigious mass of interesting
facts on this most antient national structure of ours.

(Had you by accident seen the passage in Maurice's
Indian Antiquities V:VI. p. 123, you would I make no
doubt have revoked your opinion of the small upright
stones of the inner circle: his words are. 'In the second
place, the Adytum or *Sanctum Sanctorum,* is of an oval
form, representing the *mundane egg*;' and whose remark
often quoted by Bryant and our best mythologists,
without the powerful aid of the Welsh triads, prove the
mundane egg as a principal emblem in the old patriarchial
Arkite worship.) This is also confirmed by *Aneurin* and
Talicsin in the triads describing *Iegid* the deified patriarch
as father of *Creuriug* the British Prosperine, the *token
of the egg.* The same personage as *Llywy* the *putting forth
of the egg*; in conjunction with *Hu* Noah or Aeddon.
The whole of these rites following each other, having
the clue of the celebrated *ovum anguinum* of the latter
druids and mingled with the strange tissue of the latter
british absurdities, perverted from the antient patriarchial
worship. *Gwarchan Adsbon* is the title of one poem,
in which is this line, '*The fierce youth treasured up the
gem of protection*'. What a strong allusion this is, to the
Spuma Anguini of Pliny, the *Glein Nadroeth* of the
druids! A prodigious fine specimen of which I have in my
collection, like this sketch of it. The lights, yellow. The

Convolutes, black. I am [Here is a always desirous of regulating opinion on fact; drawing of and never suffer any
theory of Hypothesis to the upper have the least sway in a
literary stricture. The side of a knowledge of producing
fossil
echinoid.]
the fittest material from antient authorities to assert
opinion, may be deemed learning; which if not obtruded
with affectation must always have weight to elucidate
the recondite truths of history. Beyond the knowledge
of antient languages, is the knowledge of the materials,
of knowing where to apply for the auxiliary in those
languages; I mean the critical study of those languages,
which is scholarship; the other, is true learning.

I am happy to find, that with me you entertain a great
respect for Stukeley. I have always considered him as
father of british antiquities.

I ought in my preceding remark on the *Glein Nadroeth*
to have sent you the citation of Mr. Davies from the
Triads, on Charms and Talismans p. 580. he says, 'amongst
the most curious productions of the antient British muse,
we may class those little poems, which are called
Gwarchanau, charms or talismans; or incantations rather.
In addition to the general lore of Druidism, these pieces
bring forward *certain mystical amulets* which were
delivered to the patriotic warriors, as infallible pledges
of the protection of the Gods; and which *were evidently
remains of the renowned magic of the Britons'.* A proof
of the earlier british rites.

I am confident when you enter deeply into the
matter which will be brought forward on the subject
of Stone-henge, that you will find no difficulty in believing
this venerable remain to have been originally erected
as a temple to the Sun, of the mithraic order. I always
could give proof of the fact and which I find is substantiated by the *triads.* In the first place, when I visited
Stonehenge with Mr. Coxe, I pointed out the single stone
115 from the circle as the stone to which the temple
was erected. I called it the *Bethylic Betyle* or stone of
adoration. It is the stone of the british *Ceres,* represented

under the character of the giantess; *Talicsin* giving an
account of his initiation, styles her *Hen Widdon Delulon,*
the old dark smiling giantress. Under this figure she
claims a monument in Cardiganshire called *Llech y Goures*
the stone of the Giantess. This was the persian prototype
of creation, the same as the single stone of Jacob to the
Deity; the God of nature. The other, that is *prostrate*
and which you think stood upright, was of *Proserpine,*
if it were upright, and in this case, synonimous to the
two stones of the *creative* and *destroying Deity*; but I
rather incline to think it always was a prostrate situation;
for I observed the earth excavated for the purpose and
the stone appeared to me not sufficiently in breadth to
compare with the *Meini Hirion* or the *Cromlech,* erect,
at 119 feet from the outward circle. In short, my dear
Sir, you will I am persuaded find *Stonehenge* to be the
Meini Ryvrival of the triads, *or the stone of the equalized
computation*; erected for solar and astrominacal purposes.
I ought rather (respecting the *single Bethyle*) to have
called it in the language of the triads, the *HIRVAEN
GWYDDOG, Ceres or the Giantess.* This stone is near the
Llech y Goures in Cardiganshire as above; a circular
erection. It is sixteen feet high three broad, and two thick.
Not far from it is a *Maen y Prenvol,* the stone of the
wooden Ark or chest. The *Llech y Goures* stands on
a rising ground in an open field as the *five stones* near
the *Rolrick Stones* in Oxfordshire, which you kindly
offered me your description of. All circular temples
had the same.

I have much to say on the celebrated barrow which
contained the *ebony bethyle* covered with *gold plate*
[presumably the famous Bush Barrow, Wilsford] as also
on the *Coelbreni* or *lots* of the antient britons found in
another barrow. In my next I will give you to a certainty
my reason, why I can safely refer *Stonehenge* to a date
of at least 1,000 years before the Christian era. I have
so much on the subject when I take up my pen that I
am sure you will excuse me for the present.

I go to work this week on the Sussex barrows—pray,
let me hear soon from you, and wishing you the great
blessing of better health. With kind compliments and
regards to your worthy family.

Dr Sir, Yours,   J. Douglas

(A friend is arrived and I finish in haste.)

P.S. It certainly is a most curious fact recorded in the
Gododin of Aneurin, that the britons were masacredd
by the Saxons at the *circus*? And the spot appointed
was in the presence of *TOR* in the *fair quadrangular area*
(the circus) of the great Sanctuary of the Dominion.
The meeting was on the first may at this spot were
temporary conveniences tents &c were erected. This
poem was written about 473 A.D. by Aneurin the bard
who had witnessed the horrid scene.

The *Gododin* also mentions the amber beads; and
Aneurin describes Hengistus as wearing a colar of them.
Pray favour me with your early letter, which I hope will
bring me better accounts of your health. Why was the
spot fixed where Stonehenge is situated in preference to
any other? There must have been a reason for this; or
why transport the stones 16 miles.

Dinas Emrys, or the ambrosial city is an appellation
common to similar erections as Stonehenge. Davies says,
the rocks on Snowdon had this name. Aurelius Ambrosius
received his name from Stonehenge. In the age of the
solar divinity of the britons, in this Dinas or Ambrosial
spot, were lodged by a son of *Beli,* or Child of the *Sun,*
the dragons. The destiny of Britanain was supposed to
depend upon the due concealment of the Mystery. Beli
was represented as the father of the brave Cassivellanus,
radiated with splender a title with that of *Prydian* to
express the *Helio-Arkite divinities* at Stonehenge. See
Welsh Archaeologia, v. II, p.g. 11. 65. 78.

Copy of a letter to the Revnd. Mr. Douglas [From William Cunnington].

Heytesbury 1810

Dear Sir,

Since I received your favor of 24th April I have spent a day and half at Stonehenge, chiefly with Sir R. Hoare—having just received your favor I made the men dig under the prostrate stone so as to examine it thoroughly, and I have now Sir R. Hoare, Mr. Crocker and an Irish Gentleman to attest the fact, that the aforesaid Stone was placed originally in an erect position—that part of the Stone which stood in the ground was rough, but those parts which were exposed were chipped like the others.—The hollow in which the Stone now lies was occasioned by digging often to see what was under.—In regard to the small upright stones within the oval, you must have misunderstood me—I never said they were circular, they are of the same form as the Trilithons viz of an egg form, but this idea does not in the least operate against your Hypothesis—but be pleased to remember that there is also a *circle* of *upright*—I think your opinions in regard to Stonehenge are very consistent, but I have not so high an opinion of the Welsh Triads as you appear to have—I think they have no authentic documents prior to the 4th or 5th Century.—I now copy a paper I wrote for Sir R. Hoare, from which you will better understand my Hypothesis [Not included.]

Arundel 26th Novr 1810

My dear Sir,

I am very much concerned indeed to hear of the continuance of your severe indisposition and I most sincerely hope you will soon experience a speedy restoration to health.

I have certainly been anxious to have some intelligence concerning my Wiltshire friends and your letter with one very shortly after from Sir R. Hoare have relieved that anxiety; who not having said any thing of his late indisposition inclines me to hope that his health is reestablished.

I am very much obliged to you for a perusal of your Northamptonshire Iter, with your account of fossil strata; the contemplation of which in all my travels, either at home or on the continent, I never neglected. I have certainly been much gratified with the system of Mr. Smith, into whose company I was invited during my residence in Suffolk, at the town of Eye, a few miles distant from my living of Kenton. He shewed me his map of England, with the designation of the fossil strata of each county; a valuable acquisition to geologic researches as founded on a correct survey, and establishing *matter of fact data*; but if I remember right, he told me that he did not enter on any system and only proposed to publish an account of the various fossil strata of our island. I differed from him on one of his assertions, respecting the deposition of our chalk hills on sarrenaceous strata; which in one instance near the sea he had I think unquestionably established; but I could not agree to its having been universally the case.

I have a pretty good engraving of the Rollrick stones which erection I consider in common with similar erections in various parts of this kingdom, to which one or more upright stones are connected, as temples of the particular principalities partitioned out to the british chieftains; who were at one particular period, united under one king and who upon national alarm or invasion, assembled perhaps at an annual convocation; and I should apprehend that many reasons can be given, that at one period Abury was the spot, and at some other distant period Stonehenge; I mean at a later period. The single detached stones I have always considered as a key to these structures, the prototypes of the deities to which the temple was raised; where ceremonies of inauguration religious and of convocation, were at stated periods established.

I have sent Sr Richd Hoare by his request some little detail of my barrow researches this summer, which perhaps on some occasion, he will show you; some few facts I have been enabled to establish although not successful in obtaining any valuable relics. One particular fact I think I may venture to adduce; which is, the erection of our large british barrows at a period antecedent to our fortified posts on these downs, similar to yours in Wiltshire &c which with some probability have been considered as Belgic.

An antiquary of considerable literary reputation has this summer been inspecting your celebrated temple; from whom I have received several sheets of recondite speculation and which I have been obliged to enter the lists against to refute his opinions. He had taken up the old Monkish fable of Geoffrey, ascribing the creation to Aurelius Ambrosius; which required no great labour to get rid of. I believe he is set at rest; for had he been encouraged, it was his intention to have given his critique a turn to a certain channel which I did not approve of.

With every sincere wish for your restoration to every mental resource or amusement, in your abstract pursuits from worldly transactions of greater moment, in which our social habits are more eminently centered and with my kind regards to Mrs. Cunnington and Miss Cunnington,

I remain sensible to your obliging good wishes, Dear Sir,

                    Yours truly,   J. Douglas.

16

SELECTION OF LETTERS TO
SIR RICHARD COLT HOARE, 1812-14

(Wiltshire County and Diocesan Archives, Trowbridge. Colt Hoare
Papers 383.907.)

Preston,
Brighton, 25th June 1812

Dear Sir Richard,

I have received your magnificent third Livraison from
Mr. Miller, the contents of which I consider as valuable
in the extreme, to the recondite study of our british
history. The plates are eminently beautiful, the objects
scattered with great taste and even to the cursory reader
I should not think they can fail of affording considerable
interest. I may possibly speak with a certain degree of
partiality from the harmony of mutual pursuit; but I am
convinced that the value of your work will shortly rise
beyond your expectations.

I consider your present, as doubly gratifying to my
feelings, valuable from the antiquarian treasure it contains
and coming from a gentleman for whom I shall always
entertain the highest regard and respect.

I think myself very ill treated by the author or rather
editor of the Quarterly. We were at a certain period of
life on intimate terms and I could mention certain serious
obligations he has been under to me. I sent him a long
answer to some of his unmannerly, inept, and puny

critiques on your ancient Wiltshire but I have received no answer from him. I can only account for this in this way: he is himself no antiquary: and were he to have shown my remarks to the learned Dr. I readily conceive he might possibly be averse to contend with argument; but I am convinced of one good which may possibly evene; when noticed by the Quarterly I think the learned Dr. will be more guarded in his jocularity.

The Duke of Norfolk and a friend of mine at Cuckfield have your work and as I am now frequently with gentlemen who are beginning to appreciate our curious researches, I shall use my endeavours to serve Mr. Miller; but they seem shy of the expence. You will now have an opportunity of sending a copy to the French institute, which I make no doubt you have already thought of; but this I earnestly recommend, as it will be the means of making it known on the continent, where I am certain, from the prevailing pursuit of similar researches it will be highly noticed.

I have been with a party, Col. 'Crips', the companion to Dr. Clarke the traveller, and several other dilitante friends, exploring some barrows near Rotten dean [Rottingdean]. They began earlier than I could attend, on a large flat british barrow without system; excavating trenches from the circumference to the center; without attacking the primary. Skeletons were discovered, and about two urns; distant after deposits; of more posterior shapes than the higher british; though of the friable pottery. These with numerous other facts convince me that comburation and inhumation prevailed at a contemporary era. The center I broke into; but time did not allow of a satisfactory ransack. This I must defer to some other day. We also opened a group of the lower british small bell fashioned barrows: a few only; urns of a similar pottery and shape of the one I sent you; with the calcined bones, small iron buckles and fragments of a brass *arferial* vessel, melted in part by an ardent fire. Similar facts I discovered in a group or groups of the same order, on Lavington hill on the down beyond

Petworth and on Bignor down. The weather has been against me just at the time I was setting off for the british intrenched hill at Poynings; where I intend breaking into a complete series of the british flat, bell and what Stukeley calls the Druid barrows (a term I do not like). These are situated a short distance from the vallum. I have attacked one of our cromlechs called the Goldstone: but my labours were blank at the time: I have not finished the research. I am fortunate in being able to get labourers always at command from the 10th Rl. HUZ [10th Royal Huzzars, to which he was Chaplain].

As you are about this time encamped at our celebrated Abury temple I anxiously expect your barrow explorations will afford the most interesting facts. I have three of the round rayed blue verditer beads of the highest period, which were once in the possession of Dr. Stukeley and mentioned in his Abury; from a barrow near the Hackpen hill, the head of the great Python, as the learned Dr. with much inginuity and I think with much colour of truth pronounces it. Most happy I should be were it possible to be of your party.

Congratulating you on the regular, expeditious and successful publication of your South Wiltshire and with the most sincere wish for the completion of your interesting labours and with every gratifying pleasure arising from them, I am, Dear Sir,

Your faithful and obedt Servant, James Douglas.

I have found the scattered remains of a very large stone cirque on our downs: [the site remains unidentified] and all the criteria of your Wiltshire Romanised british villages or posts. Samian pottery &c, &c, &c. See Gildas who speaking of his times, which must have been 90 years at least, says after the advent of the Saxons 'neither at this day, were the towns or cities of Britain inhabited, but entirely forsaken, overthrown and desolated'. The dwellings of the britons were at this time out of towns or cities. This may date about An: 500. Their desolate state lasted about 50 years. Gildas flourished An: 546. He says the Scots and Picts were the desolators and subjected the britons several years. I have some curious matters on this subject.

Preston Vicarage,
Brighton
17th Augt, 1813

Dear Sir,

On comparing the remains of the very earliest inhabitants of this island scattered over our Sussex downs, with those described in your Ancient Wiltshire, I find the greatest analogy; yet having met with some identies, which I have not noted in your County or in Dorsetshire, I am anxious to report them to you; conceiving their application may enable me to seperate them from our fortified camps, beacons or retreats, with their converging lines, as also from the large isolated tumuli in their neighbourhood. These identies are the Kistvaens on tumuli, dolmens and stone circques. The former I have, (from some convincing reasons I trust), classed with the first Belgic eruption. The latter to a far more early people; and on these I purpose very shortly to go to work. Many of these stone chests have been examined by my late friend Mr. Rooke of Woodhouse Notts; and described in the Archaeologia, as also in Borlase and other writers, but not to my satisfaction. Should you in the course of your present elaborate ancient survey of your county have encountered any of these very ancient vestigia, I should be greatly obliged for your information.

I have been employed on the etymon of the names of our County places; and though perfectly aware of the cautious ground I have to tread, lest the decoration of fancy should meander beyond the sober appeal, I feel gratified to a considerable degree, in the attempt of referring the names of our localities to the British Armoric or Cornish, it matters not which, for I find them applicable to the extended race of the most primitive languages.

Shall I give you the specimen in the name of our present gay watering place, which royalty is preparing to adorn with additional lustre.

Briththelmstone. Bryn-el-Towyn. Bryn. Brine, id.Brit. Hillock, Hill or Cliff, also Welsh or Celtic. *El/Ehal—Eal-Ail. Aigle.* see Borlase. Corn: Vocab: *High—Holy—sacred. El* or *Al* the solar God. [Hebrew: ? El] also [Hebrew: ? Elkin] Lux Matutina. *Towyn Tuya,* id. Brit. Burfy down, in Davies, *Gleba Cespes,* hence BRYN EL TOWYN. sacred promontary, on which the sacred stones are now existent, on the hill near the church; and from which the Saxon derived their appellation of *Burgh-helef-Stein* Helef —holy, sacred. *Est il vraisemblable?* If I do not trespass too much on your patience, just permit me to say that in looking over Aubrey's Misc: I find he has a very curious paper on the british names of places surrounding Stonehenge. It is worth your notice as I think you have him in your splendid library; and might I venture, if not too obtrusive, just to hint, your not passing over a thought of this in the names of places in your survey.

What with our splendid victories, the awful appearance of the approaching crash of warlike conflicts in the North, [Wellington at Vittoria: the Luddite Riots in Yorkshire] I find few persons here have a moments time to ponder on these retired chamber cogitations, especially on our great bustle for the second arrival of our magnificent Prince; and with this apprehension, I fear I must make some apology to you—for the volunteering of my antiquarian gossip; but pass all this. I have also the motive to make every kind enquiry after your health; at the same time wishing I had it once more in my power to visit one of the most beautiful places in this kingdom which the hospitable and polite reception of a Gentleman, has so forcibly left on my mind the most pleasing recollections of.

Dear Sir,

    Your very obedient humble Servant, James Douglas.

Brighton, 5th Novr 1813

Dear Sir,

For these several weeks I have been deprived of a comfortable moment to acknowledge the kind remembrances you favoured me with through the hand of your son Mr. Hoare . . . sent for to Town, to visit more than one bed of illness in my family in York Street [Lady Glode's house] and this under the greatest anxiety, where I staid about 10 days till our best hopes were revived. On my return to Preston Mrs. D was laid up with severe indisposition which turned to a fit of the gout; and this owing to the picturesque embellishment of a poor little vicarage garden in which my son and his mother presided over the tasteful hand of a gardner; transplanting of trees . . . This event brought my daughter Mrs. Tucker with my youngest son post haste to see the mother; who thank God is on her legs again and my family now jugged in a very comfortable house in Upper Rock gardens at Brighton, where I reside during the winter months owing to the uncomfortable dampness of our small vicarage house at Preston, beautiful in the fine season but absolutely not tenable in winter.

I am happy to inform you that Mr. Hoare is in excellent health and appears perfectly recovered from his most awful and perilous shipwreck on his intended excursion to the Isle of Wight . . . [The continuation of this interesting paragraph may be read on page 155.]

As to the miscellanies of Aubrey; my head must have been in a miscellaneous jumble. Hearnes Collectania ought to have come uppermost, where you will perceive a very curious tract on Stonehenge as to the etymology of places merely, in that neighbourhood. I regard not the critiques of our modern sceptical fogramites at the painstaking etymologist. Can there be a shadow of doubt, but that great light may be thrown on the modern names of places? Where local habitation and name may serve to explain and illustrate the higher periods of our british antiquities.

I think the cromlech deserves a more particular investigation; as certainly distinct from the central tolmin or obeliscal stone of the cirque; because it is most commonly affixed at a short distance from the cirques in a N.E. direction, like the Ceredwyn of the Triads at Stonehenge, and also at Rolrick and at many other cirques. The tolmen and kistvain I think are sufficiently explained or exemplified. The old british name of crumlech is not applied as I conceive to a crooked bending stone; but as a stone of adoration which Roland and Llwyd have ably illustrated; to which the bowing and adoration were paid on approaching the solar cirque; as sacred to the teme-mater, the british ceres, or ceredwyn; thus considered as the two great prototypes of creation. The sun as the great vivifier, the earth the great producer. It is the evene— Mascheith or Leviticus, or *lapidem insignem*; from [Hebrew: ? Shaklah] *incurvare,* to bow down or adore. The cromlech has been applied to several unhewn stones laid on each other, as so expressed in Haggai 2, ch: 15.2: and as Altar Stones; and also confounded with the *Lech-lever*; notwithstanding all this, I think with you that the spade and pick-axe are more likely to evince the assertion of the past *In apricum proferet olas,* than the most learned commentary and I trust your friend in wales will therefore bring to light as much information as Llwyd Roland and Borlase.have done for us. When your friend uses the spade and pick axe at the central stone perhaps it may be found sepulchral; but if he attacks the cromlech near the *Meini Gwyr* I think he will prove it to be templar.

May all things be propitious for the enthusiastic pleasure of meeting you, my Dear Sir at your head quarters at Malborough! [*sic*] I have armed myself with every thing I can rake up about our great Ophic temple. I have no theory to intrude and the longer I live the more I think with you, that fact alone is our best safeguard: yet I am still convinced that much very much is left undone, respecting our earliest memorials of british antiquities, which through the extended race of our first colonizers may be brought home to a much purer fountain than has been dreamed

of by our antiquaries, even the best of them; and with
all due deference even without any assistance from their
druidical authorities; which are very often too laughable
for common sense to repose upon.

Before I conclude suffer me to congratulate you on
your opinion of etymon. Your splendid library is stored
with celtic dictionaries &c, which on reference for the
names of modern localities will amply repay with increased
pleasure the time bestowed on the research. If you should
have an opportunity of seeing Mr. Coxe, I beg my kind
remembrance may be acceptable; and should my residence
here be in any way compatible with any commission you
wish to forward I beg you will consider me truly at
your service.

Mr. Hoare informed me you have been indisposed with
a rheumatic complaint which I shall be happy to hear is
removed and I am, Dear Sir,

                                 Yours truly, J. Douglas.

                                      Preston, 11th Augt 1814

Dear Sir,

I am very much obliged to you for your interesting
communication. Your evidence appears very satisfactory
to confirm your opinion on the comparative date of the
barrows at Abury . . . [The remainder of this personal
paragraph may be read on page 157.]

I do not pretend to be an Oedipus, but under the
indulgent auspices of your spade and pick axe, your
plans, your local surveys &c, &c, I think I should have
boldly dared to have entered the Cretan labyrinth of the
two mysterious temples; Abury and Stonehenge. I have
hoarded up several, indeed a budjet of *perhap's* and
conjectures to approach their awful precincts with all
due humility; which after all may be another 'fool's
bolt' shot at a venture. You certainly have taken a
wiser part in your incontrovertable collectanea of the de
rebus: for without your stubborn facts no clue to get

honourably out of the labyrinth will be possible. Something however has been done to purify the Augean rubbish
of some former antiquaries; and had I but the *loco motive*
power I certainly should shut my eyes against a rash
adventure.

I think we have three most strong presumable facts
in what we have been enabled to rake up, for an Abury
and Stonehenge history. To do this with a powerful
bravado at the stout fastidious criticism of the present
day, much involved enquiry is required to frame complete
and honest and clear deductions; but the course I
should pursue would be to inverse the positions of our
former antiquaries; by setting out with those facts we
do know from our more modern authorities, down to
the period of evanescent history; then I think our
presumable materials can be martialled and something
more atchieved than passive timidity may apprehend.
Certain periods we have obtained by the spade and
pick axe; analogous temples though on such stupendous
specimens, can be ascertained to elicit some meaning.
Religious customs can be inferred, and when we can
palpably ascertain, that the british chieftains, even by
their names, were at the head of the priesthood, as
was the case with most other nations, the religious and
conventual history may be with much safety combined.
This I can explain by a gold coin of Dyfnwal or Dunwallo
mulmietiano; which is in my possession and which I
send you a rough pen scratch of, from the object before
me. [It is of Dubnovellaunos, Essex type. Mr. Derek Allen
kindly tells me that the coin is without doubt one of the
specimens in the Ashmolean Museum, Oxford and that
his guess is that it was found at Colchester and not at
Dorchester, Oxon. as Evans thought.] The sacred gloins
on this coin show *perhaps* the number of temples he
presided at. They are *perhaps* the Stonehenge and Aburies
in miniature.

*Very thick gold. Roman letters from the foundation of
Rome were common through Europe.*

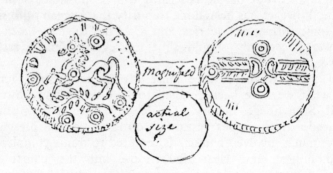

*Reverse the regal wreathe with the half moon and the
sacred gloins. I saw another coin of Dunwallo with his
name written out. from the same spot. The inscription
of mine is imperfect.*

At all events here is some thing which we can mount
upon. My favourite hobby horse. Sacred to Apollo—to
Bel—the ear of Corn to Ceres. The temple to the Sun the
upright stone beyond the circle at Stonehenge to Ceres.
The Adytum we have settled, I mean, the sanctuary stone
for Hugh. Mr. Coxe may remember I pointed out the
upright stone as the chief index to the temple of the
Cerydwin. I think we may also shoot a bolt at the
granite stones; but pray excuse a little levity to relieve
a very obscure subject. I had drawn out a long list of
names in the neighbourhood of Stone-henge which may
apply to the temple. Haradan hill—orthog: *heredun*, has
been conjectured as a belgic word, signifying the hill of
refuge for the Belgae. These were the Salic, hence
Salisburghen plain. Saxon prefix. *Rustisale—martinsale,*
from the salic also Lupale. *Mein Gaur* or *Manyng.*
Giants great stones; hence the *Manyng fords,* where
fords are at these villages. The proper name of Avon is
Manyng; the course of the river pointing to these stones.
This is a proof the britons who gave these names had lost
all knowledge of the erectors of Stonehenge and a strong

proof they existed above 100 years before Cæsar's advent: hence also *Manton* near Marlborough, from 3 large broadstones in a circular form—? are they now cognisable. ? at Seven *barroweshill* 4 miles west of Marlborough near the London road are the 40 prostrate large stones, inclosing an inner circle of 16 great stones; are any remains of these still visible? Barrows are near them. Wilton, anciently called *Llandune Ellandune,* i.e. Temple down; thus if Wilton took its name from the Temple, then the name of the county and the other Wills near Stonehenge, *Willebourne, Willfal, Williford.* Wilcot on the rivers near the Temple. If the temple was consecrated to the goddess of victory, *Andraste, Anraith* or *Andates*— supposed from *rhaid* brit. for spear one of the brass spears. vid: barrows. The name will then be retained in some proximate villages. *Androsh Lunsdon, Calling-burn Andros.* In Yarnsburie camp or vallum. *Anraithsbury*: in the *Ansties*—in Andover, *Andufur,* in the hundred of *Andeverly.* 10 *Wills* and 14 *Ans* in the vicinity, all referable to the Temple. Wills from Elil Temple—Temple to the sun Ela-or Bel consecrated to a victory and then the *Ans* from *Andrathe.* Old Badonicus Gildas, says something about the *Torvis vultibus.* May this refer to the Bull worship of the Cimri? vid: *Bulford*—the two *Blunsdons* —*Bullans downs,* i.e. Bulls Temple down—see *Willfal perhaps* orthog: Bullfal, i.e. *Bull Devil.* The *Torvis* vultibus —*nee enumerans patrice portenta ipsa diabolica—lineamen-tis adhunc deformibus.* May all this be applied to Stone-henge in the *lower british* ages? To the sites of Bachus— to the [?] tic Bruma—commemorate symbols and with *Triad* assistance, might we be permitted or indulged with a few excursions in the Labyrinth.

There is nothing here but what you can find in your library. Apropos—I trust you have a collection of the local names round Abury, for an application to your Celtic dictionary; a fine copy in your possession.

I make no doubt but you are on the eve of your exploratory tour to the Carnac in Bretaigne—where I make no doubt you will find plenty of barrow groupes sur-

rounding the dilapidated temple in strict analogy with
many of ours. I have a M.S. of Lord Winchelsea [*sic*]
who says in his time one side of the stone avenue to the
Hack-penill was remaining and most of the snakes head
on the hill. Hac-pen. brit: snake-head. ? *Beacon Hills.*
Cantock hill called Quantock—from Cangi-tock. Caves of
the Cangi in Somerset: you see there will be no end to
this—but pray do not forget the names of places round
Abury. Excuse all this ramble which I am unloading
from my disappointment—but I trust the time will still
arrive when I shall be able to visit the most ancient record;
of a powerful people who honoured this Island with their
magnificent memorials.

I think your british villages, may be elucidated by the
Saxon invasions, when the britons were driven to hills
and caves, as *Old Bede* reporteth. I mean the romanised
britons. They are scattered over our Sussex downs. You
will confer a favour by saying if you have met with any
of my small barrows in groupes on your downs; which
contain spear heads & swords of iron and umbones; in the
graves of women beads &c. Mr. Wyndham has some on
his grounds. Grose sent me a drawing of a spear and umbo
found there and an iron sword.

Wishing you a pleasant tour to Carnac, from whence I
make no doubt you will draw some real treasures to
illustrate our British antiquities and with my best regards
to your diletanti circle, I am, Dear Sir,

Your faithful and sincere servant,   J. Douglas

PLATES

3.

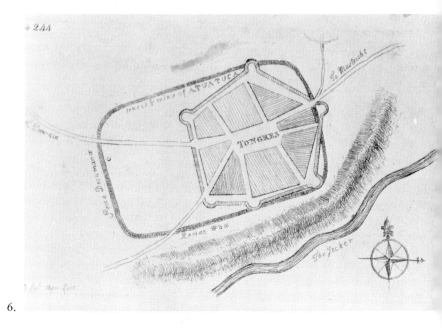

6.

7.

9.

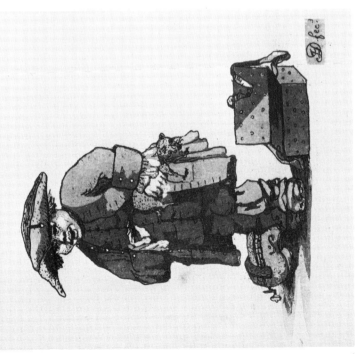

8.

10.

12.

13.

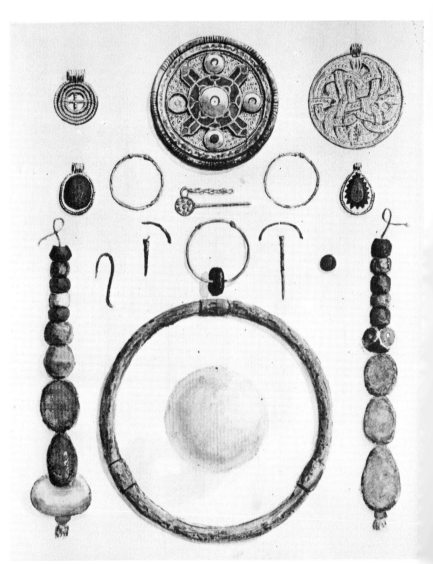

14.

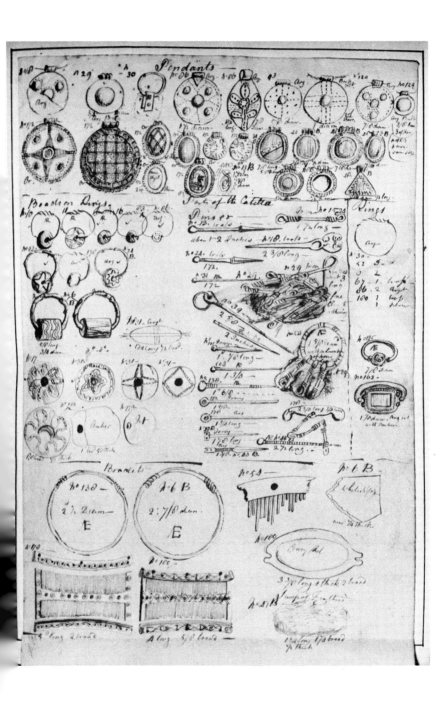

Pendants

Breast or Rings.

Parts of the Caletta

Rings

Bracelets

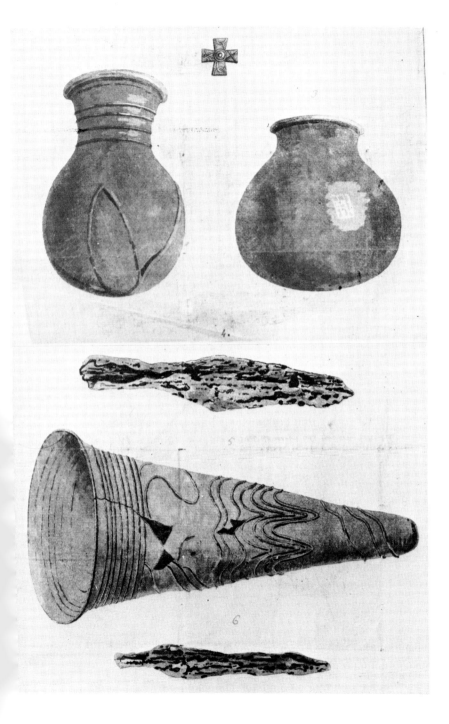

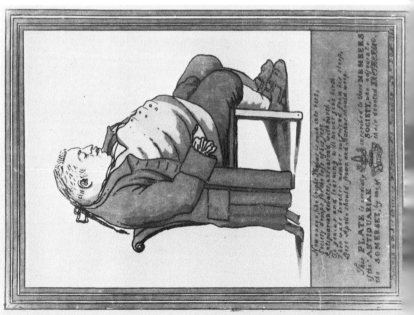

The PLATE is inscribed to those MEMBERS of the ANTIQUARIAN SOCIETY who are the SOMERSET, by one of their devoted BRETHREN

21.

23.

BARR.ws at St Margaret's in the CLIFFY near DOVER.

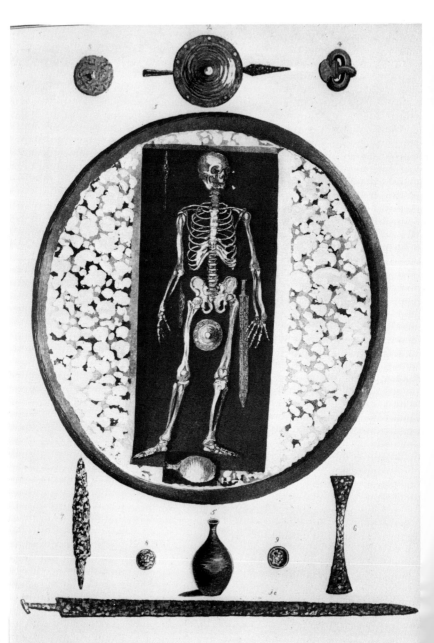

25.

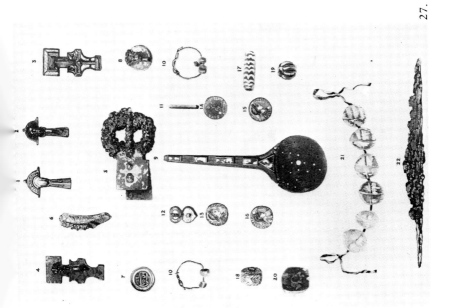

27.

26.

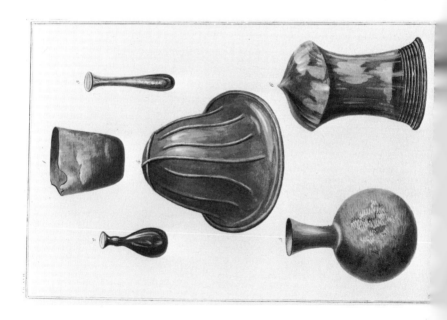

31.

32.

PRESTON near Brighthelmton

33.

DIAMETEROFTHE
N°1 LITTLE XIII
II. MEDIVM XXIII
III. GREAT XXXII

ID. MDCCXCI

34.

M · S

IACOBI · DOVGLAS · A · M ·

CVIVS · IN · NÆNIA · BRITANNICA ·

QVÆCVNQVE · AD · PRISCORVM · BRITANNIÆ · INCOLARVM ·
SEPVLTVRAM · PERTINENT · DOCTISSIME · EXPLICANTVR ·
OBIIT · V · NOVEMB · A · D · M · D · CCC · XIX · ÆT · LXVII ·

ALIORVM · SEPVLCRA · HAVD · SINE · REVERENTIA · EXTVRBAVIT ·
IN · SVO · PLACIDE · QVIESCAT ·

NOTES ON THE PLATES

1. Portrait of James Douglas by T. Phillips (1770-1845), R.A., F.S.A. Copyright Department of Antiquities, Ashmolean Museum, Oxford.

2. '*Les chongs clotiers*', the five towers of the Cathedral of Notre Dame, Tournai, the finest in Belgium. These Romanesque and Gothic towers with their pyramid spires rebuilt in the 16th century are a far-seen feature of the Tournais landscape and were often dramatised in Tournaisien folk-lore. Copyright A.C.L., Brussels.

3. Procession de la Peste, Tournai, September 1968.

(*above*) Châsse de Saint Eleuthère (1247) escorted by ecclesiastics.

(*below*) Châsse des Damoiseaux (1571-2) escorted by leading members of the legal profession passing the church of St. Brice, a 12th-century foundation rebuilt in 13th century Transitional style. It was in the destruction of a house adjoining this church in 1653 that the tomb of Childeric, King of the Franks (d. 481) was discovered. The magnificent Royal treasures then disclosed and moved to Paris in 1664 were well-known to Douglas. Both Shrines are in the Treasury of the Cathedral at Tournai.

Photograph *Nord Eclair*, Tournai.

4. Sand-pit at Ash, Kent, 1773, 1783.

This is perhaps the earliest published excavation section diagram in British archaeology. Douglas first visited

the pit in 1773, probably on his way to Dover to join a
boat for Flanders, and from children searching in the pit
obtained several glass beads which he gave to Sir Ashton
Lever for his Museum. He also recognised the 'Saxon'
character of the many iron weapons collected by the
local miller. Later he often visited the site, realised the
significance of the collections of local antiquaries Boys,
Faussett and Jacob from the same place and lamented
that the greater part of gold and silver relics had been
melted down for commercial use.

This vignette of 7 May 1783, the original in a fine
brown wash, shows the site after many years of sand-
digging. *A* represents the natural ground level, a ploughed
field. *B* is the general level of discoveries in graves about
four feet below ground level and shown in the pit by
marks of 'a factitious earth in the natural sand', again a
novel development of observation in field archaeology.
C and *D* are the windmills between which he carefully
excavated a richly-furnished barrow notable for its necklace of amber, crystal, amethyst, paste and brilliantly
coloured glass beads, a fine Kentish style brooch of
which he analysed the solder, iron work with impressions
of coarse cloth and a bulbous pot at the foot of the
skeleton. All are described in detail. *E* and *F* denote the
interior and entrance of the pit. The whole is a most
remarkable early archaeological record.

Nenia Britannica, 1793, 25-6, 35, plate 9 and head-piece
to p. 25. Original drawing in the British Museum MS. G.
6863.

5. (*above*) Chatham Dockyard and its Environs from
Fort Pitt. The site of part of Douglas's excavation is on
the extreme right hand of the picture.

After a drawing by G. Shepherd, c. 1828.

(*below*) The Great Lines, Chatham from Rochester
Castle Keep, 1973. The Naval War Memorial is on the
skyline immediately to the left of the Cathedral tower
and many of Douglas's excavations were close to the site
of the future Memorial. The fossil bones of extinct animals

described in the *Dissertation on the Antiquity of the Earth* were found in 1773 near the river bank of an area now covered by buildings seen to the right of the Cathedral tower. Douglas's house in College Yard was below the west front of the Cathedral, just out of the photograph, as is the still standing College Gate entrance to the Precincts.

Photograph by Leonard Hill, Rochester, 1973.

6. Plan of the Roman station of *Atuatuca* drawn by Douglas in 1773. From Douglas's *Travelling Anecdotes* . . . (1782). It makes an interesting comparison with Dr. M. E. Mariën's plan in his book *Par la Chaussée Brunehaut*, Brussels, 1968.

7. *Ruins of Atuatuca*, 1773. From *Travelling Anecdotes* . . . (1782).

This drawing by Douglas again makes an interesting comparison with what can now be seen from the foot-paths on the north-western outskirts of the Roman settlement with the first-century walls and later additions. Further sections which may have been observed by Douglas can be visited underground close to the entrance of the Basilica: see Plates 11 and 12.

8. A Swiss Boy. *Travelling Anecdotes* . . . (1782).

9. Monsieur Varelst. *Travelling Anecdotes* . . . (1782).

10. The two large Roman barrows at Koninksem seen by Douglas in 1773 and described in *Travelling Anecdotes* . . . (1782).

Photograph by Dr. H. Roosens, 1972.

See also 'Roman Barrows' by G. C. Dunning and R. F. Jessup, *Antiquity*, X, March 1936, p. 37.

11. (*above*) Section of Roman walling at Tongres: the earliest stone walling beside the site of a Romano-Celtic type of temple dedicated perhaps to Mercury or Jupiter, excavated recently by Professor J. Mertens.

Photograph by Professor J. Mertens.

(*below*) A section of the Roman town rampart at Tongres, weathered, and robbed of much of its material

by later builders. It was here that Douglas took his evening walks with the Abbé van Muyssen. A public foot-path now runs along part of its course. 'Le rempart romain de Tongres. *Ne pereant ruinae . . .*' as Dr. Roosens has reminded us in his forthright paper 'Préservation de sites archéologiques en Belgique' in *Helinium*, XIII (1973), p. 1, and *Archaeologia Belgica*, 149 (1973). Many of the sites he mentions were known to Douglas.

Photograph copyright Service national des Fouilles, Brussels.

12. Tongres, Basilica of *Onze Leive Vrouw* with its impressive 15th-century west tower, and the statue of Ambiorix, chief of the Eburones who offered strong resistance to Cæsar, erected in the Market Place in 1866 on a mock megalith. Both are prominent features of this ancient town of the Hesbaye. Part of the Roman wall may be seen underground near the Basilica entrance.

Copyright A.C.L., Brussels.

13. Piringen, near Tongres. Roman barrow near the Roman road from Tongres to Borgloon, near Betho, excavated by Douglas and the Abbé Van Muyssen, 1772. The Roman aqueduct, the 'Beukenberg', its course now lined with beech trees can be seen in the background.

Copyright A.C.L., Brussels.

14. Antiquities excavated at Chartham, Kent, by Cromwell Mortimer in 1730. Coloured drawing by Henry Godfrey Faussett in Bryan Faussett's original MS *Inventorium Sepulchrale*, Vol. VI, folio 50.

Courtesy of Liverpool City Museums.

15. Anglo-Saxon antiquities from East Kent, the jewellery from Sibertswold and Barfreston. Pencil and ink drawings almost certainly by Douglas from items in the Faussett Collection, but possibly by Henry Godfrey Faussett for use by Douglas. Most of the items can be identified in C. Roach Smith's edition of *Inventorium Sepulchrale* (1856). Society of Antiquaries MS. 723, folio 25 by courtesy of the Society: copyright Society of Antiquaries.

16. The Faussett Pavilion in the Garden at Heppington in 1950 shortly before its destruction. Bryan Faussett's learned Latin descriptions (1769-1775) of the remaining antiquities can be seen, together with the inscription in gable inserted by Henry Godfrey Faussett to the memory of his father.

Photograph by Ronald Jessup.

17. Proof pull of the future Plate XVI of *Nenia Britannica (1793).*

The letter from Douglas to Henry Godfrey Faussett dated 11 October 1787 is written on the reverse. Society of Antiquaries MS. 723, folio 71 by courtesy of the Society: copyright Society of Antiquaries.

18. Douglas's portrait of Francis Grose, 1785. It is described in Grose's obituary in the *Gentleman's Magazine,* 61(1791), p. 493 as 'by a well known gentleman-artist'.

19. Coston church, Leicestershire, by James Douglas, 1791. From John Nichols, *History and Antiquities of the County of Leicester,* Vol. 11 (1795), plate XXXIV. 'The Revd James Douglas, M.A. [*sic*] F.S.A. contributes this Plate.'

20. (*above*) Roman ceremonial bronze axe in the form of a bull, found near Canterbury. Length 9 cm. Weight 260.3 gms. Douglas Collection, Ashmolean Museum, Oxford.

Copyright Department of Antiquities, Ashmolean Museum, Oxford.

(*below*) Roman ceremonial axe in the form of a bull, provenance unknown. Length 7.3 cm. Weight 135.91 gms. Towneley Collection, British Museum.

By courtesy of the Trustees of the British Museum, copyright reserved.

21. (*above*) Chiddingfold, Surrey; the Old Parsonage, now the Glebe House, Douglas's home for some 14 years, It was here that he wrote the greater part of *Nenia.*

Copyright R.C.H.M. (England) by courtesy of Cecil H. J. Farthing, F.S.A.

(*below*) The house from the milestone on the London Road.

Photograph by Ronald Jessup.

22. View of Richborough Castle from the Amphitheatre, and of the Isle of Thanet drawn by Douglas, 1787. J. Nichols, *Bibliotheca Topographica Britannica* (1780-90), Vol. I, Plate VIII, p. 490.

23. (*above*) Fine water colour drawing of barrows in Greenwich Park, Kent, opened by Douglas in 1784, with the Observatory on the hill-top beyond. Douglas must be the figure taking notes. Extra illustration facing folio 89 in Douglas's own copy of *Nenia Britannica* (1793).

British Museum MS. G. 6863.

By courtesy of the Trustees of the British Museum, copyright reserved.

(*below*) Greenwich Park: the site of some of Douglas's explorations on the hill-side below the Observatory. Indication of barrows excavated and subsequently levelled during improvements to the Park are still visible. The historical coincidence that this land was once part of the Kentish possessions of the Abbey of St. Pierre on Mont Blondin in his beloved Ghent would have pleased Douglas greatly.

Photograph by Dr. C. W. T. Shuttleworth, 1973.

24. (*above*) Fine water colour drawing 'Barrows at St. Margaret's on the Cliff near Dover'. They were opened by Douglas in 1782, and again he may have drawn himself as the supervisor. Extra illustration as plate XXV in British Museum MS. G. 6863. The figures do not appear in the finished plate XXV in *Nenia Britannica*.

(*below*) Facsimile entry made by Douglas from his copy of Lord Winchilsea's common-place book noting discoveries at Boughton Alough (Boughton Aluph) Kent in 1720. This is one of the earliest of British archaeological field note-books. Extra illustrations in British Museum MS. G. 6863 as above. Modifications were made before its use in *Nenia Britannica*, plate XXV.

Both by courtesy of the Trustees of the British Museum, copyright reserved.

25. Plan of Tumulus I on Chatham Lines opened by Douglas in September 1779, the first illustration of its kind in British archaeology, with drawings of the relics. *Nenia Britannica* (1793), Plate I.

26. Contents of Tumulus II on Chatham Lines opened by Douglas in September 1779. *Nenia Britannica* (1793), p. 5 and Plate II.

27. The contents of Tumulus II on Chatham Lines (without the coins) preserved in the Douglas Collection, Ashmolean Museum.

Copyright Department of Antiquities, Ashmolean Museum, Oxford.

28. Douglas's fine original water-colour drawings of glass vessels, 1, 2, 3 and 5 from Roman cremation urns with ashes, Kent: 4 Minster churchyard, Kent, 1786: 6 Woodnesborough near Sandwich, Kent.

British Museum MS. G. 6863 as plate XVII facing folio 70. Cf. *Nenia Britannica* (1793), Plate XVII, pp. 70-1 which shows some differences from the original drawing.

By courtesy of the Trustees of the British Museum, copyright reserved.

29. Roman pottery and glass from Tongres and district, one of many signed original drawings sent to Douglas by the Abbé Van Muyssen. Lettering and scale added by Douglas. British Museum MS. G. 6863 folio 146d. Douglas's version of the drawings is on folio 146c and this he used as his plate XXXI, p. 147 in *Nenia Britannica* (1793).

By courtesy of the Trustees of the British Museum, copyright reserved.

30. (*above*) Van Muyssen's signed colour drawing of a fine samian bowl (Dragendorff Form 37) found at Offulkin near Tongres. British Museum MS. G. 6863 folio 146a. 'Fig 2' is added by Douglas.

By courtesy of the Trustees of the British Museum, copyright reserved.

(*below*) The bowl redrawn by Douglas and used by him as plate XXX and noted on pp. 146-7 in *Nenia Britannica* (1793). The three pieces of samian ware below were collected by Douglas from near Castle Field, Manchester, when he was very young and may have been the first pieces in his collection.

31. 'Group of Barrows, South of Stone Henge.' A fine water colour by Philip Crocker, Colt Hoare's draughtsman and surveyor, c. 1806. The onlookers are Cunnington and Colt Hoare; Douglas visited the site for some days in 1809.

Courtesy of Wiltshire Archaeological and Natural History Society, Devizes Museum and F. K. Annable, F.S.A.

32. The Goldstone, Hove Park, Sussex, a modern historical megalith.

Photograph by Edward Reeves, Lewes.

33. 'Preston near Brighthelmston', sepia water colour by James Lambert, 1763. The church, farm buildings and the tree-flowered vicarage can be seen.

Courtesy of N. E. S. Norris, F.S.A.

34. (*above*) 'Kitts Cotty House near Aylesford, Kent' after a drawing by G. Shepherd, c. 1828. This well-known monument was described by Lambarde in 1570 and drawn by Stukeley in 1722. The disturbances in the foreground may be in part the result of Douglas's digging in 1783; he could find no trace of a sepulchre but noted from the appearance of the soil that the place had been previously explored. The stones, he correctly observed, had been taken from the adjacent land where many were still to be seen. 'They were of reddish brown grit, and in their natural gibbous state'—no bad description of sarsen stones. In a footnote to pp. 180-1 of *Nenia* he adds details of 'another Cromlech nearby', clearly Lower Kits Coty or the Countless Stones, which had been thrown down by a farmer for road-stone.

(*below*) Fine water colour by Douglas of a labourer

digging at Kits Coty, presumably c. 1783. British Museum MS. G. 6863, plate XXIV used as a decoration to a plan of Chartham Downs in the part of *Nenia* published in 1791.

By courtesy of the Trustees of the British Museum, copyright reserved.

35. (*above*) A piece of 'fine red coraline ware, foliage of of the same' found near Tongres and given to Douglas by the Abbé Van Muyssen. It is wrongly noted under item 259 in Duncan's Catalogue of Antiquities in the Ashmolean Museum (1836) and is in fact Plate XXXII, No. 1, 7 of *Nenia* and a drawing of it by Van Muyssen is in the British Museum Grenville copy of *Nenia*. It is the well-known form 36 with leaves in barbotine on a curved rim and although Douglas goes on to quote the potters' stamps from Tongres and other items in Van Muyssen's collection, he does not specifically refer to this pottery as samian as he does elsewhere.

Copyright Department of Antiquities, Ashmolean Museum, Oxford.

(*below*) Douglas's tortoiseshell snuff-box, the lid inlaid with a small brass of Constantine which, according to Duncan's Catalogue, item 179, was found in a barrow.

Copyright Department of Antiquities, Ashmolean Museum, Oxford.

36. Memorial inscription to James Douglas erected in the church of St. Peter, Preston, Brighton by Charles Townsend, a later curate, who was also an antiquarian and a friend of the 3rd Lord Egremont.

Photograph by Edward Reeves, Lewes, by courtesy of N. E. S. Norris, F.S.A.

18

BIBLIOGRAPHY

1   Works by James Douglas

1781. *A general essay on Tactics.* Translated from the French of J. A. H. Guibert by an Officer [Lieutenant Douglas].
2 vols. (London).

1782. *Travelling Anecdotes, through various parts of Europe.*
In 2 vols. Vol. I [all published] (T. Fisher, Rochester).
2nd ed., by J. D. (London, 1785).
3rd ed., by James Douglas (London, 1786).
4th ed., Preface signed James Douglas (Dublin, 1787).

1785. Engraved portrait of Francis Grose, F.S.A., with verse and decoration. (London, W. Stores, 3 Piccadilly.)

A Dissertation on the Antiquity of the Earth. (London, with reversal of date at end of Dedication to read 1758.)

Based on a paper read to the Royal Society 'Dissertation on some animal and testaceous Petrefections with some Inferences on the Cosmography of our Globe.' *Royal Society Minute Books,* 12 May 1785.

Two Dissertations on the Brass Instruments called Celts, found near Canterbury, and other Arms of the Antients found in this Island.

In J. Nichols, *Bibliotheca Topographica Britannica*, Vol. 1 (London), No. 7. Paper No. 33.
Based on a Communication to the Society of Antiquaries, *Minute Books*, 17 June 1784. Notes and draft of paper in *Society of Antiquaries MS. 723*, 40-2 with illustrations.

1787. *On the Urbs Rutupiae of Ptolemy, and the Linden-Pic of the Saxons.*
In J. Nichols, *Bibliotheca Topographica Britannica*, Vol. 1 (London), No. 7, Paper No. 42. Douglas drew the fine view of Richborough Castle from the Amphitheatre and of the Isle of Thanet, Plate VIII.
Part of the paper had been communicated to the Society of Antiquaries, *Minute Book*, 21 November 1782.

1790. See 1797.

1792. *Twelve Discourses on the Influence of the Christian Religion on Civil Society.*
The author is described as 'F.A.S., of St. Peter's College, Cambridge and Chaplain in Ordinary to H.R.H. the Prince of Wales'.

1793. *Nenia Britannica or, A Sepulchral History of Great Britain from the earliest period to its General Conversion to Christianity . . .*
(London) in parts, 1786-93. Final part, 1793. See also **Manuscripts**, British Museum.

1795. J. Nichols, *The History and Antiquities of the County of Leicester* (London), Vol. II, part I, plate XXXIV. The exterior of Coston church by James Douglas and an illustration of a fossil oyster, 21 September 1791. 'The Revd James Douglas M.A. [*sic*] F.S.A. contributes this Plate.'

1797. *The History of Julia d'Haumont; or the eventful connection of the House of Montmelian with that of D'Haumont.*
2 vols. (London).

The author is mis-stated as of Chiddington, Sussex. In 1790 he told H. G. Faussett that he had published two small three-volume novels, *Fashionable Infidelity* and *The Maid of Kent.* (See p. 121 for a note on the latter book.)

1818. The ancient barrows observable on the South Downs near Brighthelmstone.
The Provincial Magazine (Lewes), Vol. I, page 1.

Discovery of a Roman villa in the parish of Bletchington.
The Provincial Magazine (Lewes), Vol. I, page 115.

Both were reprinted as *The Gleaner's Portfolio* . . . (Lewes), 1819.

Roman remains near Blatchington.
Gentleman's Magazine, No. 88, Aug. 1818, page 107.

---

2 Communications to the Society of Antiquaries

1782. (21 November). Roman remains found in constructing the Redoubt on Chatham Lines with details and speculations concerning the *Comes Littoris Saxonici.*

1783. (20 March). Exhibited drawings of antiquities from barrows opened under his inspection.

1784. (17 June). Exhibited some singular celts and drawings of others. The Secretary's summary fills seven pages of the large Minute Book. Withdrawn for separate publication: see under 1785 above.

1785. (27 January). Exhibited a Roman sword and Roman remains from Kingsholm near Gloucester (*Archaeologia*, Vol. 7, 1785, p. 376; *Nenia Britannica*, 1793, Plate 26, p. 133; P. D. Duncan, *Catalogue of the Ashmolean Museum*, 1836, Douglas Collection No. 249).

On a Manuscript formerly in the possession of Lord Winchilsea (*Arch.*, Vol. 7, 1785, p. 377).

1785. (7 April). A Letter on the Gypsy language. (*Arch.*, Vol. 7, 1785, p. 387.)

— (16 June). Exhibited a silver penannular brooch found near Penrith. Note in the margin of the Minute Book by the Society's Secretary 'Supposed to be a Broach'. Describes Douglas wrongly as a Doctor of Divinity.

1789. (15 January). Letter on Roman antiquities from a barrow near the Dane John Hill, Canterbury, examined by him in 1783 with description of the pottery, recognition of the site of the ustrinum on the natural undisturbed soil under the barrow, and discussion of the ritual significance of a cock's leg with spur from the burial deposit.

1790. (21 January). Exhibited two amulets, one said to be worn by Queen Elizabeth, the other by Mary, Queen of Scots.

---

3   Manuscripts

British Museum. G. 6863. Douglas's own hand-coloured copy of *Nenia Britannica* with many unpublished illustrations and manuscript additions by the author.

Additional MS. 19097. Collections for a parochial history of Suffolk [by D. E. Davy] undated, but c. 1838. See under 'Kenton' where there is much information about James Douglas.

Ashmolean Museum, Oxford. Department of Antiquities.

Manuscript list of Various Property left by the late

Revd. James Douglas—Author of the Naenia Britannica now in the care of Mr. P. Hoare at Brighton. [c. 1820.]

Bodleian Library, Oxford. MS. Num. d. 3, 9-12. List of the Douglas-Colt Hoare coin collection [c. 1819-20.]

Peterhouse, Cambridge. Admission Book, 22 October 1777.

Society of Antiquaries of London.
Minute Books.
MS. 723 'Douglas and Faussett on Kentish Antiquities'. Contains letters from Douglas to H. G. Faussett, 1781-94, chiefly concerning the progress of *Nenia Britannica,* letters, notes and drawings by Bryan Faussett and his son Henry Godfrey Faussett, many other miscellaneous notes on antiquarian discoveries in Britain, and incomplete notes and drafts of papers of Douglas.

File of 18th-century letters. Letters from Douglas to Hayman Rooke, 1784, 1787.

The Hayman Rooke Correspondence.

Historical Manuscripts Commission, Public Record Office.
W.O. 25/93. Commissions, 1778-81, Independent Corps, Sheerness, James Douglas, Ensign, 22 October 1779.

W.O. 65/29. Army List, 1779. Ind. Comp. of Invalids at Dover. James Douglas as Ensign, 22 October 1779, or as Lieutenant, 2 November [the entry has been subsequently altered].

Hampshire Record Office, The Castle, Winchester.
Ordination papers of James Douglas with details of his places of residence and ecclesiastical career.

Register of Ordination to priesthood by Bishop of Winchester, 4 March 1787, in whose Diocese Chiddingfold was then situated. Nominated by the Rector.

Ipswich and East Suffolk Record Office, Ipswich.

4 December 1813 and 19 January 1818 Licences to James Douglas to be absent from his benefice at Kenton, Suffolk, owing to its small value and the fact that he is also stipendary curate of Preston-cum-Hove, Sussex.

Lincolnshire Archives Committee, Lincoln.

Bishop of Lincoln's Register, 39, p. 393. Thomas Thurlow, Bishop of Lincoln and Master of the Temple ordained James Douglas as deacon at the Temple church, 16 March 1783.

Manchester Grammar School.

Admission Register, 5 August 1765. James, son of John Douglas, innkeeper of London, Middlesex.

Norfolk and Norwich Record Office, Norwich.

Consignation Book, Bishops Visitation to Kenton, Suffolk, in the Diocese of Norwich, 1806, VSC/15. Record of James Douglas's ecclesiastical career.

Petworth House Manuscripts.

MS. 101. Letters 1803-8 from James Douglas to the 3rd Lord Egremont, to his agent and man-of-law, to the tenant and the farmer at Middleton, Sussex.

Mr. Eric Vasmer.

Deeds and documents mainly of the 18th and 19th centuries relation to properties at Caldecote Hill, etc., Aldenham and Bushey, Herts. Private collection, not catalogued.

Westminster Public Library, Archives and Local History Collection, Buckingham Palace Road, S.W.1.

St. George, Hanover Square, Outer Ward, Rate Books.

MS. Foster, D., *Inns, Taverns* . . . *in and around London,* Vol. 34 (? 1900), p. 49-54.

Wiltshire County Record Office, Trowbridge.

Stourhead Archive 383.907. Letters from James Douglas to William Cunnington, 1809-10, and to Sir Richard Colt Hoare, 1812-14.

---

4   General Bibliography

Nils Åberg, *The Anglo-Saxons in England* (Uppsala, Sweden, 1926).

J. Y. Akerman, *Remains of Pagan Saxondom* (1855).

F. K. Annable and D. D. A. Simpson, *Neolithic and Bronze Age Antiquities in Devizes Museum* (Devizes, Wilts., Museum, 1964).

Paul Ashbee, *The Bronze Age Round Barrow in Britain* (1960), *The Earthen Long Barrow in Britain* (1970).

R. J. C. Atkinson, *Stonehenge* (Pelican ed., 1960).

George Baker, *History and Antiquities of Northampton,* Vol. 1 (1822), p. 410 for Litchborough.

William Borlase, *Antiquities of Cornwall* (1769).

William Boys, *Collections for an History of Sandwich in Kent* . . . (1792).

E. W. Brayley, *History of Surrey,* Vol. 5 (1850) for Chiddingfold.

G. Baldwin Brown, *The Arts in Early England,* Vol. 3 (1915).

John Burke, *History of the Commoners of Great Britain and Ireland,* Vol. 4 (1838), p. 601, under Douglas of Gyrn.

Alfred Cauchie, *La Grande Procession de Tournai* (Louvain, 1892).

G. Clinch, *Mayfair and Belgravia* (1892).

John Collinson, *The Beauties of British Antiquity* . . . (1779).

Sir Richard Colt Hoare, *Giraldus Cambrensis, Itin. Cambriae* (1804), *Ancient History of South Wiltshire* (1810-12), *Ancient History of North Wiltshire* (1819), *Ancient History of Wiltshire, Roman Period* (1821).

G. A. Cooke, *Pocket Directory of . . . Kent* (1810, 1816), *Walks through Kent* (London, 1819 ed.).

C. T., (Cooper, Thompson), *Dict. Nat. Biography,* Vol. 15 (1888), 332.

R. H. Cunnington, *Stonehenge and its Date* (1935), 'The Cunningtons of Wiltshire', *Wilts. Arch. Mag.,* June, 1954.

J. E. Cussans, *History of Hertfordshire,* Vol. 3 (1879-81).

J. Dallaway, *History of the Western Divisions . . . of Sussex,* Vol. 2, Part 1 (1819), p. 11 for Middleton.

Glyn E. Daniel, *A Hundred Years of Archaeology* (reprint, 1952), *The Idea of Prehistory* (Pelican ed., 1964), *The Origins and Growth òf Archaeology* (Pelican, Original, 1967), *Megaliths in History* (1972).

William Dugdale, *The Antiquities of Warwickshire* (1656).

[P. B. Duncan], Catalogue of the Ashmolean Museum (1836).

James Edwards, *Topographical Surveys of Surrey, Sussex and Kent,* 2nd ed. (1819), pp. 52-3 for barrows on Blackheath and in Greenwich Park excavated by Douglas. The binding of the work varies. [This reference is kindly supplied by N. E. S. Norris, F.S.A.]

Joan Evans, *A History of the Society of Antiquaries* (1956).

Bryan Faussett, *Inventorium Sepulchrale . . .* Edited by Charles Roach Smith (1856). The six volumes of Faussett's MS. are in the City of Liverpool Museums with the Collection presented by Joseph Mayer in 1867.

Thomas Fisher, *The History and Antiquities of Rochester and its Environs* (Rochester, 1772, 1817). Shrubsole, Denne and Wildash, all local Fellows of the Society of Antiquaries, contributed. *The Kentish Traveller's Companion* (Rochester, 1776, 1779, and Canterbury eds. with additional material, 1790, 1794, 1799).

Maurice Frère, *Tongres: Point de Rencontre Romain* (Tongres, 1958).

Gentleman's Magazine:
1786, Vol. 56, Feb., p. 150, Review of Douglas's 'Celts' Dissertation; 1786, Vol. 56, March, p. 245, Douglas's reply in eight columns; 1789, Vol. 59, July, p. 638, 'Tumboracus' contribution; 1792, Vol. 62, July, p. 648, Review of *Discourses on Christian Religion;* 1793, Vol. 63, Oct., p. 881, Douglas on the title of *Nenia;* 1802, Vol. 72, Aug., pp. 718, 825, Douglas on the Winchilsea MS.; 1803, Vol. 73, Aug., p. 785, Note on Douglas's appointment to Kenton vicarage; 1818, Vol. 88, Aug., p. 107, Douglas on Roman remains at Blatchington, Sussex; 1819, Vol. 89, Dec., p. 564, Obituary of Douglas.

J. A. Graham and B. A. Phythian (Eds.) *The Manchester Grammar School,* 2nd ed., Manchester Univ. Press (1968).

L. V. Grinsell, *The Ancient Burial Mounds of England* (1953), *The Archaeology of Wessex* (1958).

J. A. Hippolyte de Guibert, *Oeuvres militaires* (Paris, 5 vols. 1803).

F. Harrison and J. S. North, *Old Brighton, Old Preston, Old Hove* Brighton, privately printed, 1937).

Edward Hasted, *History of Kent.* Barrows opened by Douglas at Greenwich Park, Vol. I (1797), p. 377; at Chatham, Vol. IV(1798), p. 202.

D. C. Heggie, 'Megalithic lunar observatories: an astronomer's view', *Antiquity,* Vol. 46 (1972), p. 43.

H. R. Hodgkin, *A History of the Anglo-Saxons,* 2nd ed. (1939).

T. W. Horsfield, *History, Antiquities and Topography of Sussex* (Lewes, 1835), Vol. I, p. 171; Vol. II, p. 111.

Fr. Huybrigts, 'Texte de la correspondence du voyageur Douglas, voyage a Tongres et des sépultures des environs', *Bulletin Soc. Scientifique et Litteraire du Limburg,* No. 18 (Tongres, 1897), part 1, pp. 136-58.

Edward Jacob, *The History of the Town and Port of Faversham . . . Kent* (1774), *Plantae Favershamiensis . . . and a short View of the Fossil Bodies of the adjacent Island of Sheppey* (1777).

R. F. Jessup, *Anglo-Saxon Jewellery* (London, 1950, Florida, 1951, New York, 1953), 'Notes and Correspondence of Bryan Faussett: MSS. 723', *Ant. Journ.*, Vol. 33 (1953), p. 149, 'Two Monuments to a Mood: Fawley Mount and Faussett's Pavilion', *Ant. Journ.*, Vol. 34 (1954), p. 144, 'The Faussett Pavilion', *Arch. Cantiana*, Vol. 66 (1954), p. 1, 'Barrows in Roman Britain', *Journ. Arch. Assoc.*, Vol. 22 (1958), p. 1; *Latomus*, Vol. 58 (Brussels, 1962), p. 853, 'A Roman bronze ceremonial axe from near Canterbury', *Ant. Journ.*, Vol. 50 (1970), p. 348, 'The common-place book of Heneage Finch . . .', *Ant. Journ.*, Vol. 50 (1970), p. 343.

Sir Thomas Kendrick, *The Druids* (London, 1927, New York, 1966), *British Antiquity* (1950).

Edward King, *Munimenta Antiqua* (1799-1805).

E. Thurlow Leeds, *The Archaeology of the Anglo-Saxon Settlements* (1913, reprint 1972), *Corpus of Early Anglo-Saxon Great Square-headed Brooches* (1949).

C. L. Kingsford, *Piccadilly, Leicester Square, Soho* (Cambridge, 1925, for London Topographical Society).

M. A. Lower, *The Worthies of Sussex* (1865), *History of Sussex* (1870), Vol. 1, p. 252 for the Goldstone.

W. T. Lowndes, *Bibliographical Manual of English Literature,* Vol. 2 (1858), pp. 664, 954.

B. D. and T. F. Lynch, 'The Beginnings of a Scientific Approach to Prehistoric Archaeology in 17th and 18th century Britain', *Southwestern Journ. Anthrop.* Univ. New Mexico, Albuquerque, Vol. 24 (1968). No. 1, p. 33.

Samuel Lysons, *Reliquiae Britannico-Romanae . . .*, p. 3 (plates drawn 1814-19). *An Account of the Remains of a Roman Villa discovered at Bignor . . . Sussex . . .* (1815, 1820, 1839).

O. Manning and W. Bray, *History and Antiquities of*

The County of Surrey, Vol. 1 (1804), p. 653 for Chiddingfold.

M. E. Mariën, *Par la Chaussée Brunehaut de Bavai à Cologne* Brussels, 1962, 2nd ed., 1968).

J. Mertens, 'Een Romeins tempelcomplex et Tongren', *Kölner Jahrd. für Vorund Frühgeschicht,* Vol. 9 (1967-8), p. 101.

E. Moir, 'The English Antiquaries', *History Today* (1958), p. 781.

Monthly Review:
   1782, Vol. 71, Aug., p. 93, Review of *Travelling Anecdotes*; 1786, No. 75, Dec., p. 457, Review of *Dissertation on the Antiquity of the Earth*; 1787, No. 76, p. 77, Review of early numbers of *Nenia Britannica.*

Clifford Musgrave, *Life in Brighton from the earliest times to the present* (1970).

John Nichols, *History and Antiquities of the County of Leicester* (1795-1815), Vol. 2, plate 34, Douglas's drawing of Coston church.
   Literary Anecdotes of the Eighteenth Century:
   Vol. 3, 1812, p. 659 Douglas's portrait of Grose; Vol. 8, 1814, p. 685, Enquiry on author of *Travelling Anecdotes*; Vol. 9, 1815, pp. 8, 71, 88, Copy review of *Nenia Britannica,* note on paper on *Celts* and on *Twelve Discourses.*
   Illustrations of the Literary History of the Eighteenth Century:
   Vol. 4, 1822, p. 650, Hasted's view of Douglas; Vol. 6, 1831, pp. 455, 893, Brief obituary; three letters by Douglas; his clerical appointments; Vol. 7, 1848, p. 698, Short third-party reference.

Stuart Piggott, 'Stukeley, Avebury and the Druids', *Antiquity,* Vol. 9 (1935), p. 22, *William Stukeley* (1950), 'Antiquarian Thought in the Sixteenth and Seventeenth Centuries' in L. Fox, *English Historical Scholarship in the sixteenth and seventeenth centuries* (1956), *The Druids* (1968).

Robert Plot, *The Natural History of Oxfordshire* (1677).

The Natural History of Staffordshire (1686).

Whitworth Porter, *History of the Corps of Royal Engineers,* Vol. 2 (1889), p. 394.

Paul Rolland, *Histoire de Tournai* (2nd ed., Tournai and Paris, 1957).

Hayman Rooke, 'Druidical remains on Stanton Moor; Pits in Derbyshire; a barrow in Derbyshire' in *Archaeologia,* Vol. 6 (1782), p. 110; Vol. 10 (1792), p. 114; Vol. 12 (1809), p. 327.

Osbert Sitwell and Margaret Barton, *Brighton* (1935).

J. F. Smith (Ed.), *Admission Register of the Manchester School* (1837).

F. W. Steer (Ed.), *The Letters of John Hawkins and Samuel and Daniel Lysons 1812-1830 with special reference to the Roman villa at Bignor, Sussex,* Chichester, West Sussex County Council, 1966).

Alexander Thom, *Megalithic lunar observatories* (1971).

J. A. Venn, *Alumni Cantabrigienses,* Part 2, Vol. 2 (1944), p. 325.

Victoria County History:
  Herts. Caldecote Hill, Vol. 1 (1908), p. 157; *Kent.* Anglo-Saxon remains, Vol. 1 (1908), p. 339; *Surrey.* Chiddingfold, Vol. 3 (1911), p. 10; *Sussex.* Anglo-Saxon remains, Vol. 1 (1905), p. 337, The Goldstone, Hove, Vol. 7 (1940), p. 265.

T. A. Walker, *Admissions to Peterhouse . . .* (1912), p. 343, *A Peterhouse Bibliography* (1924), p. 40.

H. B. Walters, *The English Antiquaries of the 16th, 17th and 18th centuries* (London, 1934, privately published).

J. Watkins and F. Shoberl, *Biographical Dictionary of Living Authors of Great Britain and Ireland* (1816), p. 98.

Robert Watt, *Bibliotheca Britannica,* Vol. 1 (1824), pp. 1, 314.

William Wildash, *The History and Antiquities of Rochester and its Environs* (Rochester, 1772; for Douglas's work on Chatham Lines, 2nd ed., 1817, p. 333).

Kenneth Woodbridge, *Landscape and Antiquity* (1970).

INDEX

Aix-la-Chapelle [Aachen] (Germany): 32, 45
Aldenham (Herts): 15-16
Aloest [Aalst] (Belgium): 32, 37
Ambresbury, Arbury [Amesbury] (Wilts): 158, 273
Ancient Wiltshire by Colt Hoare: 143, 147, 271
Annable, F. K., and Simpson, D. D. A.: 130
Antiquaries, Society of: 22, 27-9, 53, 60, 75, 109, 171, 203, 209; *Ms.*, 723, 182-229; *Correspondence Files*, 230-42
Apsley House, London: 13
Arkwright, Sir Richard: cotton-spinning machines, 16
Arundel (Sussex): 125, 127
Ash (E. Kent): 19, 103, 105, 112, 170, 200-2, 207, 210, 283

Baggrave (Leics): 103
Barham Downs (Kent): 108, 170, 199, 221
Barnham (Sussex): 125
Barrows: Excavation, types, relics, attributed dates; *see under* Douglas, James
Bartlow Barrows (Essex): 240
Beads: 114, 116, 131-3, 171, 223, 234, 252-4
Bignor (Sussex): barrows, 148, 164, 273; Roman villa, 123, 127, 146-7, 163
Blackheath (Kent): 55, 78
Boughton Aluph (Kent): 111, 288
Boxley (Kent): 106, 111
Boys, William: 109, 200
Brassington Moor (Yorks): 231

Brighton (Sussex): library, 98; life at, 146, 152-3, 155; stones near church, 149; Upper Rock Gardens, 154
British Museum: Grenville library, 97; Towneley collection, 74
Bronze 'Bull' axes and 'Celts': 66 *et seq.*, 144, 171, 174, 237-8, 287
Brown, P. D. C.: 171
Browne, Sir Thomas: 48
Brussels (Belgium): 32, 46; Bibliothèque Royale, 97
Burial rites: 133, 145, 148, 173, 254, 262, 272
Burstow, G. P.: 161
Bush Barrow, Wilsford (Wilts): 138, 266
Caburn (Sussex): 163
Calais (France): 32
Caldecotte Hill (Herts): 15
Cambridge University: Peterhouse, 21, 30
Canterbury (Kent): bronze axe, 68; Dane John and Dungeon Hills, 59, 64, 106, 223; Roman station, 89-90; Royal Museum, 51
Chartham (Kent): 48, 104, 286
Chatham (Kent): Dockyard, 23, 284; Hill, 55, 83, 89, 106; Lines, 21, 23, 24 *et seq.*, 52, 55, 66, 92, 103, 107, 109, 118, 170, 284, 289; river-bank, discoveries, 77, 81
Chenekbury [Chanctonbury] (Sussex): 163
Chesterford [Essex]: 56, 106, 195
Chiddingfold (Surrey): 79, 88, 107,

Chiddingfold (Surrey)—*cont.*
115, 175, 287; Gorstead barrow,
225
Childeric: jewels of, 54, 100, 111,
172, 207, 217
Cisbury [Cissbury] (Sussex): 115,
163, 228
Clarke, Revd. William: 146
Coins and Inscriptions: as dating
burials, 105, 108, 114, 172,
196, 210 *et seq.*, 279
Colchester (Essex): 170
Coldred (Kent): 106
Comes Litoris Saxonici: 89-91
Coston (Leics): 60, 61, 287
Courtrai (Belgium): 32, 46
Coxe, Archdeacon: 136, 143, 262
Crundale (Kent): 50, 201
Crystal Balls: 200, 202, 210, 217
Cunnington, William: 126, 128, 129,
131-41, 144, 145; letters to, 251-
270

Daniel, Professor Glyn: 129
Davy, David Elisha: *Ms.* History of
Suffolk, 17, 125
Debbieg, Colonel (later Major-
General) Hugh: 21, 24
Denne, Samuel: 24
Devil's Dyke (Sussex): 163
Dinton (Bucks): 217
*Discourses on . . . Christian Religion
. . .*: 118-9
*Dissertation on the Antiquity of the
Earth*: 81 *et seq.*; reviews of, 87,
285
Ditchling (Sussex): 163
Douglas: Alexander, 14
— : James Bruce (infant son),
88
— : James Edward Moreton
(eldest son), 88, 155,
157
— : John (father), 13-17
— : John (nephew), 17, 126
— : Margaret (*née* Oldershaw,

Douglas—*cont.*
wife), 26, 79, 88, 124, 154,
165, 168, 276
— : Mary (mother), 15
— : Richard William Glode
(son), 88, 125, 154
— : Thomas (brother), 15, 16,
124
— : Tucker, Mrs. (daughter),
154, 169-70, 276
Douglas, James: antiquarian interests and views, 19, 24, 25, 26, 28,
43, 69 *et seq.*, 89, 102, 107, 137,
145, 162-5, 176; antiquity of the
earth and of man, views on, 59,
79 *et seq.*; astronomy and stone
monuments, views on, 107, 136,
138, 156, 158, 177, 232, 265-6,
277, 280 *et seq.*; barrows, cists,
stone circles, and views on, 24,
39, 65, 83, 92 *et seq.*, 103 *et seq.*,
107, 114, 116,'128, 131, 133-5,
140, 145, 146-8, 151, 162, 164,
172, 176, 219, 225, 231 *et seq.*,
255-9, 264-9, 272-4; birth, 12,
15; British Museum, hope of
appointment to, 144, 145; Chaplain to Prince of Wales, 79, 118,
128, 151, 159; character, 123,
127, 160, 167-8; chronology,
importance of relics in determina-
tion of, 105, 108, 143, 145, 164,
172, 176, 226; church career, 11,
17, 54, 56, 59 *et seq.*, 78-9, 88,
98, 115, 122-5, 126, 142, 146,
151-2, 159, 175, 192 *et seq.*, 221,
233, 241-50, 263; classical, antiquarian, and topographical literature, knowledge of, 11, 17, 69,
80, 89, 91, 101, 110, 111, 138,
172-3, 257; his own collections,
24, 55, 92, 109, 168-72, 191,
194, 253; death, memorials and
obituary, 165, 166, 178, 292;
education, 17, 21, 110; excavations, list of (*and see* relative

Douglas, James—*cont.*
place-names), 172, techniques of, 145, 156, 172, 175, 222; family and connections, 10, 11, 13, 14 *et seq.*, 21, 27, 57, 100, 115,154, 220, 245, 276; fiction, works of, 116, 119, 224; field archaeology, 83, 96, 162, 172, illustrations and, 109; finances, 18, 99, 100, 115, 124-5, 208, 220, 244-50; friends, 11, 24, 25, 52 *et seq.*, 130 *et seq.*; geology, interest in, 11, 18, 19, 77, 82-6, 123-4, 131-2, 139, 140, 172, 251, 253, 259, 269; on the Grand Tour, 33-6; health, 58, 100, 117, 125, 139, 145, 160, 181, 185, 221, 229, 253; marriage, 26; military career, 3, 10, 18-24, and appreciation of topography, 172; natural history, interest in, 18, 77; *Nenia Britannica*, progress of, 53, 58, 60, 92-114, 187 *et seq.*, 199, 212 *et seq.*, 226, 234; nicknames, 102, 127, 143, 175; painting, knowledge of, and sales, 33, 54, 59, 61-3, 123, 191 *et seq.*, 218; painting and drawing, his own, 7, 18, 31, 59, 92, 109, 173, 195, 207; place-name theories, 153, 155, 158, 163, 173, 198, 230, 267, 274, 280-2; portrait of, 168, 170, 283; religious discourses, 118-9; residences, 14, 15, 53, 77-8, 132, 152, 154, 183, 197, 204, 249, 263, 276, 287; Royal Society, 78, 205; snuff-box, 171, 292; Society of Antiquaries (*and see* Bibliography), 19, 27-9, 54, 65, 66; on soil and crop marks, 112, 160, 172, 235, 237; technical knowledge and experiments, 71, 77, 83, 112, 173, 222; travels, 17, 18, 31, 54, 59, 63, 88, 99, 157, 192, 216, 219, 222; (*and see* Bibliography, 293)

Druids: 107, 109, 139, 149-51, 173, 231, 236, 238 *et seq.*, 264
Dubnovellaunos, coin of; 158, 171, 279

Earthworks, 134, 141, 151, 163, 256-9, 270, 274, 282
Eastry (Kent); 56
Egremont, 3rd Earl of: 122, 124-5, 147, 152, 178; letters to, and to his agent, 243-50
Engineers: (Royal) Corps of, 21, 24

Fagge, Sir William:109, 192, 222
Fashionable Infidelity: 117
Faussett: Bryan, 19, 26, 49
— : Collection, 49 *et seq.*, 54, 92, 99, 110, 182 *et seq.*, 286
— : Henry Godfrey, 52, 54-5, 63, 92, 99, 110, 116; letters to, 182-229
Finch, Heneage (5th Earl of Winchilsea): 111, 159, 170, 201-2, 207, 282, 288
Fisher, Thomas: 24, 31
Forman Collection: 75
Frere, John: discovery of flint weapons at Hoxne, 80

Gardiner, Mary; *see* Douglas, Mary
General Essay on Tactics (Trans): 20
Gent [Ghent] (Belgium): 3, 18, 32, 46
Gibraltar: fossil jawbone from, 85
Glasgow University Library: 98
Gloucester: 213-14, 234
Goldstone, the (Sussex): 148-51, 273, 290
Göttingen: university, 75
Gough, Richard; 67, 73
Greenwich Park (Kent): 59, 105, 195, 206, 232, 288
Grose, Francis: 60, 107, 287
Guibert, Comte Hippolyte de: 20
Half Moon Street, London: 13

Hardham (Sussex): 163
Hasted, Edward: 25, 209
Hawkes: Prof. and Mrs. Christopher, 50
Heppington (Kent): 49, 51, 93, 287
Hercules Pillars, London: 13
Herderen (Belgium): 38, 42
History of Julia D'Haumont: 119
Hoare: Peter, 168
— : Prince, 161, 168
— : Sir Richard Colt, 73, 74, 107, 126, 128, 129, 135, 142 *et seq.*, 147, 157, 168; letters to, 271-282
— : Henry Colt (son), 155, 276
Hollingbury (Sussex): 163
Hunter, Dr.: 189
Hyde Park Corner, London: 13

Independent Company of Invalids (Regt.): 21
Inventorium Sepulchrale: 50, 51, 53, 93, 99, 113, 213, 286

Jacob, Edward: 24, 27, 221
Johnson, Dr., and title of *Nenia Britannica*: 101

Kenton (Suffolk): 17, 123, 125, 174, 175
Kingsholm (Gloucs): 106, 171
Kingston Downs (Kent): 52, 83, 104
Kits-Coty-House [Kits Coty] (Aylesford, Kent): 172, 231, 291
Koninksem (Belgium): 39, 285

Lambert, A. B.: 130, 251
Lausselt, Lawfeld, Laafelt (Belgium): battle of, 38
Lavington Hill (Sussex): 148, 164, 272
Leicester Militia: 21
Leicestershire: tumuli in, 194
Leman, Revd. Thomas: 143
Lever, Sir Ashton: 18, 27, 77, 84,

Lever, Sir Ashton—*cont.*
109, 186, 284
Lewis, Revd. John: 112
Lhwyd, Edward: 67
Lilliers (France): 32, 33
Lisle (France): 32
Litchborough (Northants): 79, 122, 174, 241
Little Stanhope Street, London: 14, 78
Liverpool Museums: 50, 51
Lort: Dr. Michael: 27
Louvain (Belgium): 32
Lysons, Samuel: 123, 127, 146

Maestricht (Belgium): 19, 32
Maid of Kent: 117, 121
Manchester: assembly rooms, 17; Castle Field, 19, 172, 290; constable, 16; cotton industry, 16; Grammar School, 17, 138
Mander: John (and White Lowe, Derbys), 109, 233
Mayfair, London: 14
May Fair, The: 14
Medway, River: 11, 19, 77, 82
Mell (Belgium): 32
Melville, Colonel (General) Robert: 27, 66, 87
Meneage (Cornwall): 197, 232
Mertens, Prof. J.: 41, 44, 285
Middleton (Sussex): 122, 125, 175, 243, 244-50
Mining Low (Derbys): 239
Minster (Kent): 289
Mortimer, Cromwell: 48, 104, 286

Nenia Britannica: 92-114; title chosen, 101, 143; contemporary views of, 113, 167, 178; Colt Hoare's views of, 142; progress of, *see under* Douglas, James
Nichols, John: 60, 66, 67, 101, 125
Norris, N. E. S.: 161, 291-2

Offulkin (Belgium): 289

Ordnance, Board of: 21
Oudenaarde (Belgium): 4
Oxford University: Ashmolean Museum, 48, 68, 74, 104, 130, 168-72; Bodleian Library, 171

Pendleton (Lancs): 16
Perthes, Boucher de: 51
Petworth (Sussex): 123
Petworth House Library: *Ms.* 101, 243-50
Phillips, Thomas: 170
Pinkerton, John: 144
Piringen (Belgium): 42, 286
Portslade (Sussex): 133, 255
Portchester (Hants): 161
Portus Adurni: 161
Poynings (Sussex): 148, 273
Preston (Sussex): 125, 146, 152, 159, 165, 174, 178, 276, 291-2

Redbourn (Herts): 47
Relative dating: 105-8, 143, 164, 266, 270
Richborough (Kent): 89-90, 112, 161, 288
Rochester (Kent): 24, 55, 77-8, 106
Rooke, Major Hayman: 107, 109, 173, 197, 200; letters to, 230-242
Rook House (The Rookery), Aldenham (Herts): 15, 16
Roosens: Dr. H., 286
Rottingdean (Sussex): 147, 272
Rundel [Rewell] Hill (Sussex): 134, 256 *et seq.*

St. George's, Hanover Square, London: 12, 14
St. Margarets-at-Cliffe (Kent): 56, 106, 288
Saltdean (Sussex): 164
'Samian' Pottery: 133, 255
Sarsen Stones: 138, 146, 149-151
Secondary burials: 133; first anti-

Secondary burials—*cont.*
quary to realise significance of, 173, 255
Sheffield City Museums: 201, 235
Shells in burials: 200, 205, 215, 217, 224
Shepperton (Mdx): 198
Sheppey, Isle of (Kent): 19, 77, 84
Sibertswold [Sibbertswould], Shepherdswell (Kent): 106, 286
Silbury-Mount (Wilts): 240
Smith, Charles Roach: 51, 112-3
Smith, 'Strata': 124, 140, 269
Stack House Scar (Yorks): 230, 236
Stanton Moor (Derbys): 107
Steer, Francis: 127
Stone circles and cromlechs: *see under* Douglas, James
Stonehenge (Wilts): 107, 128, 136-40, 145, 156, 158, 260-70, 278-81
Strood (Kent): 58, 77
Stukeley, William: 74; thoughts of re-publishing his work, 126, 142; 131, 132, 137, 160, 171, 240 *et seq.*, 265, 273

Thame (Oxon): fossil jawbone from, 85
Thorpe, John (Jnr.): 24
'Tiddy Doll': 14
Tinewald (Isle of Man): 107
Tirlemont (Belgium): 39
Tongres (Belgium): 4, 19, 20, 31, 38, 106, 110, 286; mineral waters, 41, 110; Roman antiquities, 39, 41, 42, 44, 46, 58, 171, 285, 289, 291
Tortington (Sussex): 126
Tournai (Belgium): 3-11, 54, 283
Townsend, Revd. Charles: 178
Travelling Anecdotes: 20, 22, 30 *et seq.*, 45, 92, 190, 285
'Tumboracos': 116, 117, 176
Twynne, John: 108

Van Muyssen, Abbé P. G.: 19,
39, 42, 58, 59, 109, 171,
196, 289, 291
Vasmer, Eric G.: 15
Vienna (Austria): 18

Wales, Prince of (Prince Regent): 79, 128, 147, 152
Walton-on-Thames (Surrey):
59, 197, 208, 233
Wessex Bronze Age: 131-2, 138
West Blatchington (Sussex):
160-2, 169
White: Benjamin and John, 101,
228
Whitehawk, Brighton (Sussex):
163

White Lowe, Winster Common
(Derbys): 201, 203, 233, 235,
237
Wiltshire Archaeological and Natural
History Society: 130
Wiltshire, County and Diocesan
Archives: 142; *Colt Hoare Papers,*
251-82
Wimbledon Common (Surrey): 172,
174, 222
Winchelsea (*sic*), Lord: *see* Finch,
Heneage
Woodbridge, Kenneth: 130, 143,
157
Woodnesborough (Kent): 289
Woolsenbury [Wolstonbury] (Sus-
sex): 163